Beat The Devil

How To Get Government Regulators
Off Your Back — *Permanently!*

Richard A. Mackie

Solution Publishing

Beat The Devil
*How To Get Government Regulators
Off Your Back—Permanently!*

© 1994 by Richard A. Mackie

Solution Publishing
1647 Willow Pass Road, Suite 101
Concord, CA 94520

ISBN No. 1-885372-01-9
Library of Congress 94-066792

Cover art by Lucija Jovanovic

Excerpts from "The Designer Plague," by Gregory Benford and from "Species Argument," by Jeff Taylor reprinted, with permission, from the January 1994 issue of *REASON* magazine. Copyright 1994 by the Reason Foundation, 3415 S. Sepulveda Blvd., Suite 400, Los Angeles, CA 90034.

Sources, when not specifically cited, derive from general circulation newspapers, particularly the *Contra Costa Times, Oakland Tribune, San Francisco Chronicle* and *San Jose Mercury.*

Note: The law is constantly evolving. While every effort was made to provide the most current and accurate information, all ideas, suggestions, general principles and conclusions presented in this text are subject to local, state and federal laws and regulations, court cases and revisions of same. Therefore, the reader is encouraged to consult legal counsel regarding any points of law. This book should not be used as a substitute for competent legal advice.

"Today there is not a man, woman, or child whose life could not be destroyed by some government agency that has declared an action of theirs to be a violation of a regulation."

Contents

Introduction

"We enact many laws that manufacture criminals, and then a few that punish them."

Allen Tucker

"It behooves every man who values liberty of conscience for himself to resist invasions of it in the case of others; or their case may, by change of circumstances, become his own."

Thomas Jefferson

Something had to be done. Rivers were so polluted they would soon catch on fire. The Great Lakes were dying a slow death from pollution. Harbors, bays and estuaries were becoming garbage dumps. Our country was discarding its unwanted materials with careless abandon, and our environment was becoming degraded.

No wonder there was little opposition when Nixon established the Environmental Protection Agency (EPA) in 1968. The EPA and kindred agencies started investigating one source of pollution after another. Pollution sources were discovered, the culprits cited and the pollution abated. Mother Nature, using her great powers of recuperation, soon had these damaged areas well on the road to recovery. The success of this program is apparent in the clean rivers, lakes and oceans we see today.

Unfortunately, these agencies were handed almost unlimited power, a new type of power that eliminated the checks and balances normally used to ensure that power is not abused. Not surprisingly, left with unlimited power and no accountability, these agencies eventually went well beyond the point of abating nuisances and became large, abusive, and bureaucratic. They now have the power to control the life and property of every citizen of this country, and they seem to have taken on this responsibility. It is essential that these agencies return to the duties for which they were created. We cannot wait any longer or they will consume us the way they have Larry Duncan.

Larry hails from Houston, Texas, and he has been in the oil-drilling business all his life. Because of his particular brand of expertise, demand for his services come from anywhere in the world where oil is produced. One day Larry made the mistake of trying to do one of his clients a favor by purchasing a piece of equipment for him. Without warning, Larry became a hostage of the U.S. Customs Service, lost his job and had over a million dollars in assets confiscated. Despite his pleas, Customs took over a year to formally notify him of why such actions were taken. In the end, it was revealed that Larry had committed no crime. Customs just wanted to "punish" him a little and knew he didn't have the $500,000 it would take to fight them in court.

While Larry is busily representing himself in hopes of regaining his life savings and his job, another government agency has initiated action that could condemn many physically disadvantaged people to remain in their beds for the rest of their lives. The disabled may lose access to the equipment that has made it possible for them to participate as active members of society. Ironically, while one government agency is depriving the physically disadvantaged of their freedom, yet another government agency is scurrying around trying to make sure that all buildings, public transportation and parking areas are made wheelchair-accessible.

This tragedy is taking place because one government agency

wants more power, even if it costs many disabled people their freedom.

However, it is not just government that abuses power. States and even neighborhood associations are quick to elbow their way to the trough when they see an opportunity. Eagle Hardware Stores in the State of Washington, for example, had never experienced trouble building their stores throughout the state because they'd been very careful to follow the thousands of government regulations to the letter; however, when they began construction of a new store in Bellevue, they discovered that there is an even greater and more unreasonable power then government: a special interest group. A group called BROIL, made up of just a few individuals, decided they did not want an Eagle Store where it was being constructed. Despite the fact that BROIL represented less then one percent of the local community, despite the fact that BROIL's claims were found to be nothing but lies and despite the fact that the store was almost finished, BROIL was able to stop it from opening. The delay in opening has cost Eagle $9,000 per day and the delay has gone on for over a year. Eventually, the courts will find in favor of Eagle. However, the entire cost of this episode will fall upon Eagle. It will cost the members of BROIL nothing.

Or take Bob Carpenter of Livermore, California. He made a mistake that could very well cost him his home. Nobody wants to lose their home but for Bob it is particularly difficult because he is retired and in no position to start over again. This loss is all the more tragic because Bob wouldn't be in this predicament if he hadn't been so conscientious about *obeying* the law. Had he ignored the law, his home would not now be in jeopardy. Bob is the victim of government regulation and a few overzealous government employees.

We'll be looking at these cases in depth later on, along with that of John Poszgai, who was robbed of his freedom and all his savings. Unbelievable as it sounds, John was sentenced to three years in prison and fined $202,000 for trying to clean up some property he had purchased. The property had previously served as an unofficial town dump for many years. John's crime was to remove about 7,000 old tires, unclog a waterway that had been plugged by years' worth of the townspeople's rubbish and then cover the entire degraded site with clean soil. Everyone agreed that he had greatly improved the property, so why the fine and jail sentence? He refused to get a permit to clean his own property.

Then there's William Gorsk, his wife and three children. They had scrimped and saved for years and years to build their dream house. When they had finally saved enough money, they were ecstatic. Five people living in a one-bedroom home had been difficult, especially since two of the children were now teenagers. Unfortunately, one very small rat not only destroyed their dream, but severely lowered the value of their property, making it impossible to sell. They can't buy land elsewhere to build a home without first selling the old place, but the government feels it's more important for the rat to have a home then for the Gorsk family to have one.

These are but a few grains of sand on the beach of tragedies that have buried hundreds of thousands of Americans who have fallen victim to the millions of regulations that have sprung up over the last forty years. Today, there is not a man, woman or child in America whose life is not in danger of being destroyed by some government agency that has declared an action of theirs to be in violation of some regulation. Other examples will appear later in this book.

Considering the cases cited above, however, it is little wonder that over two-thirds of the corporate attorneys surveyed by the National Law Journal stated that it was impossible for their company to achieve full compliance with all of the environmental laws. This is startling coming from attorneys who represent companies with annual revenues ranging from $50 million to over $10 billion.

For smaller companies, those that cannot afford a battery of full time attorneys, the regulatory problem is far more dramatic. Some have been driven out of business by government regulations and government regulators. Many have been forced to lay off employees because of some regulation or permit process. Other businesses are trying to relocate to less restrictive states, while still others are considering abandoning the United States altogether in order survive.

To the regulatory agencies, it's business as usual. Thousands of harmful actions are taken by our government on a daily basis and are obvious symptoms of a very serious illness. Like a raging, highly infectious disease, the regulatory process is out of control. If this disease is not stopped, it will consume our businesses and, eventually, our country.

There was a concerted effort by the Reagan administration to try to curb this regulatory onslaught. The President himself issued an Executive Order on March 15, 1988 ordering Federal Departments and Agencies to consider the takings implications of their regulatory actions and to act to minimize interference with private property rights to the extent permitted by law.

However, shortly thereafter, the reins of leadership were transferred to George Bush who had a totally different set of goals. To prove to the taxpayers that he was tough on crime, Bush considered any act against the environment a crime. The results were immediate and dramatic. Ninety-four percent of all the fines and all the penalties ever imposed for "environmental crimes" took place during the Bush administration. In addition, 69% of *all* prison time served for "environmental crimes" resulted from Bush's new doctrine, despite the fact that the environmental laws have been on the books since 1968.

If this is not enough to make your hair stand on end, the Clinton-Gore Administration has an even bigger mandate to protect the environment then did George Bush. As you will see in the chapters that follow, there are presently sufficient regulations on the books to throw every property owner and every business owner in jail. With the blessings of the Bush Administration, Congress passed a bill increasing the number of criminal investigators in the Environmental Protection Agency by over 400%. The Clinton Administration has shown no inclination to reduce this number.

With such an increase in EPA investigators, there is a heightened possibility that there will be an ominous knock on your door at some time in the near future. Even if you are fortunate enough to stay out of jail or avoid the enormous fines that can now be imposed, that knock on the door can be very expensive. Oklahoma criminal defense attorney Jerry McCombs estimates a competent environmental defense will cost between $250,000 and $500,000. This does not, of course, include the costs in time, anxiety and reputation that such prosecution exacts.

For reasons that will become apparent later in this book, none of these regulatory headaches are going to go away by themselves. Even though the current regulatory process is in violation of the moral, ethical, scientific and constitutional fibre of this country, regulatory agencies are not going to relinquish their power voluntarily. They will only be curbed when business and individuals in this country are fed up enough to do something about it. Businesses large and small currently have the power to curb the cancers that plague the regulatory process, stop its growth and, eventually, bring a state of reasonableness to the process. It's just a matter of knowing how and then taking the appropriate action.

This book has three major goals. The first goal is to give every business owner and every citizen of this country a complete understanding of the regulatory process: what it is, where it came from, and why it is what it is today. The reason for going into the process in such detail is that it is difficult to eliminate a problem unless you have a complete understanding of what the problem is, and you will need a complete grasp of where the regulatory process came from in order to exploit its weaknesses.

The second goal of this book is to teach every business owner and every citizen where there are weaknesses in the regulatory process and how to take advantage of these weaknesses. You will discover that almost every regulation or regulatory process violates one or more of the basic moral, ethical, legal, constitutional or scientific tenets upon which this country was built.

The third goal of this book is to encourage the development of a national coalition of businesses and citizens, organized specifically to help individuals and businesses beat back unfair and unjust regulatory practices. With a coordinated effort, America's citizens and businesses can remold the regulatory process so that it is more reasonable, less corrupt and more responsive to the moral, legal, ethical, scientific and constitutional values we hold dear.

We owe it to ourselves and to the American people to be sure that this corrupt, unconstitutional system of government is not allowed to put us out of business. Such a system can only continue to survive in its current form if we are willing to sit by and passively let it happen.

The examples cited at the beginning of this introduction were selected from among thousands of unjust government actions that take place almost daily. They are not the worst examples one can find, but were chosen because each represents the suppressive forces of a different agency and a different set of regulations. I will refer to each of these situations time and again throughout this book to make various points, and you will become intimately acquainted with the people trapped in the jaws of this merciless system so that you can protect yourself from being eaten by regulators.

CHAPTER 1

Land of the Free?

"The essence of Government is power; and power, lodged as it must in human hands, will ever be liable to abuse."

James Madison

"No man's life, liberty or property is safe while the Legislature is in session."

Gideon J. Tucker

"Unjust laws exist; shall we be content to obey them, or shall we endeavor to amend them, and obey them until we have succeeded, or shall we transgress them at once?... If the injustice is part of the necessary friction of the machine of government, let it go, let it go; perchance it will wear smooth...but if it is of such a nature that it requires you to be the agent of injustice to another, then, I say, break the law. Let your life be counter-friction to stop the machine. What I have to do is to see, at any rate, that I do not lend myself to the wrong which I condemn."

Henry David Thoreau

Most people assume that the law is basically a good thing to have around. It does, after all, help to discourage the commission of crimes and punishes those that insist on breaking the law. Like the rest of you, I believe the existence of laws are a necessity. Unlike Thoreau, I would never recommend that you break a law. However, you can sometimes have too much of a good thing. When the laws themselves become abusive, it is time to stop and re-evaluate what unregulated laws are doing to us.

Modern law and modern government are cumbersome subjects with which to deal because they have become many-headed dragons. In order to understand their complexities, I'd like to introduce you to a few situations. As we progress through the labyrinth of law and government, we will reference these situations to help you understand how they came to be and how you can avoid them.

Larry Duncan has been in the oil-drilling business for most of his life. His expertise in various aspects of drilling for oil has taken him to countries all over the world. Obviously, much of his time is spent in the Middle East, where a large portion of the world's oil is produced. To accommodate his needs and the needs of the companies who contract for his services, he often works for thirty-five straight days, then comes home for thirty-five days, then back to work for thirty-five days, etc. This is the arrangement he had with the company he was contracting with in Tunisia. Unfortunately, Larry agreed to do his employer a favor while he was on one of his thirty-five day leaves.

The company wanted an asphalt-making machine for a project in Algeria and Larry offered to purchase one for them. This involved buying parts from several vendors around the United States and shipping the parts to Algeria. Being an expert in the industry, Larry had no trouble locating the parts and starting the process of shipping them to their final destination. In total, the equipment cost approximately $1.5 million dollars; Larry invested his life savings in the equipment. However, he felt it was a good investment, and it probably was. Or at least it was until August 10, 1992.

It was on that day that a key rattled in the lock of his apartment door: the rattle that would destroy his life. Within seconds, two men, armed with guns, entered his apartment without waiting for an invitation. They waved a federal search warrant in his face and identified themselves as Special Agents of the U.S. Customs Service. Without any discussion, they begin an intense search of his apartment. According to the warrant handed to Larry, there was "evidence of a violation of 50 USC section 1701-1706."

When Larry asked what was going on, what 50 USC section 1701-1706 was, he was told that the agents were undertaking the "search" for his own good. When he disagreed, one of the agents became angry and called the Houston Police Department for back up. Five minutes later, a uniformed, well-armed police officer arrived. When questioned, one of the agents told Larry that he was not under arrest and that he could leave if he wanted. Since he felt very uncomfortable in the presence of two very aggressive agents with guns, he took advantage of the offer and departed while the two agents continued their search. When Larry returned a few hours later the agents were gone, having left behind a list of the things they had taken. They had confiscated his passport, some business and personal papers, and his diary. They did not, however, provide an explanation of how he might be violating 50 USC section 1701-1706.

Since most of his jobs are overseas, Larry needs his passport in order to make a living. He has carried a U.S. passport since 1948. In this case, he was due to report back to his job in Tunisia in a few days but he could not leave the U.S. without his passport. Therefore, he called Customs to request its return. Customs informed him that the passport had been seized pursuant to a search warrant and was now the property of the U.S. Government and would not be returned. For most people this would be just an inconvenience, but for Larry his livelihood was at stake. Therefore, broke as he was, he contacted a lawyer.

The lawyer sent customs a letter demanding the return of the passport and papers taken from Larry's apartment. Customs responded by advising Larry that if he wanted his passport and papers back he would have to file a claim under the Freedom Of Information Act. This turned out to be the beginning of a series of stonewalling actions taken by the Customs Service, apparently to "punish" Larry.

Since Larry had never received a single piece of paper or a single phone call advising him of what crime he might have committed, he tortured himself asking why he was being "punished" by Customs.

About two weeks later, the pieces begin to fall into place. Larry learned from the lawyer of one of the vendors from which he had purchased some of the equipment, that all the equipment slated for Algeria had been seized by Customs. When he called the Customs Service, he was told that the equipment had been confiscated and that a civil forfeiture suit was being filed against the "defendant equipment." Not against Larry, mind you, but against the equipment. Since his entire life savings was wrapped up in the equipment, Larry filed a claim against the government as required in such a seizure/forfeiture case. It was becoming apparent that Larry was being punished for owning the equipment.

Although Larry still had received no paperwork or other information from Customs, he finally discovered why Customs had decided to make his life a living hell. The agency, through some wierd thought process, had determined that the equipment Larry was shipping to Algeria was "really" going to Libya. Since Libya is currently on our government's list of less than favorable countries, the equipment was, in Customs opinion, destined to provide comfort to the enemy. Since they couldn't prove that Larry was in any way consorting with the enemy, they couldn't charge him with a crime. Therefore, they did the next best thing.

They took away his livelihood and all his life savings.

The harder Larry tried to get his passport back, the more Customs stonewalled and the more ways Customs found to make Larry cough up more money. Since he couldn't return to Tunisia without a passport, he eventually lost his job. Finally, in desperation, he contacted Senator Phil Gramm and petitioned him for help in securing the return of his passport. Soon thereafter, Larry received a letter from Senator Gramm which enclosed a letter Gramm had received from Customs. Customs advised Senator Gramm that they would return Larry's passport and papers right away. After six months of frustration, Larry had finally found the key that got his passport returned to him. Petition your Senator.

However, the government was not yet through with Larry. A few weeks later he received a "Warning Letter" from the Office of Foreign Assets Control suggesting that Larry "may have" engaged in unlicensed travel to Libya. The letter advised Larry that he was to refrain from unlicensed travel to Libya and that violations of this order could result in penalties of up to $250,000 in fines and 12 years in jail. This was followed by a series of questions regarding his travels to Libya. Failure to answer the questions, he was advised, could result in a $10,000 fine and five years in prison. Since Larry had never traveled to Libya and never intended to, he didn't fill out the questionnaire. Instead, he wrote a letter advising the FAC office of this fact.

Finally, almost a year to the day after breaking into Larry's apartment, the government filed its first official legal action. This action, an "in rem" forfeiture against his equipment was titled, "The United States of America, Plaintiff, v. One Portable Diesel Refining Unit, Its Accessories and Containers." This action served two purposes. First, it gave the government a legal reason for confiscating Larry's property and holding it. Until this "en ren" forfeiture was filed, Customs had no more legal right to hold Larry's property than to jail someone for a year without charging the person with a crime. Second, now that the complaint had been filed, the "defendant equipment" (through Larry) could now defend itself in court.

The government knows it has no case. However, those in charge also know that it will cost Larry at least $100,000 in legal fees to fight this action. And Larry, of course, is bankrupt. However, unlike some of us, Larry is a fighter. He is now attempting to represent himself in court on two different suits. He has filed a Civil Suit against the Customs Service for the illegal seizure of his passport. He is also trying to get the equipment forfeiture lifted so he can recover his life savings. Unfortunately, being in the right means very little in a court of law. So far, most of his petitions have been thrown out of court because of procedural errors in the filing process. Larry is fighting a large contingent of government lawyers who know how to tie things up in court for years. As we will discover later on, exhausting your funds and your patience is one of the greatest weapons the government has in beating the "little guy" into submission. It is used frequently by many of the enforcement agencies.

You may find it hard to believe that any government agency would take such arbitrary action against a citizen of this country. You may believe that Larry must have done "something" to deserve this kind of treatment. I only wish that were true. As you progress through this book, you will understand why government agencies act the way they do. What happened to Larry is typical of the action taken by most government agencies responsible for enforcing regulations, and for a very good reason. Their very existence depends upon such actions.

The wheelchairs that roll off the assembly line in a wheelchair manufacturing plant do not fit the needs of many physically handicapped individuals in this country. While a standard issue wheelchair directly off the assembly line may be perfectly adequate for someone being released from a hospital with a broken leg, it hardly fits the needs of a quadriplegic or even most paraplegics. Therefore, it has fallen upon *Wheelchairs of Berkeley* and other small companies across the country to modify the assembly line wheelchairs so that they can accommodate the individual needs of each physically handicapped person. In most cases, these modifications include the addition of special footrests, or the addition of special reclining backs or similar additions that allow the user some independence. Each person bears a different handicap, so each chair will vary to accommodate these differences. First the individual's needs are assessed, then special parts are ordered from manufacturers, then the parts are attached to the wheelchair based on the assessed need. In a sense, the modifiers work very much like an orthopedic physician does when fitting an individual with an orthopedic device to straighten a deformed leg, or like an orthodontist works when designing individualized retainers to straighten teeth.

This has worked very well for the handicapped individual. He or she can get a wheelchair specifically modified at an affordable price. Small companies like *Wheelchairs of Berkeley* have been able to accomplish this for the handicapped by keeping their costs to a minimum. However, if the Food and Drug Administration has its way, this will no longer be true.

I don't know what the real problem is—maybe the FDA has too many inspectors with not enough to do—but whatever the reason, the FDA suddenly decided to investigate these little companies. Someone, somewhere in the FDA Center for Medical Devices determined that these little wheelchair-modifying companies are manufacturers and, as such, are subject to the relevant FDA regulatory requirements.

Unaware that all this was taking place, *Wheelchairs of Berkeley* went about their business of helping the handicapped deal with the world the rest of us built for them. However, on April 27, 1993, the owners of *Wheelchairs of Berkeley,* Andy and Doe Caytling, received a very loud wake-up call. This wake-up call had the ominous heading "WARNING LETTER." The contents, which I have edited for purposes of brevity, were as follows:

> Dear Mr. and Mrs. Caytling:
>
> During an inspection of your establishment on March 18 through 31, 1993, Investigator Eric W. Anderson of this office found significant violations of the Federal Food, Drug and Cosmetic Act (Act) as they pertain to your wheelchair products, which are devices within the meaning of Section 201(h) of the Act.
>
> Your products are misbranded within the meaning of Section 502(o) of the Act in that they are manufactured in a facility that is not currently registered as required by section 510 of the Act. The products are further misbranded within the meaning of Section 502(o) in that pre-market notifications have not been provided to the Food and Drug Administration in accordance with Section 510k.
>
> Your products are adulterated within the meaning of Section 502(h) of the Act, since they are not manufactured in accordance with Current Good Manufacturing Practice regulations specified in Title 21 Code of Federal Regulations (CFR), Part 820, as follows:

(At this point the "Warning Letter" lists six different Sections of the code that *Wheelchairs of Berkeley* was said to be violating. I won't waste your time with this detailed listing.) The letter continues:

> Additionally, the above stated inspection revealed that your devices are misbranded in that your firm failed to submit information to the Food and Drug Administration as required by the Medical Device Report-

ing (MDR) regulations, as specified in 21 CFR Part 803.

...Within ten days of receipt of this letter you must furnish the written MDR reports for the incidents identified above. You must also submit written reports for each MDR reportable incident...

(Here follow pages of jargon.)

This letter is not intended to be an all inclusive list of deficiencies at your facility. It is your responsibility to assure that all requirements of the Act and regulations are being met. Until these violations are corrected, Federal agencies will be informed that FDA recommends against award of contracts for affected products.

You should take prompt action to correct these violations. Failure to promptly correct these deviations may result in regulatory action without further notice. These actions can include, but are not limited to, seizure, injunction, and/or civil penalties.

The Caytlings were dumbfounded when they received the Warning Letter. They had no idea you could misbrand a wheelchair or why someone would want to. Like you, they had always associated branding with a bunch of cowboys around a campfire heating up the old branding iron. They were also rather surprised to learn that a wheelchair could be adulterated. The fact that they had been accused of doing the adulterating made it all the more bewildering. Like me, they thought the Food and Drug Administration was involved with foods and drugs which, we all know, *can* be adulterated and misbranded (mislabeled?).

However, they knew this was no time to quibble over such unfathomables. The last two paragraphs of the letter made it rather apparent that they would be out of business in short order if they didn't do something and do it quickly. They did the only thing they could do under the circumstances. They called a lawyer.

The Caytlings soon learned that they were the forerunners, the trial balloon so to speak, for the entire wheelchair-modifying industry nationwide. Whatever happens to them, it seems, will happen to their counterparts all over the U.S. There is the distinct possibility that not just the Caytlings, but the entire industry will be put out of business.

As you may have already surmised, the parties that will suffer the most are not the Caytlings or their counterparts around the country. The real losers will be the people who have depended on this industry. In the future, the physically handicapped could be permanently confined to their beds because the costs involved in purchasing wheelchairs "manufactured" to fit their specific handicap will be astronomical.

Eagle Hardware Stores likes to build their retail outlets in areas zoned for warehouse and distribution companies because their activities relate more closely to warehousing and distribution then to typical retail situations. They do not have a great number of people coming to the store at any one time like a retail grocery would. Their principal customers are home improvement buffs and the occasional small contractor. Customers often need something with more capacity than a car to haul their purchases home and some customers even require delivery. This type of retail sales does not fit well within a typical shopping mall environment.

They were delighted, therefore, when they had the opportunity to buy an existing building in the middle of a large area of warehouses and distribution centers. The building they purchased was originally a candy factory that could be converted to an Eagle retail outlet with relative ease. A six lane freeway passed within a few hundred feet of the property, and there were on- and off-ramps at the main cross street close by, making the store quite accessible to their customers. The presence of the freeway and the on- and off-ramps had prompted the construction of three- and four-story office buildings around the freeway. The closest residential area was almost a quarter mile away and was separated from the store site by the freeway and the office buildings.

As required by law, the company filed the required environmental impact statement and acquired the appropriate permits from the city of Bellevue. In the course of constructing the store, the company followed every directive of the city of Bellevue, Washington to the letter. They even chopped off thirty feet at one end of the building to keep the building the required fifty feet away from a recently identified "wetlands" on an adjacent property. The store, which was scheduled to open in February of 1993, was nearly completed when the company was served with a court injunction ordering the company to cease and desist any further activity.

The injunction, it turned out, was issued at the behest of a group of citizens who call themselves Bellevue Residents Opposed to Illegal Land use (BROIL). In reality, BROIL consisted of a small group of homeowners that lived in the residential area on the other side of the freeway and the office buildings. It was the contention of BROIL that the store was going to increase traffic in their neighborhood, attract additional retail stores and lower property values. (Obviously, none of the BROIL members were interested in home improvement.)

It had been part of the permit process to study how the store would affect traffic patterns in the area, and this study determined that the store would increase traffic on the neighborhood's through streets by 2% or 3% on Saturdays but would have no impact on other days of the week. The store would have absolutely no impact on other streets in the neighborhood. A second study, demand by BROIL, came to the same conclusion.

The second and third objections were found to be equally invalid. As for the second objection, there is no place to accommodate any additional retail stores in the area nor has there been any retail companies that have expressed any interest in opening a store in the area.

The third objection, when viewed at face value, can be considered little more than a hoax. The six-lane freeway might impact the value of the homeowners' property because of the noise and traffic congestion it creates. The proximity of the three- and four-story office buildings may have a little impact. The movement of large trucks in and out of the area from the many wholesale and distribution companies could possibly wrinkle an eyebrow or two. However, in light of the above, to suggest that one retail store is going to lower property values is ludicrous. Such an addition to the neighborhood is more likely to enhance property values.

Unfortunately, an injunction such as this can be very expensive. Every day that their store opening was delayed cost Eagle $9,000. That's $63,000 per week or $270,000 per month. Under the circumstances, Eagle decided to appease BROIL rather than enter into a protracted court battle. They agreed to file another environmental impact statement and, in addition, agreed to pay for $530,000 in additional traffic control improvements in the area. Their goal, obviously, was to get the project on its way once again.

However, it soon became apparent that BROIL's real concerns were not traffic problems or property values. They just plain didn't want the Eagle Hardware store at all, not under any circumstances. The organization filed an Administrative Appeal in court requesting a permanent injunction against the store opening. Eagle had just wasted $530,000 on unnecessary civic improvements. Their store still isn't open.

As we continue our voyage through the labyrinth of confusing government regulations, you will discover just how effective special interest groups have been in imposing their will and how unconcerned they are about robbing you of your constitutional rights whenever it serves their purpose.

When Bob Carpenter and his wife Edna purchased their home in 1971 they had no idea this purchase would become their worst nightmare twenty years later. They had, after all, purchased the house in anticipation of being able to spend their sunset years in the peace and quiet of the pleasant little valley just outside of Livermore, California.

The house the Carpenters bought was an old ranch house that had been constructed in 1928, some 43 years previous to their purchase. At the time the Carpenters purchased the home, they were advised by the current owners that there was a riveted steel tank buried in the backyard about 7 feet from the house. The tank, Bob was told, had held diesel fuel which was used to heat the house many years ago. They further advised Bob that the tank was no longer in service and that it hadn't been in service since 1932, when the current owners had moved into the house. (We're talking sixty years ago.)

Bob's first mistake was remembering that the tank was buried in the ground behind his house.

The people who sold Bob the house also advised him that they had kept track of the level of diesel fuel in the tank since 1954, and that the level had remained constant. Bob decided to continue measuring the level of diesel fuel in the tank periodically to make sure the tank didn't start to leak. During the ensuing thirty-seven years between 1954 and 1991, the level in the tank remained constant. No diesel fuel was lost, even through evaporation, much less through leakage.

Bob discovered that the area above the tank had been used as a parking place for cars for over forty years. This action, of course, was allowing oil and gasoline from the cars to drip onto the soil above the tank. Bob, being a somewhat environmentally concerned individual, didn't like the idea of the soil being contaminated with oil and gasoline so he decided to cement over the area where the cars were being parked. However, before doing this, he decided it would be expedient to remove the tank. After all, once the cement pad was poured, the tank would be rather inaccessible.

This was Bob's second mistake.

Bob hired a contractor to remove the tank and, in the process, met his first government employee. The result of this meeting was the requirement that Bob file a ten-page report with the county health department specifying exactly how the tank was going to be removed and where it would be disposed of. It also required that soil samples be taken and sent to a laboratory for analysis. Poor, innocent Bob had no idea what ramifications this last request would have.

Not only had automobiles been dripping oil and gasoline onto the ground above the tank for forty years, but rain runoff from the paving in front of the garage had been carrying oil, gasoline and transmission fluid to this same area ever since the first car was parked there in 1928. The soil sample, quite naturally, showed that the soil contained petroleum hydrocarbons. The Health Department assumed that the petroleum hydrocarbons had come from the tank and, based on that faulty assumption, issued its next edict. Bob was now required to dig down three feet below where the bottom of the tank once sat, remove all this soil and then take some additional samples. All these samples came back negative. There was no sign of petroleum hydrocarbons in the soil three feet below where the tank had sat. Bob heaved a sigh of relief. It had cost him an *additional* $8,300 to remove the extra three feet of soil and have the samples tested, but it was worth it. At least now he could pave over the area with a clear conscience. Or at least he could proceed with the paving just as soon as the Health Department signed off that the project was completed. Bob waited for a year but heard nothing from the Health Department. Finally, in desperation, he contacted the agency and asked them to close his file so he could get on with his cement-laying project.

This was Bob's third mistake.

In response to his request, Bob received a letter from the Health Department stating that there was still concern that some contamination might have reached the water table beneath his property. Therefore, he was being required to start a new sampling program. This program would require that sample holes be drilled all the way down to the water table and that samples be taken every five feet. The agency also required that he hire a reputable environmental consultant to oversee this entire project. When Bob added up the costs of this new requirement, he knew he was in trouble. The cost of removing this small tank was now exceeding the current value of his house. The Health Department never provided a reasonable explanation of how it was possible for the diesel fuel to travel all the way down to the water table without leaving traces of diesel fuel in the three feet of soil directly under the tank that had already been sampled and found free of diesel fuel.

The original project had nearly exhausted his savings. He did not have the funds required to undertake this additional testing. His only resource was the house and he could neither refinance or sell the house until the project was completed. He was tempted to just walk away from his retirement home. However, in a last ditch effort to salvage his dream, he hired a lawyer. Three years after his ordeal started, the situation is still unresolved.

When John Poszgai left the oppression of Communism in his

home country of Hungary, everyone assured him that when he reached the United States, he would be in the land of the free. He was aware, as we all are, that acts such as murder, robbery, and other violent crimes are forbidden acts, even in a free country. However, it was impossible for him to understand that it can be a serious crime in his new "free" country to improve a piece of property that you own. After all, even in Communist Hungary, this is not a crime. It was his failure to believe that such a ridiculous law could exist in such a "free" country that ultimately got John in big trouble.

People from the nearby town had been dumping their trash on the fourteen acres that John bought, and had been doing so for many years. In all those years, no person and no government agency had said a word to any of these dumpers, even though the dumping was blocking an intermittent waterway. John had great expectations for the property, and immediately begin removing the years of rubbish the town had donated to the property. This included, among other things, 7,000 old tires. Once the area was clean of trash, John's next project was to cover over all the contaminated soil with a fresh cover of clean soil.

Unbeknownst to John, while he was busy cleaning his property, the Bush administration was busy redefining the meaning of a "wetland." Once the new definition was in place, certain government employees were assigned responsibility to reassess the area to determine what new property could now be declared a "wetlands." One such employee spotted John's freshly cleaned property and thought it would make a lovely new "wetlands." John was advised that his property was now a "wetlands" and, as such, he would have to get a permit if he wanted to continue improving his property. John looked all over his property but could not find a "wetlands" anywhere. Therefore, he refused to believe there was a "wetlands" and refused to get the permit. This is, after all, the land of the free. Isn't it?

Despite several warnings, John held firm to his beliefs. To the regulators, however, he was just an obnoxious law breaker that needed to be punished, not just for failing to get a permit, but for his attitude. John was marched off to court where he was fined $202,000 and sent to jail for three years. That's a very big price to pay for wanting to clean up an old dump and revitalize a piece of property that had been abused for years. In viewing similar cases, one can only assume that the major portion of the sentence was meted out, not for his violation of the law, but for his insistence that his property was not a "wetlands" and, therefore, did not require a permit.

Many would agree with John. Even some of the most avid environmentalists. For instance, a reporter for the "Audubon Magazine," when shown around the property, wanted to know where the "wetlands" was. However, the crowning blow in the John Poszgai saga came when the case was appealed to the Supreme Court. At that time the Solicitor General of the United States admitted that the prosecutor in the case had lied to the jury and had misrepresented some evidence (a photograph) in his attempt to get a conviction.

Welcome to the land of the free, John.

William Gorsk, his wife and their three children, two boys ages fifteen and thirteen, and a daughter ten, have been crammed into a small, one bedroom residence on their twenty acre ranch for many years. The only thing that enabled them to keep their sanity was the knowledge that, in the near future, they would be able to build their dream home on their land. When they finally saved enough money to begin construction on their new home, William, with a song in his heart, applied for a permit with the county.

However, things had changed appreciably since William had built the first small house on their property. While he was busy saving money to build a larger house, the Fish and Wildlife Service had been busy taking control of 78,000 acres of land in the area. The Fish and Wildlife Service had determined that this 78,000 acres was the home of the Stephen's kangaroo rat, an endangered or threatened species. Since there is no specific criteria for declaring a plant or animal "endangered" or "threatened," this is a relative simple job. However, it made life anything but simple for William. His twenty acres fell within the 78,000 acres being protected.

The County advised William that it could not issue him a permit to build on this now sacred land and, furthermore, that any activity that might injure the rodent could bring about as much as $100,000 in fines and some jail time. William, obviously, was not a happy camper. His only option, he was advised, was to spend upwards of $5,000 to hire a biologist to survey his property. If the biologist found his property to be rat free, William would be allowed to develop his property if he paid the government "mitigating fees." The "mitigating fees," he discovered, amounted to about $40,000 which the government would use to purchase land elsewhere for a rat preserve.

The Gorsks are still in their tiny, one bedroom house, but their dream is gone. What's more, they are trapped. Property values have plummeted and "For Sale" signs surround their property. Any hopes of selling the ranch and buying a larger home have gone down a rat hole. Their home is almost valueless.

There are currently about 800 species of plants and animals on the endangered species list and another 3300 are under consideration. Any citizen or group can petition the Fish and Wildlife Service to place a species on the list. In addition, environmental groups such as The Fund for Animals, Defenders of Wildlife, and the Sierra Club Legal Defense Fund have sued the Fish and Wildlife Service to expedite the process.

One might suspect that there is a contest between the agencies that control the Clean Water Act (which identify "wetlands") and the agencies that control the Endangered Species Act, to see which agencies can take control of the most private property in the shortest period of time.

The mere existence of laws and government agencies that can inflict such severe punishment on citizens of the United States who have committed no crime is unsettling. The fact that agencies carry out this deprivation upon individuals and small businesses with such careless abandon and with such a lack of concern for the rights of these people is extremely discomforting. The knowledge that our only recourse against these injustices is through a court of law is terrifying, as the courts have yet to find such abuses of enough significance to stop the agencies from plying their reign of terror.

However, the most alarming prospect we must all face is the change in attitude that has taken place in the last few years. The George Bush administration mentality brought with it the perception that the best way to prevent any potential violations of regulations is to make any such activity a crime punishable to the full extent of the law. Their perception is that the prospect of a jail sentence is a great deterrent in the breaking of any regulations. Judges, who previously questioned whether moving a shovel full of dirt in a "wetlands" should be considered a crime, were encouraged to "kill the bastards." This is why, during the forty-plus years environmental laws have been on the books, 94% of all fines and penalties and 69% of all jail time for environmental violations has occurred in the last four years.

As a result of this change in attitude, courts have meted out severe sentences, even to those who were not aware they were violating an environmental regulation. The fact that you meant no harm or did no harm by moving a shovelful of dirt from one side of your yard to another, no longer protects you from receiving the most severe penalty permitted by law.

In 1994, the U.S. Sentencing Commission will hand down a new set of environmental guidelines. One of the advisers to this Commission, Jonathan Turley, recently wrote in the "Wall Street Journal" that "Environmental criminal penalties punish individuals and corporations by correctly labeling them as criminals. Nothing serves to concentrate the business mind more than a potential prison stint, even a brief one."

However, the worst is yet to come. Representative Schumer is, at the time of this writing, ready to reintroduce his own environmental crime bill. His bill would increase the penalty for violating certain environmental crimes to as high as $1 million and prison terms as long as fifteen years. In addition, his bill would permit enforcement agencies to award bounties of as much as $10,000 to citizens who turn in violators. This bounty system should certainly help neighbors get along with each other.

Until the Bush administration, criminal sanctions were reserved for protecting persons and their property. Now criminal sanctions are used whenever there is an affront to weeds, rocks or mountains. Human life has taken a back seat to every aspect of our natural surroundings.

If Representative Schumer has his way, it will be a greater crime to dump a wheelbarrow full of dirt onto your own property than to rape a woman or to open fire with an Uzi on a playground full of school children. With a $10,000 bounty available, we will have the "Salem witch hunts" all over again. Only this time the "hunt" will be nation wide and the victims will be the very people and small businesses who keep this country afloat.

In the next chapter, we will discover how this came to be.

CHAPTER 2

The Nature of the Law

"Power will intoxicate the best hearts, as wine the strongest heads. No man is wise enough, nor good enough to be trusted with unlimited power."

Charles Caleb Colton

"Justice is a commodity which in a more or less adulterate condition the State sells to the citizen as a reward for his allegiance, taxes and personal service."

Ambrose Bierce

While all of God's other creatures seemed to get along very well just obeying the laws of nature, man has not been so fortunate. Because man is a social animal, every human culture on earth has found it necessary to develop a set of rules to govern what that culture considers to be unacceptable behavior. These rules must be obeyed by all the members of that culture except, strangely enough, some of the leaders. Anyone who violates the rules of the culture is administered some form of "punishment," which is also generally administered by the "leaders." In the early days, these rules or "laws" were relatively simple. For the most part, the rules or "laws" adopted by different cultures around the world were very similar from culture to culture, even though most cultures had no contact with others. The "forbidden acts" were all basically the same. "Thou shalt not" kill another person or steal from another person or covet another person's spouse or, basically, do anything to another person that you wouldn't want done to you.

Everything was rather simple and straightforward.

These basic laws or "truths" have run like a river through virtually every society that ever existed on earth. No society has ever permitted one person to wantonly kill others, or to steal from others, or to commit any of the other "forbidden acts" we are all familiar with. Another common thread among all societies is that whenever the society is "threatened" by an outside entity, that outside entity is identified as an "enemy" and the rules are changed. The society then determines that killing this outside entity and stealing from it are not only okay but are often necessary. The society creates a "Government" to take care of such unpleasantness. Under the banner of a "government," the society can then kill, rape and pillage the enemies of the society with a clear conscience.

The problem that continually arises, however, is determining what constitutes a "threat" and determining who the "enemy" is. In some societies the enemy may be anyone who worships a different God, while in another society it may be someone with different colored eyes or different colored skin. Certainly, anyone who speaks a different language must be approached with great caution. In societies ruled by a single person, such as a kingdom, a monarchy or dictatorship, the "threat" and, thus, the "enemy" can be anyone within or without the boundaries of the society who disagrees with "management." In those places where the citizens of the society have no power, the citizens themselves are often the enemy and are summarily put to death for such vile acts as disagreeing with those in power.

So we now have two sets of rules. We have one set of rules to govern our behavior towards those people who are members of our society and a different set of rules to govern our behavior towards those people who are perceived as threats to our society.

In every society, it seems, there must be leaders and these leaders are responsible for carrying out the societal functions previously discussed. The first function, that of protecting the society from external enemies, gives the leader(s) command over the society's enforcement group (generally labeled "army" or "police," etc.). The second function gives the leader(s) control over the actions of all individuals living within that society. It is in the exercise of this second function that leadership seems to go to extremes.

With leadership comes power and, as Henry Kissinger so succinctly pointed out, power is an aphrodisiac, and absolute power is the ultimate aphrodisiac. Since the beginning of recorded history, every known leader, even the most benevolent, has been unable to resist this aphrodisiac and has eventually abused his or her power. This is particularly true when one individual assumes power and there are no safeguards to protect the members of society from the abuses of the leader. The leader can, at his or her whim, decree any law. Since the leader also controls the "army" or "police," the law must be obeyed. Those not obeying the law suffer the wrath of the leader and whatever punishment the leader decides is appropriate for the "crime." When the leader's abuses become severe enough, civil war ensues and a new set of leaders is set in place. The new leaders then assume power and the cycle begins again.

There are two important factors one needs to understand at this juncture. The first factor is that power comes from two sources. The ability to make laws and the ability to enforce these laws. The only purpose of a law is to control human behavior and, with the passage of every law, the leader gains more power. The second factor that must be understood is that leaders become leaders because they crave power. Left to their own devices, every leader is going to gather more and more power by passing more and more laws.

Unfortunately, with the passage of every law, the leadership gains power at the expense of the members of society. With every law, the citizens lose a few more rights and a little more freedom. Regardless of how benevolent and well-intentioned the leadership might be, with every law there is a transfer of control from the members of society to those in leadership roles. As human societies have evolved, the people within these societies have come to realize that they cannot leave their fate totally in the hands of their leaders and expect to be treated fairly. They have discovered that they must have some control over their own destinies and can only do this by placing some limits on those in power.

Some of the most basic human rights currently enjoyed by citizens of the United States originally came from a place called Runnymeade in the year 1215. It was here that King John was held at swordpoint until he signed the Magna Carta, a document which guaranteed the people of England some very basic human rights. While the Magna Carta provided the citizens of England with many basic rights, it did not establish an effective means of preventing the leadership from finding ways around the restrictions placed upon them. Before long, England's leaders were again abusing their powers. Nowhere was this abuse more extensive than in their abuse of overseas colonies. Our Revolutionary War was a result of this abuse of power.

The framers of our Constitution were very aware of the history of abuses by leaders and were determined that it should not occur in the newly-formed union of colonies. They were well aware of the Magna Carta and the formation of the English Parliament and the English Bill of Rights of 1689. In developing a Constitution they drew upon such sources as Greek philosophy and the Roman Republic as well as the evolution of the English democratic process. They embraced the writings of such philosophical giants of the seventeenth and eighteenth centuries as Rousseau, Kant, Voltaire, Locke and Hume.

It is apparent to anyone who takes the time to study the discussions that took place during the development of the Constitution of the United States that one thing was foremost in everybody's mind: the protection of the individual from the tyranny of government. While recognizing that government was a necessary evil, they did everything they could to eliminate unnecessary governmental powers and, further, to divide the remaining powers so no one individual or branch of government would gain too much power.

First on their agenda was the separation of the law makers from the law enforcers. By separating the power to make laws from the power to enforce laws, it was believed that there would be less likelihood of either power being horribly abused. Our forefathers were also knowledgeable enough to know that both entities would try to abscond with powers granted to the other and, of more importance, try to take power away from the citizens. In an effort to keep these abuses to a minimum, our founders created a third branch, the Judiciary. The Judiciary was created, in part, to resolve disputes between the law-making and law-enforcing branches. However, the crafters of the Constitution made it abundantly clear that the most important responsibility of the Judiciary was to protect the rights of the individual citizens of this country from government abuses.

When the Constitution was finally in place, the following "checks" and "balances" had been established:

THE EXECUTIVE (PRESIDENT)
POWERS

- Approves or vetoes federal bills
- Carries out (enforces) federal law
- Appoints judges and other high officials
- Makes foreign treaties
- Can issue pardons and reprieves to federal offenders

- Acts as Commander-and-Chief of armed forces

CHECKS

- Congress can override vetoes by two-thirds vote
- Senate can refuse to confirm appointments or ratify treaties
- Congress can impeach and remove the President
- Congress can declare war
- Supreme Court can declare executive acts unconstitutional

THE LEGISLATURE (CONGRESS)
POWERS

- Passes federal laws
- Establishes lower federal courts & number of federal judges
- Can override the President's veto with a two-thirds vote

CHECKS

- Presidential veto of federal bills
- Supreme Court can rule laws unconstitutional
- Both houses of Congress must vote to pass a law

THE JUDICIARY (SUPREME COURT)
POWERS

- Interprets and applies the law by trying federal cases
- Can declare laws passed by Congress and executive actions unconstitutional

CHECKS

- Congress can propose constitutional amendments to override court decisions (if ratified by three-fourths of the states)
- Congress can impeach and remove judges
- The President appoints and Congress confirms judges

Many scholars who have studied the discussions that took place during the development of the Constitution of the United States believe that the framers of the Constitution felt that government had only one purpose. That purpose was to protect the rights of the individual. Certainly, if this was not the sole purpose of the Constitution, it was the main purpose. However, as one might expect, those in power have had a different agenda.

The individuals who have assumed leadership roles in the United States have now had a little over 200 years in which to find ways to circumvent the Constitution, and they have done an excellent job. During those years Congress has managed to pass several million laws. While some of those laws have been aimed at curtailing the activities of the executive branch of government (especially if the President is from an opposing political party), most have been directed at taking rights away from you and me. While the Supreme Court has held some of the acts of Congress in check, it has done little to stop the erosion of certain of our civil rights.

In his book, *Grand Theft And Petit Larceny: Property Rights In America,* Mark L. Pollot does an excellent job of pointing out how government has managed to acquire the physical property or services of hundreds of thousands of citizens in direct violation of the Fifth and Fourteenth amendments to the Constitution. Unfortunately, this action has been taken with the consent of the Judiciary. Why the Judiciary has allowed the other two branches of government to tromp all over our individual rights will be discussed in more detail in the next chapter. This is a key issue in your battle against unjust regulations.

It is the perception of most people, I am sure, that laws are in place to prohibit an individual or group of individuals from doing something that causes harm to another. Just as in days of yore, we tend to assume that modern day laws are in place to prohibit such acts as murder, assault, theft, mayhem, rape, etc., and to mete out punishment to those who undertake such acts against others. We all want protection from the violent individuals in our society and we want those who insist on injuring, maiming, killing or stealing from others to be punished and/or removed from society. We expect no less from our leaders.

Most of us are aware that our leaders have stepped far beyond these simple measures in controlling what individuals can and can't do to other members of society. Congress has attempted to protect us from our naiveté by making it illegal for others to defraud us, whether it be through some money making scheme or by making false claims about a product or by taking advantage of our lack of expertise in a particular area. (However, Congress has never prohibited itself from defrauding the public.)

Taking things a step, further, Congress has also decided that it must protect us from ourselves. Laws prohibiting the use of drugs, laws against suicide and similar laws are examples of our leaders' perception that we are unable to make appropriate decisions about our own personal lives.

Then there are the nuisance laws. These are laws that prohibit us from being a nuisance to our neighbors. If your neighbor doesn't like the smoke from your barbecue or the color of your house or where you wash your car you could very well be a nuisance to your neighbor. It is in this area that our Legislators have found a virtual bonanza for controlling our lives and our property. As Mark Pollot points out in his book, *Grand Theft and Petit Larceny*, it is the provision of nuisance laws where Congress has made great strides in depriving us of those rights granted us under the fifth and fourteenth amendments to the Constitution.

For the first one hundred or more years after the founding of our country, most Americans lived on farms or in other rural environments where several miles separated one neighbor from another. There was little likelihood that the activities of one person was going to be bothersome to another. Even if someone did something that troubled a neighbor, the disagreement was generally resolved between the two without interference from the government.

During the last 100 years or so, there has been a growing migration of people from rural environments to the bright lights of the city. Apparently these people did not bring with them a tolerance for close neighbors or an ability to settle their differences without an outside referee. Rather than working with their neighbors to settle their differences, they turned to government. Those in power were delighted to oblige.

In an effort to keep our pesky neighbors under control, Americans willingly gave up more of freedoms and more property rights. While the numbers of felonious crimes one can commit are rather limited, (murder, rape, assault, theft, etc.), the number of nuisances one can commit are almost limitless. After all, it is almost impossible to function in this world without irritating someone. For those in power the opportunity to control nuisances is irresistible. Any time one group complains about a particular action taken by another group, those in power are happy to draft a law prohibiting such action. With each new law they gain additional power while each of us loses a little more freedom and has less rights to the use of our property.

With our permission, government grew at a phenomenal rate as it attempted to take action against those of us who created a situation that our neighbors considered a nuisance. In some cases we even encouraged those in power to decide what a nuisance is and what to do about it. Now we were not only losing more freedoms and losing more use of our property, we were also being hit rather severely in our pocketbooks. Creating new government agencies to enforce new laws is not cheap. Take it from someone who ran such a government agency for a number of years.

However, it was not until the advent of "Enabling Legislation" that government found a way to take a sledgehammer to the Constitution and pound it into a bloody pulp. It was with "Enabling Legislation" that Congress, hand-in-hand with the executive branch of government, was able to secure tremendous power. With "Enabling Legislation" government could, at the whim of those in power, control the actions of every single business and every single person in this country.

You will note that to this point we have made no mention of Larry Duncan, Bob Carpenter, the Caytlings, John Poszgai, Eagle Hardware, or the Gorsk family. You would think, considering what happened to them, they must have committed some rather serious crimes. However, you will not find the laws they have violated among the laws we have already discussed. This is because they have not committed a crime against their fellow man. They have not even created a nuisance. Their only crime was that the government suspected that they might commit a nuisance at some point in the future. It was this suspicion that cost Larry his livelihood and life savings, Bob his house, threatened to put the Caytlings out of business, has kept the Eagle project on hold for over a year, threw John in jail and took the Gorsk family's dream away.

Enabling Legislation

For obvious reasons, people have a difficult time discerning the difference between other forms of law and "Enabling Legislation." However, it is critical that the differences be crystal clear in your mind, so bear with me as I try to explain the concepts.

To this point we have been discussing laws where government is only allowed to take action against you if you commit a felony or nuisance against another member of society. Commit a crime against your fellow human and suffer the consequences. Kill someone and you will be arrested, tried by a jury of your peers and, if found guilty, punished. Create a nuisance, and you will be cited. If you don't think you are guilty, you can ask for a trial or, if you don't want to be bothered with a trial, you can forfeit bail (or, as most of us think of it, pay a fine).

Regardless of what you do, government can take no action against you until you have committed an illegal act against another and are arrested (or cited) for this transgression. At that point, you are entitled to a trial before a jury of your peers who will determine your guilt or innocence. If your crime is of a very minor nature, you may choose to forfeit your right to a trial and forfeit bail (pay a fine) and go on about your life. The two things to remember here is that (1) government is not allowed to take any action against you until you commit the transgression and (2) you are innocent until proven guilty before a jury of your peers.

Enabling Legislation deprives you of these two very basic rights. By means of Enabling Legislation, a government entity can take action against you on the suspicious that you might commit a transgression against another human or the environment or whatever, *not that you have committed a transgression, but that you* might *commit a transgression.* As we move along, the full significance of this will become staggeringly apparent. It is difficult to grasp in its entirety in just one sitting.

When you can be punished for something a government agency thinks you might do, three things become obvious. First, you can now be punished for a crime you didn't commit and probably never will commit. John Carpenter, for instance, was punished because the government agency decided he might contaminate the water table. However, there was no evidence that a water table existed under his property or that it was contaminated. Even if those two conditions had occurred, the preponderance of evidence indicated that the diesel fuel tank was not the source of the petroleum hydrocarbons found in his soil samples.

The second tragedy of Enabling Legislation is that you are no longer considered innocent until you are proven guilty. And the third tragedy is that you are judged guilty without benefit of a trial by a jury of your peers.

I have no idea who originated this new form of legislation, I only know what it does. In simple terms, Enabling Legislation allows Congress to express an "intent" and then can order the enforcing agency to write the regulations necessary to carry out this "intent." As an example, some years back Congress passed a law that gave the Environmental Protection Agency the authority to write any regulations it deemed necessary to carry out the "intent" of the law. In this case, the intent of the law was to "protect the environment." This opened up an incredible can of worms.

Depending on one's perception of "the environment," anything we do has an impact on it. Mowing your lawn, sweeping your porch, building your house, riding your bike, eating a meal, growing food, making clothing, and breathing the air all have an impact. Because we are living creatures, everything we do impacts the environment in one way or another.

With Congressional approval, the Administrator of the Environmental Protection Agency had the power to write any regulations deemed necessary to protect the environment. If, as Administrator of the Environmental Protection Agency you, in your wisdom, decide that humans are not a natural part of the environment, you may determine that any human activity "threatens" the environment. You now have the power to decide what things and what actions "might" have a negative influence on your new charge. You may now prohibit businesses and people from taking any actions that have the "potential" of creating a problem. It is the words "might" and "potential" that have played such a big role in how the intent of the law has been carried out.

In an effort to make things crystal clear, let me provide a simple analogy. For this purpose, lets assume that Congress has mandated that you write and enforce any regulations you deem necessary to prevent the use of guns in the commission of a murder. Your mandate is to create a society where zero killings take place through the use of guns. Your first thought, most likely, will be to ban all guns. However, with further evaluation, you come to the realization that this will turn out to be a fruitless task. Since guns are manufactured in countries all over the world, the likelihood of stopping guns from being smuggled into this country and used by those intent on killing another are virtually nil. Therefore, you decide to take a totally different approach. You decide to identify those people who are likely to commit murder and toss them in jail before they have a chance to commit the crime. Toward this end, you contract with some research institute to identify those characteristics commonly found in murderers and then write regulations making these characteristics illegal. With the authority granted you by Congress, you now have the power to jail any person having any or all of the identified characteristics of a murderer.

Some of these characteristics might be rather obvious: hired assassins for instance. Many murders could be prevented by jailing hired assassins before they commit their crimes. The odds are pretty good that you would stop some murders by jailing these individuals. However, your scientific resource also points out that the rate of murder in the inner city ghettos is three times the rate of murder in the suburbs. Perhaps only one person in a thousand who lives in an inner city ghetto will commit a murder but, since you have no idea which of those people will eventually commit murder, your only option for preventing these murders is to jail everyone living there. Now this might seem a little drastic, but how else is one to prevent murders from taking place in the ghettos? The fact that 999 innocent people will be jailed to prevent that one person from committing a murder can be justified based upon your mandate from Congress. The power to take this action is found in the regulations you wrote under the authority of the "Enabling Legislation" which mandates that you prevent all current and future murders that might be committed through the use of guns.

Obviously, not all murders by gun occur in ghettos, nor are all such murders committed by persons living in ghettos. Your research institute, in reviewing the statistics on murders by gun, discovers that one in every three murders is committed by someone with blue eyes. To carry out your mandate successfully, you must now jail everyone with blue eyes. Next, the institute discovers that three out of every four murders are committed by males, etc. And so it goes. You soon discover that almost everyone has one or more of the characteristics the research institute has discovered can lead to the possible commission of a murder. As administrator of this program, you must decide where to draw the line. Should you risk allowing those people to go free where the odds are one in a thousand that they will commit a murder? What about those where the odds are one in a million that they will commit a murder? If you fail to take action against a particular trait (such as blue eyes) and a person with blue eyes commits a murder, have you failed to carry out your mandate?

You are probably thinking right about now that this entire discussion is ridiculous. I only wish you were right. However, this is the same thought process that has gone into the development of many of the regulations that are being enforced today. Mandates such as the one cited above can be found everywhere. We have already mentioned the Environmental Protection Agency which has a mandate to prevent you and me from damaging the environment. Mandates have also been issued to Health Departments and the EPA to "protect the Public Health"; to the Occupational Health and Safety Administration to prevent "work related injuries"; to the California Coastal Commission to "protect the California Coast line"; to various Building Departments of cities and counties to prevent "poor construction of buildings"; and to thousands of Water Quality Boards or Commissions whose job it is to protect "water supplies" or "natural water ways." The list is almost endless.

Each of these agencies has a mandate from Congress or some other legislative entity to "prevent" some occurrence from taking place. On the surface, this sounds relatively reasonable. However, we just need to look at what we had to go through to prevent a murder from taking place through the use of a gun to understand that preventing an event from taking place is like chasing your tail. It is going to happen somewhere, sometime, regardless of how many regulations you write or how many people you throw in jail. Certainly you may be able to prevent some of these murders from taking place by jailing all those with the "characteristics" of a murderer. But at what price? How many innocent people must be jailed to prevent one murder?

Bob Carpenter is likely to lose his house because the California Water Commission and its regulatory arm, the Health Department, have decided that the removal of the tank in his backyard "might" contaminate a water supply. The agencies have made this determination even though all the evidence indicates that there is no possibility this could happen. However, even proving that the tank will not contaminate any water supply does not relieve Bob from the regulatory process. The regulations give the inspectors from the Health Department the authority to require whatever they deem necessary to ensure that the water supply will *never* be affected by the removal of that tank. If Bob goes bankrupt in the process, the agency will tell you that's an unfortunate but necessary part of protecting the public water supply.

Prior to the advent of "Enabling Legislation," the Health Department would have been required to afford Bob the same legal procedures accorded a murderer or a rapist. The Health Department would have first needed to determine that a crime had, indeed, been committed. In this case, they would need to determine that a water supply had been contaminated. They would then need to trace the contamination back to its source which, in this case, wouldn't have been Bob. Once the crime is discovered and the culprit identified, the Health Department would then be required to take the perpetrator before a jury of his or her peers for trial, just like we do for those who commit violent crimes against people. In Bob's case, they would have needed to determine that a water supply had been contaminated and then they would be required to trace this contamination back to Bob's diesel fuel tank. With "Enabling Legislation" the government doesn't need to discover that a crime has been committed in order to destroy someone's life.

Andy and Doe Caytling had been modifying wheelchairs for the handicapped for many years without creating any problems and without regulation from the Food and Drug Administration. However, the Food and Drug Administration decided that, since the Caytlings had many years of experience with the handicapped and the FDA had none, the handicapped would be much safer if the Caytlings operated under the detailed scrutiny of their organization. Therefore, the FDA, under the provisions of regulations they wrote themselves, labeled the Caytlings' operation as a manufacturing process that must comply with all the same regulations that any manufacturing plant is required to follow. No handicapped individual was ever harmed because of the Caytlings' operation nor was it necessary that the FDA determine that someone was. The FDA just had to decide that someone "might" be harmed at some future date. If the Caytlings are forced out of business because they must comply with very expensive regulations, the FDA decision could very well harm all the physically handicapped people in the United States. The FDA will tell you, however, that their action was necessary to prevent someone from getting hurt.

John Poszgai, of course, was the victim of a different form of "labeling." Just like Bob Carpenter's situation, nobody was able to demonstrate to him or to the reporters covering his situation just where the "wetlands" was or what damage his activities were doing to the newly labeled "wetlands." Nevertheless, the new label meant that John's property was now covered by regulations that required that his activities be supervised by one of the regulatory agencies. However, unlike Bob Carpenter, John decided to defy the ridiculous regulations and continue improving his property. This made John a criminal. Therefore, he was entitled to not just go bankrupt like Bob but he was also entitled to three years in the "pokey." We are still trying to find the "wetlands." John did not commit a crime against the environment. However, he did raise the ire of a powerful agency and this can be the greatest "crime" of all.

Eagle Hardware had to deal with a multitude of regulations and dealt with them well. They paid for and filed an "environmental impact statement" as required and met the requirements of zoning laws, building codes, health regulations and environmental regulations. They met the requirements of every law on the books even though many were unnecessary and others were downright repressive. However, despite their perfect record, the government allowed a private citizens' group with their own special agenda to take control of Eagle's property. The citizens group has been allowed to do this without fear of retribution. This country is in deep trouble when one neighbor can accuse another of a crime and the accused can be found guilty without an investigation or a trial.

While we may not be very tolerant of a government agency that throws a person in jail on "suspicion of being a potential murderer" we seem to tolerate a person's property rights being taken from him or her on the presumption that the person will misuse the property. We have tolerated the EPA's restrictions on the use of property on the assumption that it might be used in a fashion that "could adversely affect the environment." We also seem to tolerate the same abuses of our rights to the free use of our property if some agency proclaims that the use "might" endanger the public health, or "adversely impact a natural water source" or whatever other mandate is circulating around the nation at the moment.

There are probably a few of you who are thinking, "what the hell, it can't be that bad." If you think for a minute that it can't, go back and read the beginning of the chapter again. Notice how everyone who has the power to write laws and enforce those same laws always abuses that power. And I don't mean that the person is bad or incompetent. However, even the most benevolent is going to abuse such power. To do less would be to fail to carry out the mandate. When you read the chapter which talks about the enforcement of these regulations, you will understand why severe abuse of power is a natural by product of "Enabling Legislation."

Their Day in Court

Returning once again to your "mandate" from Congress to stop all murders committed with guns, you are going to find that some people are VERY upset at being thrown in jail just because there is one chance in a million that they are the blue eyed person who will commit a murder. They are going to want their day in court, and those with the patience and the money will get their day. However, they should not expect too much from the courts. This person will be tried on the basis of whether he or she is in violation of your regulations, not on whether he did or did not commit a murder. Since your regulations specifically make it a criminal offense to have blue eyes, the person is guilty. The only chance that person has is to prove that he will never commit a murder with a gun. Thus far nobody has been able to prove that an event will not occur at some point in the future. This is the final "catch 22" of the "Enabling Legislation" process.

Sounds ridiculous doesn't it? Yet this is exactly the authority given to all the agencies previously mentioned. The employees of these agencies do not have to prove that you did some form of damage. They only need to prove that you violated one of their regulations. This process does not test whether or not justice has been done. This process does not determine if the regulation was or was not a just regulation. The assumption is that jailing people with blue eyes as potential murderers *is* a just regulation. It is your fault you are in jail. After all, you have blue eyes.

There is no doubt that such a process is in total contradiction with the intentions of the Constitution of the United States. "Enabling Legislation" places far too much power in the hands of the executive branch of government and takes away most of the checks and balances that the Constitution provides for. First, it gives one branch of government the very duplicity of powers that the Framers of the Constitution were so fearful of. "Enabling Legislation" allows an agency in the Executive Branch to write its own regulations and then allows this same agency to enforce them. This is a direct violation of the separation of powers. However, this new form of law takes the process of acquiring power one giant step further.

Since you can be accused of a crime and be found guilty of that crime without benefit of a jury trial, the checks and balances provided by the Judicial Branch of government are also usurped. The actions of the executive branch are no longer subject to review by the Judiciary and it can, therefore, take any action it wants without the prospect of the action being declared inappropriate or unjust by the judicial branch.

The Labeling Game

The final lynch pin in the government's lust for power and in the lost of our rights to freedom, liberty and property comes from another activity called "labeling." Planning departments have used labeling to control how you use your property for years through the use of "zoning laws." You can only use your property for the uses for which it is zoned (read labeled). Although no one has ever been able to demonstrate that zoning laws have improved anything, most of us obediently follow them without question. However, government has now found a way to render your property completely useless with an entirely different set of labels. These "labels" include such things as "wetlands," "endangered species habitat," "coastal environment," etc. By clamping any one of these labels on your property, a mandated government agency can prevent you from using your property for any purpose. We will address this issue in more detail in the next chapter.

The greatest benefactors of "Enabling Legislation," however, are not the Executive Branch of Government but, rather, Congress and the hundreds of special interest groups that have your Congressperson in their pockets. The Framers of the Constitution devoutly wanted to protect the citizens of the United States from the evils that could take place if the majority was allowed to impose its will upon the minorities. Conversely, they did not want a minority of citizens forcing their will upon every other citizen of this country. With the "balance of powers" originally decreed by the Constitution, it was virtually impossible for one group to impose its will on the rest of the nation. However, "Enabling Legislation" has ended all that.

In order to get the needed guarantee that they will stay in office, the members of Congress have discovered that they must cater to the whims of "special interest" groups. As long as they meet the demands of these groups, they are assured of the funds necessary to run for office and of the votes required to get elected. Who can resist such a deal?

Should the United Organization of Cajun Chefs want their cooking protected from impostors, Congress will be happy to provide that protection assuming the group is large enough and well enough endowed financially so it can help a particular Congressman get re-elected. Should the International Association of Persnickety Homeowners want all houses in the U.S. properly landscaped and they have the appropriate financial and membership clout, Congress will give them what they want.

To satisfy the Cajun Chefs, Congress will merely enact "Enabling Legislation," declaring that it is the "intent" of Congress to prevent impostors from cooking Cajun food. Congress will then empower some department within the administrative branch of government to write whatever regulations it deems necessary to carry out this "intent." Likewise, to appease the persnickety homeowners, Congress need only pass "Enabling Legislation," the "intent" of which is to ensure that all houses in America are properly landscaped. The appropriate executive agency is then empowered to write the necessary regulations and enforce them. In many cases, the special interest group forcing their will on the rest of us is also allowed to have a hand in the writing of the regulations. "Enabling Legislation" gives special interests the opportunity to impose their wills on the rest of us.

Congress will most likely tell you that "Enabling Legislation" is good because it permits the development of regulations that could never be passed by both houses of Congress. For instance, it would take Congress 150 years to resolve all the differences of opinion that would occur if both houses tried to reach an agreement on all the tiny wrinkles and details that go into making up the massive amount of regulations being enforced by the EPA. What Congress won't tell you is that this is the exact reason why we have two houses of the Legislature. The Framers of our Constitution didn't want these kinds of knit picking regulations on the books!

Congress loves "Enabling Legislation" for another very important reason. It removes them from the Legislative "hot seat." They can impose legislation without taking responsibility for its outcome. If the regulations imposed by the enforcement agency become so abrasive that a large number of people start revolting, Congress can plea innocent. After all, they did not write those regulations. "Enabling Legislation" allows Congress to abrogate their primary responsibility; writing our laws and taking full responsibility for their outcome.

One would hope that in such an abusive, unconstitutional system there would be some means of finding justice. This is, after all, a country that was built on the premise that every individual has the right to life, liberty and "the pursuit of happiness." You would think that somewhere in this labyrinth of darkness called government there must be a glimmer of hope.

The next few chapters of this book will explore some of the weaknesses in this system of government, how you can recognize these weaknesses, and how you can exploit them. You will also learn how to gather the ammunition you need to "Beat the Devil." In one chapter, you will learn how to react to government inspections of your business or property, what to say and not say, as well as to whom you should and should not talk.

Also, in a different chapter you will learn where you can turn for further assistance if you feel you are being unjustly regulated by any government agency or its representative.

This book is intended only to be a guide and should not be used as a substitute for good legal advice. However, it should give you a good deal of help in evaluating your chances of beating the system and in gathering the information needed to prepare for a possible court case. It should also help you to evaluate the type of background you need from the attorney you want representing you. Your success in and out of court will depend, to a great extent, upon selecting the right attorney

CHAPTER 3

Constitutionally Speaking

"Don't interfere with anything in the Constitution. That must be maintained, for it is the only safeguard of our liberties."

Abraham Lincoln

"From the beginning of our history the country has been afflicted with compromise. It is by compromise that human rights have been abandoned."

Charles Sumner

The perception that it is unconstitutional for the administrative branch of government to devise its own laws and then enforce them is not new. Justice Hugo Black once wrote that, "Since Article I, however, vests 'All Legislative Powers' in the Congress, and no language purports to vest any such power in the President, it necessarily follows, if the Constitution is to control, that the President is completely devoid of power to make laws regulating passports or anything else. And he has no more power to make laws by labeling them regulations than to do so by calling them laws. For Congress to attempt to delegate such undefined law making was (quoting Justice Cardoza) "delegation running riot." No such plenitude of power is susceptible to transfer."

With such profound damnation from a justice of the Supreme Court, you might rightly wonder why Congress flaunts the Constitution and continues to delegate its responsibilities. Part of the problem lies within our court system which has allowed this delegation to proliferate unchallenged. As you will recall, one of the responsibilities given the Judiciary by the Constitution is to declare unconstitutional any inappropriate laws passed by Congress. If the concept of "Enabling Legislation" has been challenged in court, the Judiciary has either chosen to ignore this area of responsibility or has overridden the mandates of the Constitution and declared this form of law making to be acceptable. The Congress could not continue to pass "Enabling Legislation" and the executive branch could not continue to write regulations without permission of the Judiciary. This form of Legislation can only exist if there is a conspiracy among all three branches of government. Should any one of them refuse to cooperate, "Enabling Legislation" would die a natural death.

Unfortunately, you and I must depend upon the courts to protect us from those in government that are determined to strip us of the rights granted us by the Constitution. The courts have done an excellent job of protecting certain of the rights granted us by the Constitution but have been less diligent in protecting other of our rights. For instance, those individuals accused of committing felonies such as murder, rape, assault, armed robbery, etc. are well protected. Not only can they escape prosecution if any one of their Constitutional rights are violated, they will be freed if any small procedural error occurs during their trial. On the other hand, people such as Bob Carpenter, Larry Duncan and our other abused friends have been stripped of almost all their Constitutional rights. They were accused of a crime, found guilty and punished without being able to exercise their most basic right: the right to a fair trial. For allowing such events to occur, the Judiciary cannot be excused.

I want to make it abundantly clear that I am not advocating that those who commit felonies should be thrown in jail, even if their rights are being violated. What I am advocating is that the courts protect *everybody's* rights equally and I want it done without prejudice. However, when I see John Poszgai serving a three year jail sentence for making our environment more pleasant, while a serial killer continues to prey on victims because a procedural error in court has set him free, I know this is not happening.

The reason for this will become more apparent as we work our way through this book. However, for now it is enough to know that some of our courts have viewed this as an issue of the public's interest versus the individual's interests. Where the court senses that there is a conflict between the rights of the individual and the rights of the public, some courts have found in favor of the public. In such cases, the rights of the individual have been sacrificed for the "public good." However, you will note that the courts are only concerned with the public's interest when it comes to violating the rights of the Larry Duncans, Bob Carpenters, Gorsk families, John Poszgais, and Caytlings of this world. The courts seem totally disinterested in the "public good" when it comes to violating the rights of killers and rapists and releasing them into the community. Our goal in this book is to recover the rights of Larry, Bob and the thousands of others who have been equally abused by our current system of government.

Property Rights

As unlikely as it may seem, the avenue to recovering these rights lies in the area of "property rights." This is because it is in this arena that government as been able to attack our individual rights without interference from the courts. It is also in the area of "property rights" that special interest groups have had the greatest influence on Congress.

There are a number of areas within the Constitution and its amendments that address the issue of "property rights" in one fashion or another. The contracts clause of Article 1, section ten of the Constitution; the privileges and immunities clause found in Article IV, Section 2; the privileges and immunities clauses of the Fourteenth Amendment; and the due processes and just compensation clauses of the Fourteenth Amendment all address this issue. However, in an effort to regain our rights, we are going to ignore all these rights guaranteed to us by the Constitution and just focus on one. The one we will focus on is the "just compensation" clause of the Fifth Amendment to the Constitution of the United States.

This clause, often referred to as the "takings clause" is very short and to the point. "Nor shall private property be taken for public use, without just compensation."

The Framers of the Constitution understood that there were times when the government was going to need to take private property in order to carry out its functions. After all, government is responsible for building roads for public transportation, building reservoirs for public water supplies, building training facilities and housing for the country's military forces, etc. As much as the Framers may have wanted to keep property under the protection of private ownership, they knew government had some legitimate needs for owning property. Therefore, they had to "permit" government to "take" private property when a legitimate need arose. However, they wanted to make sure that the owner of this property received "just compensation" for this "taking" of property. Thus came the "taking clause" of the Fifth Amendment, "Nor shall private property be taken for public use, without just compensation."

The reason this provision is so vitally important is found in the interpretation of "property." Over the years the concept of "property" has been tested and retested in our courts. It is now well established that "property" consists of anything you or the government considers to be of value. Therefore, "property" is not just real property, but consists of less obvious things such as contracts and agreements, businesses, personal possessions, and anything else that can be bartered, including services provided to others for a fee. When one examines this interpretation, it becomes obvious that the proper interpretation of the "takings clause" of the Fifth Amendment to the Constitution is vital to everyone's interests. It not only determines that government pay "just compensation" for taking your real property away from you but must compensate you for taking other things of value such as a contract or your business. Likewise, government cannot force you to provide services to the government without compensation. In effect, this interpretation of "property" is a major deterrent in any government effort to take away your property and force you into slavery by making you provide services without compensation.

The *obvious* intent of this provision of the Fifth Amendment is to make sure that the government isn't allowed to arbitrarily steal property from a private citizen, but must pay that person "just compensation" regardless of how much government professes to need the property. However, many believe that this provision also has a *less obvious* but equally important purpose. This belief holds that if the government is required to pay "just compensation" for any property it "takes," it will use better judgment in the "taking" of property and will be less apt to "take" property on a whim. It is further suggested that government will also take better care of property if it must sacrifice something to acquire it.

As we make our way through this chapter we will disclose some of the ways government has found to "take" property from its citizens. We will examine how the "taking" agency views the "taking" and how the courts view such "takings." We will also help you identify which "takings" seem to violate the basic tenets of the Fifth Amendment's "just compensation" provision. Our goal here, is to help you identify situations in which a government action might entitle you to "just compensation" for the action taken against you or your property. The only thing that will ever deter government agencies from "taking" all our property is the fear of having to pay "just compensation" for what they take. Without this threat, there is nothing to stop them from taking it all.

In this chapter, I have relied heavily on the experts in land use law and, most particularly, on Mark Pollot and his book, *Grand Theft And Petit Larceny*. If, after reading this chapter, you feel you have a situation in which your right to free use of your property has been abridged without "just compensation," I strongly urge you to read Mark's book so you can make a more in depth evaluation. If, after reading Mark's book, you continue to feel you are entitled to "just compensation," we present some ideas in later chapters of this book on how you should proceed.

"Taking" Your Property

Government learned a long time ago that you don't need to own a piece of land or own a business outright in order to control its use and its operation. All government needs to do to control land use and business operations is to write regulations giving itself that power. Obviously, the more control the government takes of your property or your business, the less control you have. The less control you have over how your property is used or how your business is run, the less value it has for you. The "just compensation" clause of the Fifth Amendment says that this is a "taking" and you are entitled to "just compensation" for the reduced value of your property or business. However, government has no desire to compensate you for your loss nor does it wish to give up its power. Later on we will discuss some of the methods governments uses to circumvent the "just compensation" clause.

In order to be eligible for "just compensation," something of value must have been "taken" from you by the government. There has been a lot of haranguing in the courts throughout the last 100 years as to what constitutes a "taking." In most cases, the courts have agreed that a "taking" occurs when you are deprived of the full use of your property. Most of the time the courts have agreed that a "taking" has occurred even when you are deprived of the use of part of your property. Also the courts generally agree that a "taking" has occurred if the value of your property decreases as a result of some government action. Again, I must remind you that property has generally been defined as anything of value and can include a business or a contract or, in some cases, a service.

A "taking" can occur in numerous ways. One way would be for government to take over ownership of part or all or your property outright through an offer to purchase or through condemnation procedures. This form of "taking" usually occurs if the government wants to build a road, dam or other physical structure on property you currently own. However, this is not the common form of "taking."

A more common form of "taking" is for the government to prohibit you from carrying out the activities you intended to undertake when you bought the property. You may have, for instance, purchased a piece of property on which to build your home or on which to build a new factory for your business. Suddenly the government decides that you are about to build your home or factory on a chunk of real estate that they have (after the fact) determined to be a "wetlands." Because the government has designated your land as a "wetland" you are not allowed to proceed with your building plans. While the government may, rightly or wrongly, stop you from building your dream home or new factory, it may have to pay you "just compensation" for depriving you of that right. While you still own the property, it is no longer nearly as valuable as it once was. The government may owe you the difference between its value as a home site and its value as a "wetland" as "just compensation" for its ruling.

Government has found a virtual bonanza in this area. Armed with a fistful of labels, various agencies have been interfering with the free use of property everywhere. By identifying a piece of property as a "wetlands," or as "the site of an endangered plant or animal," or as a "national, state or local landmark," or as some other public asset, it can restrict the use of your property to those activities of which the government approves. It was through the exercise of labeling that the government was able to take control of John Poszgai's property and the Gorsk family property. John's property was suddenly labeled a "wetlands" and the Gorsk property was labeled a "habitat" of a threatened or endangered rat.

A government agency may also perform a "taking" by having a negative impact on the production of a business. If government takes an arbitrary action that hampers your ability to produce goods or services at your usual rate, you *may* have a right to "just compensation" for your loss of productivity and income. Many environmental laws fall into this category. This, of course, is the action the FDA used in taking over the operation of the Caytlings' wheelchair modification business. Actually, the FDA first labeled the Caytlings' business a manufacturing firm and then it imposed its control over the operation of the business. The Customs Service used a similar tactic with Larry Duncan. However, in Larry's case Customs didn't even bother to advise Larry of what Customs laws he may have violated. Customs exercised its police authority, and confiscated his property outright without filing a complaint. Should Customs determine that an actual law was broken it might file an action at some later date. Meanwhile, Customs just held onto Larry's property and "dared" him to try and get it back.

Government has, for many, many years taken partial or complete control over the property of individuals by declaring the property or business to be a "public nuisance." Nothing has done more to open Pandora's box of hideous regulations than when government acts under the guise of preventing a "public nuisance." It is not difficult for any agency, so empowered, to label whatever activity we undertake as a "public nuisance." Obviously, everything we do has some impact on others.

While individual property owners must deal with some rather obnoxious restrictions regarding the use of their property because of regulations prohibiting the creation of "public nuisances," the entity taking by far the biggest "hit" is business. Nuisance laws are most frequently the creation of special interest groups. All our environmental regulations, for instance, have come through the activities of special interest groups. In order to force their will upon the rest of us, these groups need our support or, at a minimum, our tacit agreement. Special interest groups have discovered that they will get little public support for their programs if they try to take too many rights away from the general public. Therefore, they have made "big business" the bad guy. They have worked diligently to make the public believe that business is some sort of evil monster whose primary goals are to pollute the environment, destroy wildlife, and endanger the public's health. The success of this brainwashing by special interest groups can be measured by the number of regulations that exist to control the actions of businesses in this country. As BROIL proved, even when a company has complied with every regulation the government could invent, a special interest group can make life hell for a business.

In Contra Costa County, California, there are currently 26 government regulatory agencies trying to keep from falling all over each other as they attempt to regulate one small chemical plant. This has occurred because business has become the whipping boy for all this country's environmental, pollution and public health woes. As we will learn in a subsequent chapter, every agency wants as much of this regulatory pie as possible. Their survival depends upon it.

It is in the area of "public nuisances" that regulatory agencies have taken full advantage of "Enabling Legislation." It is here that agencies have written mountains of legislation to prevent a crime from occurring. The twenty six agencies that are crawling all over the small chemical plant in Concord, California are not there because a "public nuisance" has occurred. They are there on the assumption that their regulatory actions will *prevent* a "nuisance" from occurring. From the statistics I have been able to garner, the opposite is probably true. The number of "nuisances" that have occurred around such factories seem to have increased in direct proportion to the increase in the number of regulatory agencies that profess to be preventing "public nuisances" through regulation.

However, that is not the real issue here. The real issue is, as we discussed in the last chapter, whether a government agency has the right to accuse you or your business of *having the potential* to commit a crime and then making you financially and legally responsible for preventing that potential crime from taking place. In addition, another issue must be addressed. When a government agency requires you or your business to comply with hundreds of regulations that are intended to prevent a public nuisance from occurring can this be considered to be a "taking"? It is the belief of many property rights lawyers that this does, indeed, constitute a "taking" and that the owner of the business is entitled to "just compensation." Unfortunately, this is one area where government has been allowed a free hand at "taking" property with few challenges. Therefore, there have been few precedents established within the courts regarding when such government actions constitute a "taking" and whether the over regulated business has a right to "just compensation" from the regulatory agencies.

I consider this unfortunate on several counts. First, I believe that this form of regulatory action is just as blatant an invasion of property rights as is throwing a person in jail because he has certain characteristics that we have attributed to a murderer.

Second, this injustice is compounded by an even greater evil. As we will learn in a later chapter, the justifications these government agencies have used for invading our property rights are built on foundations of salt which can be toppled by any reasonable man. To justify their actions, these agencies have resorted to distorting virtually every principal that proper science has put into place to prevent the misrepresentation of facts and theories. Then they have used these distorted principals in a most deceitful fashion in an effort to prove the unprovable. By discarding every scientific principal that was ever established to safeguard science from corruption by politicians, they have managed to prove that you *are* capable of committing a crime.

Only a government agency would be so egotistical as to publicly declare that they can predict the future with such absolute certainty that they are willing to prosecute you based upon a prediction. Likewise, only government would have the audacity to present grossly false research to back its claims. In coming chapters, you will be provided with enough ammunition to prove that it is *they* and not you who are committing the crime. Here, more than anywhere else, the powers of the regulatory agencies need to be challenged.

Government is not above performing a "taking" through other forms of subterfuge as well. Perhaps the most devious form of subterfuge is the permit process. The permit process is the government's way of telling you that you had better not do anything with your property without first getting a permit to do so from your government. Certain agencies have discovered that if they make you jump through enough hoops for a long enough period of time, you will eventually give up any attempt to develop your property or your business. The Army Corps of Engineers, the EPA, and many local Planning, Zoning and Building Departments are especially adept at this. They have also found that by delaying your project for a year or two, they can bankrupt your project. In recent years some courts have ruled that such tactics constitute a "taking" and the agencies causing these unjust and extensive delays have been required to pay "just compensation." Therefore, many of the current permit systems are vulnerable to challenge as a violation of property rights. Although there have been few challenges at this point, the court rulings have generally favored the individual or business. This is particularly true where the government's requirements for a permit have been based on rather frivolous concerns.

Unfortunately, one of the groups most severely damaged by the permit process has, thus far, been unrepresented in this particular "takings" procedure. This group consists of the poor and the homeless in this country. Many studies, including some by government agencies, have proven that the permit process and similar regulations have added upwards of 50% or more to the cost of construction. This means that a house that might otherwise cost only $50,000 will instead cost $75,000 or $80,000. These additional costs often place home ownership out of the reach of a large number of people in the middle to lower income groups. These same regulatory costs have a similar impact on the construction of apartment houses and low cost housing for the poor. In many cases, the additional rent that must be charged to compensate for the cost of regulations and permits will condemn a poor family to a smaller, more crowded apartment or will even place the apartment out of the reach of a poor family and force the family onto the streets.

The regulation plague is by no means on the decrease. There were more the 63,000 pages of new, revised and proposed regulations issued in just the year 1990 alone. When I wrote to the state of Texas with a request for a copy of the law that established "The Texas Water Commission" and for a copy of their Rules and Regulations, I received a phone call from one of their employees. They would be happy to meet my request, I was told. However, I needed to pay them up front because it would cost thousands of dollars to make me a copy of all their rules and regulations. She suggested, instead, that I consult a local law library because the Rules and Regulations of the Texas Water Commission would take up so much room that I might not have the space available to store them.

To understand the true enormity of this example, you need to digest a few additional facts. The Water Commission is just one of thirty or more state regulatory agencies in Texas, all with similar sets of regulations. In turn, Texas is just one of fifty states, all with similar state agencies. However, for every state agency, there are a hundred or more city and county agencies, many with their own independent sets of rules. Then, of course, there are the Feds and all their regulations. Is it any wonder the Library of Congress is the largest library in the world?

The Public Interest

Government has been able to get away with the "taking" of private property because it has declared that it is acting in the "public good" or on behalf of the "public interest." The "public good" or the "public interest," as interpreted by the various agencies, seems to be whatever that agency decides it wants domain over at any particular moment in time. For instance, the "public interest" with relation to the Federal Water Pollution Control Act has evolved numerous times since its inception. This evolution has taken place, not through acts of Congress, but because the Army Corps of Engineers and the EPA wanted to increase their powers over your property rights.

The original act was intended to give these two agencies the power to stop the deposition of pollutants into navigable waterways. However, these agencies have been very busy expanding this act, through regulation, to the point where it now encompasses any area that they define as a "wetlands." "Wetlands," in their eyes now include millions of acres of land, some of which is wet only when it rains. In addition, they determined that controlling just "navigable" waters was not enough. They needed to expand their powers to protect other properties that might serve the "public good" or the "public interest." Over the years they have expanded "navigable waters" to mean any "wetland" that might be used as a "wildlife habitat," or as a "natural flood control device," or as a "water filtration device," or as an "area of food production for wildlife," or as a place for "recreation," or as a place for possible "scientific research." If you own a piece of property somewhere in the United States that currently does not meet any of these definitions, don't get your hopes up. They have a vivid imagination and an unquenchable thirst for power. A new definition that will include your property is probably just around the corner.

Personally I think they've already got your property covered. They just haven't discover your property yet. For instance, I live in a condominium with a small balcony and, as I look at this balcony, I suspect that it meets two or three of these classifications. We feed wild birds in a small plastic dish that sits on the floor of the balcony. We also have a hanging plant where the wild birds like to build their nests. I'm sure a government employee with a little imagination could "discover" that the plastic dish is an obvious "area of food production for wildlife" and the hanging plant must, by definition, be considered a "wildlife habitat." In addition, there are a lot of other wild creatures that inhabit my balcony from time to time. Therefore, it is most likely a candidate for classification as a place that can be used for "scientific research." If you're in doubt, just remember that any government employee, so empowered, can make such decisions. He or she doesn't need my permission to declare my balcony a "wetlands," he or she needs only a little imagination.

Unfortunately, where the "public good" or "public interest" comes face to face with individual property rights, individual property rights have generally come out the loser. Over time, the courts have tended to rule that it is all right for government to tromp all over one's property rights and the Fifth Amendment to the Constitution if it is for the "public good."

This has been the area where the people of the United States have lost more rights than in any other area. The public often becomes irate at the actions of our courts because it feels the courts are coddling vicious criminals. In reality, the courts are only protecting those rights guaranteed to all of us by the constitution. Unfortunately, when these rights are accorded a serial killer the public gets upset. Particularly, if the killer gets off for what the public perceives as a "technicality." Personally, I have no problem with this. I want *my* rights protected.

However, I want *all* my rights protected, not just selected ones. Unfortunately, when it comes to property rights, the courts have done a less than admirable job. Someone once remarked that the thing we must be most wary of is not the villains of this world but those people who are well-meaning. This could very well apply to our court system. In their well-meaning attempt to do some "public good," they have allowed government agencies to trample all over our property rights.

This has become very much a philosophical debate. There are judges that firmly believe that the "public interest" should have strong precedence over the constitutional rights of the individual, while other judges feel that we are entitled to *all* the rights granted us by the constitution, *including* property rights. Those judges that have ruled on the side of "public good" are often the same judges that are so determined to protect our other rights. Even to the point of setting a murderer free on a "technicality." One might ask, if a judge is so concern about the "public good" that he or she is willing to deprive us of our property rights, why isn't that same judge equally concerned about the "public good" when they put a killer back on the streets because the killer's rights were slightly abused?

This brings forth other issues. First and foremost, if these government actions are really for the "public good," why doesn't the public pay for them? Why doesn't the government purchase the property rather than just take over control of the property? Why should one individual be expected to pay all the expenses for something that the entire public is going to benefit from?

The government's answer, obviously, is why pay for something that you can get for free? Government is not stupid. Those in control know that few people are going to challenge their authority. Out of several thousand "takings" only a few owners are going to challenge the government's actions. Even if the government loses every challenge, it comes out way ahead. If only one "taking" in a thousand is challenged, the government need only pay for one "taking" out of every thousand. The only way to correct this inequity is for more property owners to challenge the "takings." If the government is required to pay "just compensation" for *all* its "takings," it will back off very quickly. However, don't expect anything to change as long as they know they can bluff you into giving it to them for free.

The next issue involves the cost of maintaining a property after it is declared to be a "wetlands" or a "historic landmark" or a "public nuisance" or whatever. After government has taken control of this property to serve the "public good," government often expects the owner to continue to maintain the property and pay taxes on it. This, of course, provokes the same questions as before. If, indeed, this "taking" is for the "public good" why isn't the public responsible for maintaining it and paying taxes on it? Why should one individual be required to pay for *all* the taxes and for *all* the maintenance for something that benefits everyone? The answer is that government probably *is* responsible for these costs. However, government will never accept this expense voluntarily. Recent rulings by the courts have indicated that making a property owner pay these costs is probably a "taking" and that the owner is entitled to "just compensation." Nevertheless, government will never volunteer this information. Again, don't expect such things to change as long as property owners continue to allow government a free ride.

Perhaps the most important thing one must understand is the difference between a "public interest" and a "public right." We must all recognize that absolutely everything we do is of "public interest." It is impossible to own something or to do something without involving the "public." Building a house, for instance, obstructs a view, eliminates a wildlife habitat, increases road and sidewalk traffic, consumes water, uses the public sewer system, etc. Likewise, mowing your lawn creates noise, sends pollen and other "pollutants" into the air, disrupts wildlife habitat, etc. Also, driving your car causes wear and tear on the roads, causes air pollution, and can endanger the lives of others. The public, therefore, has an "interest" in everything you do.

This does not mean, however, that the "public" has a right to regulate everything you do just because your actions are of "public interest." However, many agencies would like this to be the case. There are a number of interesting questions that arise when one starts to deal with the concept of "public interest." Among the questions that arise when determining whether or not something is of "public interest" is in determining just who or what the "public" is. Does your action or property directly involve the entire public or just a few people? If it affects just a few people, how many people must be affected before it become of "public" interest? What if the "public" consist only of a "special interest group"? Since many regulations are written to appease a "special interest group," this question is of particular importance. However, the details regarding such issues are beyond the scope of this book. If you are interested in exploring these issues further, Mark Pollot's book discusses them in more detail and he also provides you with a listing of many other good resources.

At the present time the whole issue of "public interest" remains somewhat unresolved. However, the important thing to note here is that if something is taken under the guise that it is for the "public interest" or the "public good," labeling it as such does not relieve the "taking" agency from the responsibility for paying "just compensation." Most courts have ruled that an agency taking such a tactic is confusing the "public interest" with the "public right." No one will disagree with the premise that the public has a "right" to take property from an individual for public use. However, the Fifth Amendment has made it obvious that the public must pay "just compensation" for exercising this "right." Labeling the property as being in the "public interest" does not relieve the government of its responsibility for paying "just compensation."

New Tactics

The "takings" without providing "just compensation" game is a very high stakes game and the government is not going to change direction unless it is forced to. Every time an agency is brought to court, it resorts to another bag of tricks in hopes that the courts will see things their way. If an agency can't convince the court that their "taking" shouldn't require "just compensation" because it is for the "public good," they will try other tactics.

Some agencies have tried to convince the courts that they had to take the property because a public emergency existed. This immediately brings to the front two issues. First, what constitutes an emergency when it comes to "taking" someone's property? Second, can an agency avoid paying "just compensation" just because the property is taken for emergency purposes? While various aspects of this "taking" still need to be tested in court, the general reaction of the courts has been to tell the agencies to pay up.

Some agencies have tried to defend their failure to pay "just compensation" on the basis that they can't afford it. "We really need to 'take' this person's property for the 'public good,' your honor, but we can't afford to pay for it. Therefore, we feel that you should allow us to take it without paying for it." I don't know about you, but the fact that the courts would even consider such a defense scares the hell out of me. What's more frightening is that there are a few very liberal judges out there who will buy into such an argument.

Some agencies have found ways of "taking" your property and convincing you to take something of lesser value in exchange. Some have even offered to loosen the controls it has on one piece of property in order to convince an owner to accept tighter controls on another piece of property. This, perhaps more than any other government action, is an affront to me. If the regulations are so damned important that the agency is willing to take away my property rights, how can they arbitrarily allow me to violate these same regulations on another piece of property? Either the regulations are critical to the "public good" or they're not. They can't have it both ways. Some agencies have tried to get property owners to buy other property and "donate" it to the government in exchange for being allowed to develop the property the owner wishes to use.

This is what the government calls "mitigating fees" and is what was offered to the Gorsks. "We will let you build on your land if you will purchase another parcel elsewhere, at a cost of $40,000, and donate it to the government as a wildlife habitat." Where I grew up this was called extortion. Unfortunately, government agencies are allowed to try such things without fear of being prosecuted as extortionists.

In the opinion of most lawyers who specialize in property rights, *all* these government actions are just a bunch of government "hocus pocus." When all the hyperbole is swept aside, it is hard to find any situation where the Constitution allows our government to take private property without "just compensation." However, there is going to be no permanent change in the actions of government until such actions are challenged in court. Property rights lawyers cannot make this happen, only you and I can. Therefore, we all need to take responsibility for making the appropriate lawyers aware of situations where we believe that government has acted in violation of our property rights. Let these professionals evaluate the situation and determine if your situation has the potential to be a precedent-setting case. In a later chapter, we will talk about what you should do to prepare for this eventuality.

Before moving on, I want to assure you that it is not necessary to go to court every time the government tries to procure your property illegally. In fact, this should seldom be necessary. As you will discover in the following chapters, there are many other successful ways to challenge the activities of these over-zealous agencies without court action. Just having a basic knowledge of your rights as property owners will keep most of the wolves from your door. Hopefully, everything you learn in this book will go a long way toward keeping the regulators at bay without resorting to our courts.

However, the sooner we can get the courts to establish some favorable precedents, the sooner government will be forced to change its attitude about who should control property in this country

CHAPTER 4

The Personnel Factor

"He who is firmly seated in authority soon learns to think security, and not progress, the highest lesson of statecraft."

James Russell Lowell

"The nearest approach to immortality on earth is a government bureau."

James F. Byrnes

B efore we begin a discussion about how to beat this repressive regulatory system, we also need to know and to understand the people and the agencies who are enforcing these regulations. I spent twenty-two years writing and enforcing regulations and I feel it is important that you understand just who you are dealing with so you will know how to deal with them appropriately. Once you have this third component in place, we can get into the specifics of how you go about attacking the regulations that are currently making your life less than pleasant.

Who Are They?

There has been a long standing tradition in our society to blame many of the inadequacies of our government on its employees.

Whenever we find ourselves standing in line waiting for some disinterested government employee to give us a little service, we want to reach across the counter and throttle him or her. When we try to get the "inspector" to tell us why we have to disrupt our lives to comply with some useless regulation, we get aggravated when we're told they're just doing their job. When we have to fill out a thirty page questionnaire just to get a permit to build a fence, we want to scream at someone. We are not interested in hearing that the employee is "just doing his or her job." We want service!

Unfortunately, this is as good as it ever gets. The problem lies not with the employee, but with your perception. You have been led to believe that the employee is there to serve you, the taxpayer. This is why you have been paying a large portion of your income to this money-gobbling machine called government, is it not? You have been paying this money so you can get, when needed, a little help. Right? Believe it or not, most government employees, myself included, were led to believe this very same thing. We thought we were hired to serve the taxpayer. It took me quite a while to realize that I was actually there to carry out the mandates of "the system." Should any employee attempt to do anything different, such as serve you, it would only lead to his or her dismissal. To help you understand why you will never make any headway in your battle against government abuses by attacking an employee, allow me to give you their view of the world.

It Comes From Personal Experience

My first job was as an Agricultural Inspector, where I was to enforce the Agricultural Code of the State of California. I was led to believe that you, the taxpayers, were paying me my somewhat meager salary to make sure that you received nothing but the very best of everything that our hard working farmers had to offer. Like a knight on a white horse, I went charging out into the world determined to protect you from buying anything that wasn't pure, wholesome and safe. For quite a while, I knew that was exactly what I was doing. I was so proud. I was working for you and you were getting your money's worth from me.

Then one day, after working there for about three or four months, I saw some things that were just not right. I discovered that what I was doing was not always in the best interests of you, the taxpayer. Therefore, like any good employee, I recommended to my boss that we make the appropriate adjustments. After all, those wonderful taxpayers were paying my salary and they deserved my best efforts on their behalf. You can imagine my amazement when I was told to shut up and do my job. I thought I *was* doing my job.

And so it was, as time moved on I begin to observe that more and more of the things I was being required to do had very little to do with serving *you*. What's more, every time I tried to do what I thought was right, I got thoroughly chastised. I was even reminded that I risked losing my job if I continued to *care* about what was right and what was wrong. It was then that I made a most astonishing discovery.

I discovered that everything a government employee does is mandated by law. I mean everything (short of what you eat for lunch and when you go to the bathroom). Now this may not seem particularly important but, believe me, it is. Perhaps if laws were perfect or, perhaps, if laws were written with *your* best interests in mind, this would not be such a big deal. Unfortunately, however, they never are. No, that's not an exaggeration. *Never* is the appropriate word.

Such laws not only define what a government employee can and can't do, they provide the employee with the ultimate in protection. You may have stood in line for three hours only to find out that you were standing in the wrong line. However, it does little good to get mad at the government employee. He or she is totally protected as long has he or she has followed the mandate of the law that created her function to begin with. The only possible way a government employee can get into trouble is to make an exception for you. No government employees in their right minds are going to try to help you when it means they might lose their jobs. As long as they carry out their duties in strict compliance with the law, they are untouchable.

Operating under a legal mandate creates a great tool for ensuring absolute discipline and absolute uniformity among all government employees. After a good deal of frustration, you may have tried talking to the employee's boss only to get the identical response. If you have ever wondered why a government employee seems so unmoved by your impassioned plea or when you threaten the employee with bodily injury, that's why. There is no way to threaten a government employee. You have absolutely no power over them as long as they are performing as prescribed by law. The scariest part about *all* this is that the government employee may be aware that his action could create a severe hardship for you, or even cause your death, yet he is better off letting you die. He would never be indicted for murder if you died, but he could lose his job if he made the *exception* that saved your life.

This was an overwhelming discovery for me. Somewhere in my upbringing I had been taught that if I did the *right* thing I would be rewarded. Now I was not only forbidden from doing the *right* thing, I was being punished for trying to do it. The law does not reward creativity, only obedience. The message every government employee receives is, don't think about it, just do it.

However, it was my second discovery that really gave me reason for concern. In the world where I was raised, there was another axiom that I had taken to heart. I was taught to believe that while everything might not always turn out exactly right, I sincerely believed that the heart was in the right place. Therefore, I was convinced that, although the law required that I do some things that were not in your best interest, the laws were filled with the best of intentions. Silly me. I soon discovered that, while you were paying me a somewhat generous salary to make sure everything you bought to eat was wholesome and *all* that stuff, I wasn't acting on your behalf at all. What's more, it was never intended that I should. The law made sure I was nothing more than a pawn to be manipulated by those with the most political power. Were I to try to break the shackles of the law and act in favor of the consumer or taxpayer, I would just be replaced by a more obedient servant of these power brokers. I was beside myself. You, the taxpayers of America, were paying me to aid and abet the very entities that I thought I was protecting you from.

I was not thrilled with enforcing regulations that were so blatantly unfair so, after eighteen unproductive months with the Department of Agriculture, I finally found a position where I could really put my six years of college training to good use. I joined the Department of Public Health as their Public Health Entomologist.

By the early 1900's, preventive medicine had begun to emerge as a new and exciting field. Science discovered that it was not necessary for millions of people to get sick or to die from certain devastating diseases, as had been the case for hundreds of centuries. We had discovered how to get rid of such menaces as plague, malaria, yellow fever, dengue, encephalitis and other diseases by the simple mechanism of controlling the insects that carried these diseases to us. (Hooray for Public Health Entomologists.) Moreover, such scourges as cholera, typhoid fever, parasitic worms and other enemies of our digestive tract could be eliminated by the simple practice of proper sewage disposal and by cleaning up our water supply a bit. (Hooray for Public Health) This was a field that really excited me and I set forth in my new position ready to cure the world of these many ills. At last, the taxpayers of America were going to greatly benefit from the salary they paid me.

Unfortunately for me, my predecessors had done a pretty remarkable job of eliminating most of the menaces in the swamps and other "natural environments" around my chosen place of employment. What they left me with were the less appetizing problems that had been created by my fellow countrymen. As one might expect, there are laws against a person creating such health hazards, and this turned out to be my first big disappointment. I had to enforce these laws.

Now I must tell you that being an enforcer of the law isn't easy. I have a great deal of sympathy for those government employees who function in a regulatory capacity. In a perfect world, we could quickly inspect every property in the country looking for possible health hazards. And in the perfect world, the owners of these properties, wanting to do their bit for humanity, would immediately take care of the problem and thank us for our astute observations. In other words, if this were a perfect world, we wouldn't need any laws. Property owners would simply correct any problem we discovered because we both knew it was a problem.

However, most people don't think of themselves or their property as public menaces. Because of that, you can already sense the problem we face. People are not too interested in letting us onto their property to make an inspection to begin with. For some reason our very presence can generate a bit of hostility. Then, in the event we do find something that is in violation of the law, the property owner is not likely to view the situation in the same manner as the law does. Almost invariably, they are going to react in the same fashion that any normal human being would. Regardless of what the alleged "hazard" happens to be, they expect that any reasonable inspector will realize that the property owner is living closer to the "hazard" than anyone else. If it doesn't bother the owner, why should it bother anyone else?

What the property owner doesn't understand is that the inspector is not there to pass judgment. He or she is only there to enforce the law. If the law says it is a hazard, it is a hazard. If the law says it isn't, it isn't. The law is not interested in yours, mine, the inspector's or the property owner's opinion. Obviously, when the laws are written in response to the demands of a "special interest" as most of ours are, the person enforcing them is seldom welcome on anyone's property.

This is the principle that got John Poszgai in such big trouble. He failed to realize that the government employees he was arguing with were absolutely invulnerable to reason. They were totally disinterested in his opinion about a "wetlands" or about how he had improved his property. Their mandate was to ensure that he functioned under permit from their department, and nothing was going to prevent them from enforcing this mandate. John thought the issue had something to do with right and wrong. Little did he realize that it all had to do with ensuring that the government employees involved in his situation kept their jobs.

There are two important lessons to be learned at this point. First, the "inspector" who is inspecting your property has neither the authority nor the desire to change the law on your behalf. His only function is to inspect your property or business, write up the violations, advise you about them and tell you what needs to be done to comply with the law. Therefore, don't disagree with the inspector or argue with him. You will get absolutely nowhere. Second, make life easy for the inspector. The only thing he has any control over is how hard and long he looks. Every inspector has a different personality, but it has been my experience that if you make the inspector's life difficult, he will reciprocate. I have discovered that most inspectors will get out the "fine toothed combs" and the "white gloves" if you give them a hard time. With hundreds of millions of regulations on the books, they are bound to find a lot of problems if they look hard enough. Don't do what John Poszgai did; don't give them reason to look that hard.

Complaints are a Resource

Sometimes, the visits the inspectors make are the result of one neighbor complaining about another neighbor. It is amazing how many people have discovered that the best way to annoy a neighbor they don't like is to complain to a government agency. This is bound to add a good deal of spice to the life of anyone enforcing the law. The complaint usually revolves around an unsettled dispute between the two neighbors. Undoubtedly, the person the inspector is about to regulate isn't too happy to see the poor inspector. He knows you are there because his neighbor has "blown the whistle" on him and he is justifiably irate. However, rather than try to find some neighborly compromise, he generally tries to extract some revenge against his complaining neighbor by finding something equally obnoxious about that person to complain about. So now you have two people complaining about each other. This makes absolutely nobody happy. About the only thing you accomplish as an inspector is to redirect their anger. The neighbors are now so busy hating you, they have forgotten they hate each other. They have found a common enemy.

Generally, it takes every bit of a regulator's diplomacy to keep from cultivating *two* enemies whenever two citizens have a dispute. It is little wonder that most regulators encircle themselves in a shell of indifference. They would not survive otherwise.

However, from an agency point of view, this is ideal. It is the conflicts between neighbors that provide the fertilizer upon which an agency survives and grows. Every agency head is aware of this and will happily pounce upon every complaint as a potential excuse for writing additional regulations. Even I was guilty of keeping track of every complaint my department received as possible fodder for justifying the need for additional regulations. I did this, of course, on the assumption that I was working for the public good.

"Special interest groups," the ones who strongly believe that everyone in America should conduct themselves in accordance with their "special interest" standards, love complaints as well. It is such complaints that enable them to run to their politician or a regulatory agency and demand that the laws and regulations controlling your conduct be strengthened to prevent further affronts to their specific code of conduct.

The best way, obviously, for an individual to help the government regulatory process grow is to file complaints against every neighbor and every business in the community that is the least bit irritating. With any luck at all, they will reciprocate, and then some able bodied government employee can run *all* your lives.

Everything by the Book

I was always a rather nice person and didn't like the idea of cultivating enemies, but it was something I could deal with if I had to, especially knowing that, in the end, I was working for the public good. What really discouraged me was that I couldn't use the skills I learned during those six studious years in the halls of academia. Laws don't permit that. A little experience in the court room soon teaches the government employee that, above all else, he must follow strict procedures and treat each problem as entirely equal no matter how unequal they really are. There is no room for judgment or for six years of especially acquired knowledge in the field. The only thing that is important is that you know how to issue the appropriate citations, that you follow the proper enforcement procedures, that you gather the proper evidence and that you know how to testify in court. And that, I discovered, is the way it is with laws. The human factor does not count at all.

You must learn this lesson well. In the eyes of the law, there are no big infractions and small infractions. Whether you spill a pint of a forbidden liquid or 1000 gallons, you are equally guilty in the eyes of the law and the inspector. It is up to the courts, not the inspector, to determine if your infraction is severe enough to warrant some form of penalty. One of the first things you learn in law enforcement is not how to detect an infraction of the law, but how to lawyer-proof your enforcement procedure. Just as the police officer must read you your rights according to the Miranda Act and must follow certain other arrest procedures, so the inspector sent to you by a government agency must follow strict enforcement procedures. The major concern of the inspector is to be sure that he follows the proper enforcement procedures, not whether you have a big or small infraction. As long as the inspector issues the citation properly and advises you of the actions you must take to eliminate the infraction and how long you have to eliminate the problem, he is on safe ground. His inspection is safe from attack by your lawyer.

Unfortunately, despite what we see on "Matlock" and "Perry Mason," most lawyers try to defend clients on the basis that the enforcement procedure was in some way improper. If your lawyer can't find a hole in the enforcement procedure, you are pretty well out of luck. Government agencies have known for years that this is the line of attack most lawyers will follow and have built strong defenses against this form of attack. Therefore, you must anticipate that the inspector currently inspecting your property or place of business is following the proper procedures and is lawyer-proofing his inspection. If your lawyer suggests attacking your problem in this manner, I suggest you look for another lawyer. Few cases are won by proving that the government inspector didn't follow the proper procedures. In the next chapter we will talk about what you and/or your lawyer *should* do.

Going To The Top

With *all* the laws and regulations I enforced throughout the years, I would like to believe that I kept a few people from getting sick and, perhaps, even saved a life or two. However, I know I could have accomplished the same things without creating the hardship, court expenses and animosity that laws and regulations invariably cause. For every worthwhile problem I eliminated, I had to antagonize many people and, in most cases, had to create a hardship for a multitude of industrious people whose only sin was trying to make a living. I discovered that for every "sinner," a thousand honest people must suffer the indignities of being regulated.

Despite these disappointments, I continued to work within the confines of the government. I was still convinced that I could "make a difference." I just needed to became more intricately involved in the system. I knew I could make "the system" work for the people who paid my salary.

Despite my disagreements with the "system," I must have done a few things right. I eventually became a Chief Public Health Officer, which meant that I was a big honcho in Public Health. In this position, I was now the one authorized to write the regulations, and develop the enforcement procedures that would keep the lawyers at bay. I was also responsible for *all* of the Public Health employees and for all of the money budgeted to support all of our Public Health programs.

As things worked out, I was in the throes of becoming the Director of a Health Department at just about the time Congress decided to completely duck its responsibilities and use "Enabling Legislation" as a means of resolving almost all our country's perceived problems. I believe I can speak on behalf of Health Directors and Department Heads everywhere in assuring you that people such as I were delighted. We now had all the tools we needed to correct any public health problems and, in addition, we had the power to stomp on the toes of anyone who stood in our way. Basically, the Legislature had given us the legal authority to write our own laws and then enforce them. Not even the cops could do that. More important however, Congress gave us the tools to ensure that our departments (and our jobs) would live on in perpetuity, and that they would grow and flourish. Congress gave agencies such as mine immortality.

The only real losers in this deal were the taxpayers. Not only were they about to be regulated by a bunch of power-hungry Department Heads, but they were going to pay very dearly for it through their pocket books. One cannot write more laws and enforce them effectively without adding a good deal of personnel, and personnel cost money. We Department Heads now had the power we needed to build an empire. Henry Kissinger was right. It's quite an aphrodisiac.

The Legislature, in its benevolence, gave those of you who were about to be regulated an opportunity to participate in the development of the regulations. After we (government officials) have written the regulations, each of us "regulators" is required by law to hold a public hearing before we begin actual enforcement procedures.

In all the years I held "public hearings" involving regulations I wrote, I seldom found them to be really "public." Inevitably, the special interest groups that wanted the regulations passed were there in great number. However, those who were about to be regulated were seldom there to voice their protests over the prospect of being further repressed by a government agency.

There was a very good reason for this. The law requires that all such public hearings be announced in a newspaper of general circulation. However, the selection of the paper and the location of the announcement is pretty much up to the agency head. It is not difficult to place such an announcement in a place where few of the "soon to be regulated" will see it. Since the special interest groups already know there is going to be a "hearing," they need only pick up a phone to find out when and where it is going to be held. It always amazed me to see how many people from these "special interest" groups could get off work to attend these "hearings."

While this imbalance in representation is not unexpected, it is something that is in critical need of change. As long as those that are being regulated have no say in the process, special interest groups are going to continue their campaign for political power and for domination over those they perceive as enemies. James L. Payne of Yale University and researchers from John Hopkins evaluated the testimony given before Congress. Their results say it all. "Overwhelmingly, Congress' view on spending programs are shaped by government officials themselves. Of the 1,060 people providing testimony on spending issues 47% were federal administrators, 10% were state and local government officials, 6% were U.S. Senators for a total of 63%. Of the remaining 37% all but 4% were lobbyists of special interest groups with definite government ties." What chance does the average citizen or small businessperson have?

The final portion of the law states that the "regulator" shall take "under advisement" all comments offered by the public at the "hearing." In reality, "under advisement" means we can ignore all comments if we so desire. Therefore, your appearance at my public hearing will have as much or as little significance as I determine it will.

Getting Recourse After the Fact

If you are one of those who suddenly has another regulator knocking on your door as a result of my new regulations, you are probably not too pleased with my latest intrusion into your private or business life. You will most likely be required to take actions that don't make a whole lot of sense to you and could cost you quite a lot of money. Like any normal human being, you need to talk to someone about this ridiculousness. After all, why would anyone want you to do something that is totally contrary to the normal operation of a business? Once you plea your case, you know any reasonable person will realize that you shouldn't be required to undertake such meaningless and expensive activities. Therefore, you might take your grievance to your Congressperson or to some other politician you voted into office. They are, after all, responsible to you, the voter.

As I discussed in Chapter 1, by passing "Enabling Legislation," Congress and other law passing entities, no longer need take responsibility if something doesn't work. They can smile their sly little smiles and tell you, in all honesty, that they have done their job. They gave the Health Department all the authority it needs to take care of the problem. If things aren't working out, go yell at the Health Department.

So, you traipse off to the Health Department in an effort to get your problem resolved. The Health Department, like every government department, is set up so that the first person you encounter is a Clerk with absolutely no authority. The clerk can take your money and give you forms to fill out but cannot make any decisions. If you're persistent, you will get to talk to the Clerk's boss who also has no authority to make decisions. Little do you know that I, as the Department Head, am the only one with the authority to make the kind of decision you need. Am I accessible? Of course I am, if you have an unlimited supply of patience, and the persistence to fight your way through the many layers of bureaucracy that lie between me and the Clerk that you first met.

There is a wonderful reason why I am the only one who can make the decision you need. As we discussed at the beginning of this chapter, any government employee who risks trying to help you by making a decision that is not in direct accordance with the regulations can get into all sorts of trouble. No one wants to be in trouble, so no one is going to help you. The only person who might grant you an exception is me. However, I have little incentive to make an exception in your case either.

There is only one person that any Department Head need fear and it certainly isn't you. You have no power over me whatsoever. The only person I need fear is a lawyer. However, even the lawyer has no power over what I do unless I make an exception for you. As long as I make you abide by the regulations I wrote, I am untouchable. Only if I make an exception on your behalf am I open to possible legal action. Therefore, I don't really care if what you want to do is going to have *no* impact on anyone's health. I am not likely to grant you an exception when it could very well invite some action from a lawyer. If you are going to violate a regulation, let it be on your head, not on mine.

The lesson here is, I hope, rather obvious. Even going all the way to the top dog in an agency in an effort to get something changed is unlikely to do any good. You and your lawyer can rattle your sabers all day, but you will accomplish little. You are, after all, trying to get me to do two things that will endanger my position. First, you are trying to get me to grant an exception to the law when granting such an exception would bring me nothing but legal troubles from every other lawyer in town. Second, you would be asking me to undermine my employees.

While the law often provides that you can appeal the enforcement actions of an inspector to his or her superior, an appeal is generally a waste of time. Should a supervisor or Department Head not support his or her employees, the word would soon get around. If inspectors know that their supervisors aren't going to support them, the inspections will soon stop. No Department Head can afford to let this happen. Therefore, a Department Head is going to support his or her employees regardless of what took place.

This is, most likely, the phenomena Bob Carpenter ran into, head on. There is no doubt that the government employees enforcing the regulations had gone overboard by requiring that Bob take samples all the way to the water table. There is little doubt that the employees could have "overlooked" this absolutely ridiculous requirement. After all, they had ignored Bob for over a year. However, neither the employees' supervisor or the Department Head is going to overrule the employee. However, if Bob raises to much of a stink, they can heap on more requirements.

Other Things You Should Know

In private enterprise, a company normally rewards an employee for doing outstanding work by offering incentives such as pay raises and promotions. If they don't, an employee who feels he or she is not being properly rewarded by her current employer can move to another company that is more appreciative of the work ethic of that employee. However, no such system of rewards exists within Civil Service. There is no reward for excellence and, obviously, there is no other government to work for if this one is unappreciative of an employee who puts out that extra effort. Therefore, the incentive for a government employee to perform above minimum performance levels must come from the employee himself. Fortunately for us, there are many government employees who are motivated to carry out their responsibilities above the minimum level because they want to feel good about themselves. However, we are expecting a lot to assume that this attitude will continue for the twenty or thirty years an employee works for government when there is never an external reward.

Quite obviously, there is an even larger number of employees who feel that a minimum effort is more than adequate. With no external incentive, they see no reason for providing more service than the minimum requirements dictate. It can be stated without fear of retribution that, in government, the greatest reward goes to those employees who are mediocre at best.

Determining salaries and levels of responsibilities is only one of several responsibilities of the Civil Service Commission. It also serves as the citadel of protection for all government employees. In private enterprise, an employee can be dismissed (fired) by his or her boss for any reasonable violation of company policy, apparent incompetency, lack of cooperation, etc. However, once a government employee passes "probation," it is almost impossible to get rid of an incompetent employee. To begin with, the employee's manager must have documented and filed every one of the employee's foul ups. The manager must also prove that he or she has counseled the employee regarding each alleged deficiency. The manager and the employee must also attend a Civil Service Commission hearing where the employee has the opportunity to deny everything and claim that the manager is trying to get rid of him or her because of some personal prejudice. The Civil Service Commission views its job as one of protecting the employee, so if the documentation isn't perfect the manager generally loses. Since the manager receives no reward for managing a well-run organization, there is limited incentive for removing bad employees.

Under the circumstances, you need not bother complaining about a bad employee. If that employee's manager is unable to get rid of the employee, you can be sure you will have no chance whatsoever.

There are some other things about this system of government that should make you equally excited. First, you need to know that in 1977 Congress passed the Sun Shine Act which requires that we government types make our records available to you taxpayer types. As amazing as it may seem, some government agencies were quite reluctant to let the general public look at the minutes of their meetings and refused the public access to other records that were considered public domain. Apparently so many organizations outside of government got on Congress' back about this problem that Congress bent to the public pressure and passed this act.

California went a step further and passed the California Public Records Act way back in 1968. This law requires not only that you have more access to public records but that, if requested by you, the agency must send you a copy of the thing you requested. This is an important piece of knowledge that you must keep stored in your head or elsewhere. Most likely, there will be times when you will need copies of the paperwork the agency has in your file. You are entitled to examine this information and to make copies of it. However, don't expect the agency to volunteer this information. You will have to actively pursue it. In certain instances, people have had to threaten court action in order to get access to their files. Just remember, the Sun Shine Act gives you the legal right to this information.

Several studies conducted in the last twenty years have shown that government agencies comply with these laws less than 45% of the time. Not only that, but when they do comply, it was found that they charged you an exorbitant price for being one of the privileged few who got the information you requested. By way of comparison, should any company being regulated by a government agency comply with the government regulations only 45% of the time, that company would be put out of business so fast it would make your head spin.

The important lesson here is to be sure you keep records of every contact you have with a government employee. Always be sure you get a copy of everything a government employee fills out regarding you, your property, or your business. Don't put yourself in the position of trying to get a copy from the agency at some future date even though the law says they must furnish it to you. Larry Duncan can tell you how effective government is at "stonewalling" when they don't want you to have something.

This may come as a shock to you, but not everyone gets poor service from government agencies. Some years back, the Office of Consumer Affairs financed a $450,000 study (using your money) to see how well you were being served by your "public servants." Following are just a few of the findings of this $450,000 investment:

- In most agencies, serious complaints receive low priority, while trivial, *congressionally referred* complaints consumed substantial resources.
- Many of the agencies studied do not have adequate policies for handling complaints received by phone.
- Regional and field personnel receive little guidance on their responsibility for complaint handling.
- The task of mail screening is often assigned to low level clerks who have little knowledge of the complaint handling procedures.

"Don't call us, we'll call you."

Finally, as one might expect, with hundreds of agencies out there pumping out millions of regulations, they frequently run headlong into each other. This is especially thrilling if you are the one being regulated. Not infrequently, some poor company will be caught between two warring agencies, each with its own agenda of regulations that demand compliance. The regulations developed by one agency will require that the company do one thing while the other agency's regulations will require just the opposite. I can't tell you for sure which agency might eventually win, but I *can* tell you *who will always lose*. The regulated company never stood a chance.

Looking For Intent

I know that early in the game, public health had some very specific direction and some very specific goals. It was this direction and these goals that were responsible for the elimination of most of the scourges that killed our ancestors at a very early age. We were able to measure the obvious reduction in cases or completely eliminate such diseases as typhoid fever, cholera, malaria, smallpox, diphtheria, pertussis, whooping cough, polio, measles, mumps, tuberculosis, plague, rabies and other diseases that were the terrors of our recent ancestors. In less than a century it was no longer necessary to bare six children in order to ensure that two would survive to reach adulthood. Public Health established some very specific, measurable goals. We met the challenge and the public benefited mightily.

Today things are a whole lot foggier. As I delve into the thousands of regulations that exist in today's world, I have a very difficult time determining just why most of them exist. Certainly, somewhere in antiquity there was some "Enabling Legislation" that permitted the enforcing agency to write the regulations they now enforce. Hopefully, this "Enabling Legislation" expressed an intent. However, I see no specific goals. I see no measuring sticks with which to determine if all this enforcement is, indeed, accomplishing something. Finally, there appears to be no penalty if the agency fails to meet whatever goals might have been established.

My hunch is that these million or so employees who have been hired to carry out the enforcement of all these regulations are accomplishing very little. However, we will probably never know for sure. It is difficult to measure accomplishments when there was no specific direction to begin with. Without direction, without some idea of where you want to go, it is very difficult to determine when you have arrived. None of the government programs I have looked into recently have arrived, or if they have, they are not aware of it. Come to think of it, why would they want to arrive? If they established some goals and then accomplished what they set out to do, someone might suggest that they were no longer needed. That, of course, would defeat the primary goal of every government agency. You know, the primary goal of every government agency is to exist in perpetuity.

A little earlier, I suggested that you try to determine who the real enemy is. I encouraged you to find out what "special interest" groups sponsored the legislation and who is benefiting from it. With that knowledge in hand you can generally determine what the original intent of the legislation was. This can be very important information when you are seeking justice from the regulatory process.

For twenty two years I worked within the system. I wrote regulations that I hoped would make more sense than the existing ones. I stood before various political organizations such as Boards of Supervisors and Legislatures to argue the merits or pitfalls of proposed legislation. I advanced up the ladder of leadership until I was managing a territorial health agency with hundreds of employees. I worked with Health Officers from all the other states and territories of the union. I dealt with the heads of nearly every other kind of government agency our Legislators could invent. And I dealt with these entities of government at the local, state and federal levels. Finally, I had the opportunity to view things from an International level when I served as a Country representative to the World Health Organization.

I learned a lot about our government in those twenty two years. The most important thing I learned is that it is going to continue to grow and proliferate unabated unless the citizens of this country take action. There is absolutely *no* chance that government is going to take action against itself voluntarily. I also learned that no one in government will ever be able to provide you with the services you deserve. Finally, with the help of others, I discovered how you can beat the system. Therefore, as my legacy to you for paying my salary for those twenty-two years, I now offer you opportunity to take advantage of this knowledge.

CHAPTER 5

The Path Toward Justice

"A little rebellion now and then—is a medicine necessary for the sound health of government."

Thomas Jefferson

"Experience should teach us to be most on our guard to protect liberty when the government's purposes are beneficent."

Louis D. Brandeis

Hopefully, as you struggled through the last four chapters, ideas begin to formulate in your mind. You should, by now, have some idea of how to proceed against any repressive regulation that is laid upon your door step. The primary purpose of this chapter is to help you understand exactly where you stand in the regulatory process, what your goals should be and, finally, the step by step process for reaching those goals. In addition, it should help you organize the information you've acquired in the last four chapters and help you put this information to practical use.

The Big Mistake

The biggest mistake everyone (especially lawyers) makes is trying to take the regulations or the regulatory process head on. In order to be successful in this area, you would have to prove one of two things. You either have to prove that you didn't violate the law or you have to prove that the regulations were improperly enforced.

When dealing with "Enabling Legislation" it is almost impossible to prove that you didn't violate the law. As we discussed in the first chapter, you don't need to have created a public nuisance, a murder or a health hazard to be in violation of the law. You just need to possess some factor that the regulations have determined has the potential to create a public nuisance, a murder or a health hazard. If the law states that you are a potential murderer because you have blue eyes, having blue eyes is a violation of the law. The inspector doesn't have to prove that you are the one blue eyed person in a million that will commit a murder, he or she just needs to state that you have blue eyes. Likewise, the inspector of your restaurant doesn't have to prove that your dirty floor may spread germs, he or she just needs to decide your floor is dirty. The regulations have assumed that a dirty floor can, at some point, become a public nuisance or health hazard. Therefore, you are in violation of the regulation.

If you think your eyes are not the right shade of blue or that your floor is not really dirty, it becomes your word against the word of the inspector. In a court of law, the court will generally consider the inspector to be the authority in this matter and will rule in favor of the agency. Agencies also have "experts" on their staff to provide expert testimony in support of the inspector. As a Public Health Entomologist, one of my responsibilities was to provide expert testimony in support of the health inspectors in our department. Under the circumstances, there is little hope that you will convince the court that your eyes are not the right shade of blue or that your floor is not dirty. The judge will go with the expert testimony.

If an inspector determines, during the course of an inspection, that your home or your business is in violation of the regulations, *don't argue*. It will do no good. The fact that it is creating no problem is irrelevant. The regulations do not require that a public nuisance or murder or health hazard exist in order to determine that you are in violation of the regulations. Besides, as you will see later, you shouldn't really be concerned. In the end, it is the agency and not you that will pay for these violations.

As we discussed in the last chapter, you will also have no success challenging the enforcement procedure. The first thing every inspector is trained to do is to enforce the law *properly*. Each group of regulations has its own enforcement procedure and, as long as the inspector follows this procedure, his or her enforcement process is immune from attack. If you are interested in the enforcement process, you can generally get a copy of the procedure from the enforcement agency. Most of the processes are fairly similar and will follow somewhat the same procedure unless a real public nuisance, health hazard or murder exists.

BEWARE

The biggest mistake you can make, however, is the mistake that John Poszgai made. He refused to comply with the law, and in so doing became subject to criminal prosecution. At one time this was not such a critical circumstance, as there was a good deal of rational in the enforcement of environmental regulations. However, Bush changed this dramatically. The Bush Administration declared that a polluter is a criminal who has violated the rights and the sanctity of a living thing—the earth's environment. The goal of his administration was to send a strong message to would be polluters that pollution of the environment would not be tolerated. This message was to be sent through more arrests and prosecutions, stiffer penalties, and a wider range of crimes.

His administration has even influenced the courts to accept the premise that the prosecutor need not prove *mens rea*, or "guilty mind" as is required in all other felony cases. Therefore, you can now be convicted of a felony for affecting the environment even if you did not intend to or even if you did not know you were "harming" some aspect of the "environment." In all other felonies, the prosecutor must prove that a person meant to harm others, but with this new environmental mentality the prosecutor does not even need to prove that anyone was actually harmed by your actions.

The Procedure

You may already be somewhat familiar with what happens when an inspector from one of our many regulatory agencies visits your home or place of business. However, I am going to discuss it in some detail so that you will not only be able to tell that it is being done properly, but will know how to react.

Every inspector is required to identify himself before starting any inspection and let you know what agency he represents, and the purpose of the visit. Every inspector is required to have proper identification. Ask for it. This not only lets the inspector know that you are aware of your rights, but also prevents some phony from entering your property or place of business by pretending to be the new "health inspector" or whatever. If the inspector doesn't have proper identification, you are not obligated to let him enter. However, always be polite and cooperative regardless of the situation. There is no need to get anyone upset.

Most regulations require that inspections take place during "regular working hours" which are usually defined as between 8:00 am and 5:00 p.m. If someone arrives on your premises and wants to inspect your property or business at other than regular working hours, you have the right to refuse them entrance.

However, they have the right to call you and arrange to meet with you at "odd" hours. If they make such a request, you should agree to the request unless it creates some inconvenience that can be justified in court.

Do not refuse to allow an inspector entrance to your property or business during normal working hours unless you have a very compelling reason to keep them at bay for a short time. The inspector will have little difficulty getting a court order demanding that you open your doors to inspection by the agency. If you force them to get a court order, be prepared to see them arrive with that court order and a covey of armed policemen to enforce it. If you refuse entrance at this point, you will be charged with contempt of court and will be arrested on the spot. When in court, the judge will want to know why you refused to allow an inspector with the proper identification entrance to your property for a legally authorized inspection. I can't think of many excuses that will exempt you from a contempt charge. On top of everything else, you will have an inspector or two who are upset at being required to get a court order and they are going to inspect more thoroughly and find more "violations" than they would have if you had let them in to begin with. Refusing an inspector the right to inspect your property during reasonable hours is a *never* win situation for you.

In light of the above, I strongly recommend that you let the inspector onto your property or place of business unless you have a dead body in the freezer or a ton of "crack" hidden somewhere. Trying to stop a legally authorized inspection is *not* the way to win the regulations battle.

Accompany The Inspector

You have a legal right to accompany the inspector on his tour of your property or place of business and I strongly suggest that you do so. If you cannot accompany the inspector for some reason, have someone else who is well trained regarding the regulatory process accompany the inspector. You want someone accompanying the inspector who can cover all the bases for you.

One of the main reasons few people or businesses win the regulatory battle is that they fail to prepare themselves. Remember, the minute the inspector walks through your door, he or she will be acting in accordance with the enforcement procedures outlined in the regulations he is there to enforce. Every action he takes is done on the assumption that this inspection will end up in court. Therefore, everything he does and every action he takes will be guided by the enforcement procedures outlined in the regulations. Those procedures are his shield against losing to you in court in the event you decided not to comply with the regulations. This is the place where agencies have always been attack in the past and it is the place they expect to be attack in the future.

Unfortunately, until now, the person or business being regulated has never been trained on how to handle being inspected. Therefore, they are always at a great disadvantage when the inspector arrives. One of the purposes of this book is to help you get yourself as well prepared as the inspector. However, you will not be preparing yourself for an attack against those areas where the inspector and the agency are so well fortified. You will not be looking for errors in the enforcement process nor will you be looking for situations where you might be able to deny that you have broken the law. After all, at best it will be your word against his, and the court will look at his opinion as the expert testimony. Instead, you will be preparing to attack the agency in an area where it has absolutely no protection. You will be preparing to attack the agency in its budget.

Advise the inspector that you will be accompanying him or

her on the inspection. If there is some concern about this, just advise him that you are going along so that you can see first-hand what needs to be done to comply with the regulations. Bring along a tape recorder and be sure the inspector is aware that you have it. If you are asked, say that you are bringing the tape recorder along so that when a violation is found you can record exactly what you are told the problem is and what needs to be done to "bring it into compliance." Always use the words "bring it into compliance" when discussing any situation that the inspector feels is a violation of the regulations.

While this may seem like a technicality, using words like "correct the problem," makes it sound like you have admitted there is a problem. However, when you agree to bring something "into compliance," it means only that the inspector has found something that he feels is not in compliance with the regulations. Because most regulations are written to prevent a problem from occurring, being "out of compliance" does not mean that there is a problem. It only means that you are in violation of a regulation the agency wrote which is intended to prevent a problem from occurring at some time in the future.

One of the main reasons for bringing the tape recorder is to get, on tape, an agreement between you and the inspector that whatever he has found is not currently a problem but just "not in compliance" with the regulations. You also want him to tell you on tape exactly what needs to be done to bring the situation into compliance. He will probably tell you that you don't need to tape the conversation because he will be giving you a written order to correct all situations that are not in compliance. Assure him that you like the tape recorder because it gives you detail that would not be found in a written order. Some of the specifics you discuss will be missing from his or her written version.

Each time the inspector finds a violation, ask the following question about the violation:

"Can you explain to me why there is a regulation against having (a dirty floor, blue eyes, etc.)?"

You want the inspector to explain to you and to the tape recorder that the situation could create a (problem, nuisance, health hazard, etc.) at some time in the future. There is no way the inspector can demonstrate that the dirty floor has actually caused anyone to get sick. However, he can state that someone could (or might) get sick because the floor is dirty. By so commenting, he has stated to you and the tape recorder that a "nuisance" does not currently exist.

If the inspector uses the term "nuisance" or "health hazard" or "environmental hazard" or anything else that would indicate that the violation in question is or could become a nuisance or danger to the public or could become a danger to the environment, ask the following:

"Is your concern that this might become a "public nuisance" (health hazard, environmental hazard) at some time in the future?"

You are looking for either a yes or no answer here. You don't care. In either event, the inspector is stating that the situation is *not currently* a problem but could be in the future. This is what you want to hear. Don't press the issue any further.

If the inspector indicates that it might already be causing a problem to the public or to the environment, ask these questions:

"Has anyone of the public been adversely affected by the situation (dirty floor) yet?"

"Has anyone of the public claimed to have been damaged in any way by this situation? If so, who?"

"Has the environment already been damaged in some way by this situation? If so, in what way?"

Chances are that the inspector will backtrack and indicate that an actual "public nuisance" (health hazard, environmental hazard) does not exist at this time but will in the future if the situation is not corrected. This, again, is what you are looking for.

Remember, almost every regulation on the books is there to prevent an occurrence (nuisance). If a real nuisance of some sort is taking place, the inspector would be taking an entirely different approach. For instance, the inspector supervising Bob Carpenter's tank removal was not there because the water table below Bob's property was being contaminated by the tank. Therefore, there was no public nuisance. Presumably, the inspector was there to assure that the removal of the tank did not cause such a problem. However, in reality, the inspector was there to make sure Bob followed all the regulations regarding the removal of the tank. The idea that removing the tank might contaminate the water table was the justification for the existence of the regulations. While this may seem like splitting hairs, hopefully you will soon see why this differentiation is so important.

In the unlikely event that the inspector insists that the situation is already a "public nuisance" (health hazard, environmental hazard), even though he is unable to present any evidence to this effect, don't push any further. You are dealing with a thoroughly brainwashed individual who cannot distinguish a potential problem from a real problem.

Follow this same procedure throughout the entire inspection process. You want to be sure that you have on tape the inspector's opinion about each violation that is discovered. If everything goes well, the inspector will have uncovered several violations of the regulations but will have uncovered no "public nuisances" or "health hazards" or "environmental hazards."

The inspector's next responsibility in the enforcement process is to give you written notice of all the violations found, what must to be done to correct the violations and when the corrections should be completed. The written notice has only one real purpose. By issuing a written notice he can prove that you were properly informed of the violations and what to do about them, in the event you and he should end up in court. Again, the primary goal of the inspector is to follow the proper enforcement procedures. Often, the inspector will write up the notice before leaving your premises and will discuss it with you at that time. Be sure to tape this conversation as well. If possible, get him to agree again that these are measures that need to be taken to prevent a (nuisance, hazard, etc.) from occurring.

"Just so I understand completely what we are doing here, let me be sure that I have everything straight. I am complying with these regulations in order to prevent a (nuisance, hazard, etc.) from occurring. Is that correct?"

Look at the things that need to be done and the amount of time you have been given to correct them. In many instances, the regulations require that the violations be corrected within ten days or less. If some of the corrections require that you undertake some major work, don't be afraid to advise the inspector of this fact. Ask for additional time to complete that particular project. Let the inspector know that the other projects will be completed at the agreed upon time but that you need additional time for that one especially difficult task. In most cases they will be very reasonable about such things.

If you are asked to sign the inspection form, do it. You are only signing that you have received the form, not that you agree with the contents or with the inspector's findings. A refusal to sign is generally viewed by the agency and the courts as a sign that you are uncooperative. You want to always be cooperative.

Before the inspector leaves, you should both agree upon a date and time for him to come back for a reinspection to be sure all the items he found in violation are now in compliance with the regulations.

Inspectors with some agencies don't give you a written report at the time of the inspection, particularly if it is going to be a long report. In such cases, the report is written up in the inspector's office and is then mailed to you. This is generally considered to be proper notice and should be treated with the same respect as the notice received at the time of the inspection. If you need additional time for some task, call the inspector on the phone and ask for the additional time. Generally, the mailed report will include a time for the reinspection. Confirm the time for reinspection during the phone conversation or ask for another time if necessary. Always be cooperative.

When the time comes for the reinspection, accompany the inspector as you did before, with tape recorder in hand. Also have the original report or "notice" in hand so that the inspector can check off each item as "okay" after it is reinspected. The tape recorder can be used to get his verbal agreement that the violation is now corrected and, if possible, to get the inspector's comment that with compliance the threat of a possible public (nuisance, health hazard, etc.) is gone.

In many instances, such as with John Poszgai, you will be required to get a permit in order to take any action on your property. It is possible that a permit may be required even if the action you are taking has been ordered by the government agency. As an example, you may be ordered to "repair" the septic tank in your yard or business location because it is not in compliance with current regulations. However, just because the agency ordered the "repair" doesn't mean you are exempt from getting the permit. The reason for the permit, obviously, is to make sure the "repair" is accomplished under the agency's direction and inspection. When the "repairs" are completed, the permit will be "signed off" indicating that the "repairs" were completed properly.

When working with an agency under such conditions, the

principals are basically the same. Always tape record your conversations with the inspector involved in your project. As before, the main thing you want on tape is an admission from the inspector that a nuisance does not currently exist. This project is being required to prevent a public nuisance from taking place. Even if your septic tank is overflowing onto the surface of the ground, it is no more a hazard than the dirty floor in a restaurant. It has the potential to be a "public nuisance" but currently has made no one sick. Therefore, you are taking preventive measures to protect the public from what may be a nuisance at some future date.

It is important to understand that anytime you are required to get a permit from a government agency in order to do something on your property, the justification for requiring this permit is to prevent a "public nuisance" from occurring. In most cases, you will be told it is for your own good. Nevertheless, to justify the presence of the regulation, it must exist for the "public good." As always, the permit is the government's way of requiring you to not create a "public nuisance" at some future time.

Although it might seem like a stretch of the imagination, the situation with the Gorsks is identical. They want to build a new home on their property and need a permit to do so. However, in the eyes of the Fish and Wildlife Service, protecting the Stevens Kangaroo Rat is in the "public interest." Therefore, destroying the home of this creature is a "public nuisance." By stopping the Gorsks from building, the agency is stopping a potential "public nuisance."

Keeping Tally

Don't do a slipshod job when complying with the notice or written order. If you are going to do things, do them right. As you and or your employees work to bring the violations into compliance, keep track of all your expenses. Keep separate records for each item that must be "brought into compliance." You want to be sure that the costs for complying with each violation is separate from the costs of all the others. All actual costs should be included: employee salaries and benefits, administrative costs, support costs, costs of materials and other financial outlays that are incurred. Also, any documentable loss of production, loss of time or loss of real property should become a part of this cost analysis. Don't forget the costs the agency charged you for its permit.

It is now time to separate those violations that were cited because the situation could become a problem in the future, from those violations that the inspector cited because the situation is currently causing a problem to the public. Review each violation critically. Review the written notice and the tape recordings.

Existing public (nuisances, health hazards, etc.) might include any situations where the inspector has been able to demonstrate to you that a condition is *currently* causing a problem to the public. Generally, there will be no such violations unless the inspector is responding to a complaint from someone outside of your property or business. If there is no compliant, how is the inspector going to demonstrate that the condition constitutes a "public" nuisance?

However, a complaint in and of itself does not establish the existence of a public (nuisance, health hazard, etc.) either. It must still be demonstrated that someone or something is being damaged by the situation. For instance, someone may complain about the dirty floor in your store or restaurant and this may constitute a violation of the regulations. However, it doesn't prove that anyone got sick as a result of its existence. If the "public" is not being impacted, there is no public problem. It is important that you understand this concept thoroughly before we move on.

This might be a good time to go back and review Chapter 1. When you do, you will note that none of our beleaguered friends was creating a "public nuisance." However, this did not exempt them from inspection nor did it exempt them from complying with the law. As we look at each situation, we can now see how each might have been helped considerably by following the procedure outlined above.

Had Larry Duncan taped his initial conversation with the Customs Inspectors and asked the proper questions, he probably would have slowed them down considerably. Telling Larry it was none of his business would not make any points for the Customs Agents in a court of law. He also needed to have a tape recording which showed that he was being fully cooperative. He would only be exercising his constitutional rights by politely inquiring as to what laws he might be violating. To protect themselves, the Customs Agents would have needed to keep Larry well informed of what was taking place. Because he didn't ask the right questions and tape record the answers it is now just his word against theirs. This is not the best fodder to have at your side when suing the government.

I'm sure that, in retrospect, the Caytlings would love to have a tape recording of the inspector explaining to them how a wheelchair can be "misbranded" and "adulterated." Also it would be nice to have the inspector's interpretation of what constitutes "manufacturing." Certainly, an admission that the regulations are there to prevent the possible occurrence of a public nuisance would be very helpful. The Caytlings desperately needed this admission on tape.

In the case of Eagle Hardware, it would have been nice to have the president of BROIL on tape confessing that their real goal was to prevent the store from ever opening. They were just "using" the courts and the government agencies as a means toward this end. Such information would provide Eagle with plenty of ammunition in the event it decided that BROIL should share in the extra expenses BROIL created for Eagle.

Had Bob Carpenter followed this procedure, his adventure would have ended with the removal of the tank. He would have had no trouble getting the government employees to agree that the cars parked on the area over the tank had left the petroleum contamination in the soil, not the tank. This is all he would have needed in order to take the next step in the fight against over regulation.

John Poszgai, of course, is the antitheses of what should have been done. His $202,000 fine and two years in jail are evidence enough of why one doesn't fight the government in the area where it is best prepared. The fact that he created no "public nuisance" had no bearing on his case. Only his conduct. Once he refused to get a permit, he turned complete control of the situation over to the government. He attack government where it is strongest.

The Gorsks, of course, never got to meet their inspector. The declaration that their property now belonged to the Stephens Kangaroo Rat was made with the stroke of a pen in some government office. The cost of developing their property was placed well beyond their reach by a clever agency "policy." It would seem that their only recourse is to fight the policy through the courts, another expense they couldn't afford. However, as we proceed, we will discover that there is still plenty they can do. For them, it might not be too late.

Once you have sorted those violations that were intended to prevent a problem (which we hope is all of them), from those that are actually causing a problem (which we hope is none of them), you are ready to proceed. However, before moving on, be sure that the inspector has completed his or her reinspection and has verified that everything is now in compliance.

Once this is completed, you are ready to attack the agency in the one area where it is most vulnerable. The place where it has no legal right to act. The place where it has no legal protection.

CHAPTER 6

The Demand for Compensation

"You have a God-given right to kick the government around—don't hesitate to do so."

Edmund Muske

"Ultimately property rights and personal rights are the same thing."

Calvin Coolidge

You are now about to prepare for your attack on the agency. The time has come to inform the agency that it has violated your Fifth Amendment rights and, by so doing, has performed a "taking" that entitles you to "just compensation." As was discussed in Chapter 3, a government agency has most likely performed a "taking" by enforcing regulations which have a negative impact on the value of your property or business. This, of course, is why you separated those violations that were preventive in nature from those where an actual public nuisance (hazard) was occurring. A "taking" occurs only if you are not currently creating a *legitimate* public nuisance (although even this may constitute a "taking" under certain conditions). For our purposes, however, we are going to assume that the only time a "taking" occurs is when you are required to comply with regulations that are intended to prevent some problem from occurring or where the nuisance is not truly "public."

This is not the time to begin worrying if you should proceed. Many people feel threatened at the thought of taking on "big government." If you are feeling this way, there are a few things you should understand. First, there are many people just like yourself that have gone after the government in this fashion and most of them have won. Even those that lost made out much better than if they had done nothing at all. Second, you are going to be far better prepared than those that preceeded you because, by following the procedures in the previous chapter, you prepared yourself from the very beginning of the inspection. Most of the others had no such preparation. They only went after the government when things got so bad that they had to call for legal help just to keep from losing their property or business. They did not have the documentation concerning the actual inspection that you have. Therefore, they were confronted with the situation we are avoiding: your word against the government inspector's. You have the entire inspection process on tape and in writing. There can be no doubt about what took place during the inspection. Third, as a person with twenty-two years experience enforcing regulations, I can assure you that the agency personnel are just as wary of you as you are of them. They will never have met anyone as well prepared as you and they are going to be squirming. You will be hitting them in an area where they have no preparation and few defenses. In most cases, it will be the agency rather than you that is looking for a way out of this dilemma.

Finally, if you are concerned about the possibility of landing in court, don't be. The roles between you and the agency have now been reversed. Under the old procedure, it would be the government deciding whether to take you to court. Under this program, you will be the injured party and will determine whether you want to prosecute the government agency in a court of law. In other words, the decision will be yours and not theirs. Furthermore, should you decide to pursue matters in a court of law, you might well have a contingent of experts to guide you in this matter at no cost to you. In a forth coming chapter, we will discuss how you might go about getting free legal advice and how you might get court representation free of charge.

However, whether or not you eventually receive compensation from the government should not be your primary objective. By taking the action recommended here, you will have notified the agency of the responsibility it has assumed when it determined to arbitrarily inspect your property. By taking such action, you will slow the enforcement process considerably because, should the agency attempt to take any punitive action against you at this point, it will appear as if the agency were seeking revenge. The agency cannot afford the "appearance" that it is vengeful for several reasons. Congresspersons and other political entities will not support an agency that is suspected of an impropriety. Without this political support an agency would soon wither and die. In addition, even the most lenient courts absolutely abhor any entity that acts out of revenge. The agency would not only lose the battle to avoid paying just compensation but could very well open itself up to a liability suit. Finally, an agency head is not going to enter a confrontation where he or she has nothing to win and everything to lose. Therefore, your demand for just compensation will serve as a protective wall that the agency will only enter with utmost caution. Any further inspections it makes of your property or business will be done with due respect for your rights and the knowledge that it may be liable for the costs the inspection incurs.

The Taking

In proceeding, you must operate under the assumption that the government performed a "taking" when it ordered you to comply with its regulations. You were, after all, creating no public nuisance. Under the circumstances, you are going to be requesting "just compensation" for this "taking." The demand for just compensation should be made in the form of a letter sent to the agency head with copies to whomever else you think should be aware of your action. I will have some suggestions in this regard later on. This letter can be drafted by either yourself (which I recommend) or by a lawyer (which probably isn't necessary at this point). The letter should cover several important points, and should be sent "return receipt requested" so you have proof that the agency received your letter.

First, the letter must advise the agency that you have determined that their actions constitute a "taking" as defined by the Fifth Amendment to the Constitution of the United States of America. As such, you are demanding "just compensation" for the expenses you incurred in complying with its regulations. You will also demand compensation for the loss of productivity (or time or income or real property) that occurred as a result of the agency's action as well as the costs of any permits you were required to get.

Second, the letter must be accompanied by a detailed breakdown of the actual expenses you incurred in complying with their regulations and the details of any other loses you suffered, such as a loss of productivity or income.

Third, the letter should include a due date by which such "just compensation" must be paid, and the penalty that the agency will incur if payment is not made by the due date. The penalty usually amounts to charging the agency interest at the going rate on all moneys not received by the due date.

Adding Some Valuable Options

There are a number of optional items that can be included in your letter, some of which are designed to send little beads of sweat down the forehead of the agency administrator. First, you might advise the administrator that the courts of the United States have already determined that actions such as those taken by his agency do constitute a "taking" that is entitled to "just compensation." Further, you can advise the administrator that these same courts have, from time to time, determined the following (pick whatever suits your situation):

1. That police power regulations can destroy the use and enjoyment of property just as effectively as formal condemnation or physical invasion of property. (In other words, enforcing regulations is just as much an invasion of private property as physical invasion or formal condemnation.)

2. That government cannot avoid liability by claiming that it did not mean to take property.

3. That compensation is due even if the regulations are determined to be valid.

4. That the court is open to hearing from any party who contends that the Legislature went beyond its constitutional powers and that the court is free to engage in a searching analysis as to the statute's purpose. (We will discuss this aspect in detail a little later.)

5. That the courts may explore the statute's purpose, its operative provisions, the extent to which other means could have been used to achieve the same purpose, and the rights it sought to abridge in the process.

6. That although the court will assume that the agency acted in good faith (such as when an emergency exists), the assumed emergency does not save the action from being a taking.

7. That the courts can exercise their independent judgment as to whether the action taken by the agency served a public purpose or was truly the abatement of a public nuisance.

8. That strong public desires do not support a violation of the constitutional protections provided under the Fifth Amendment. (In other words, it will do the agency no good to

claim that it is acting upon the demands of the public.)

9. That, even though we could anticipate that we might be regulated at some time in the future, this did not exempt the agency from paying just compensation.

10. That a "taking" occurs even though only a portion of the "property" (production, income) was taken.

11. That to avoid paying compensation, the agency must prove that the nuisance is truly a *public* nuisance.

12. That while every person ought to contribute his portion for public purposes and public exigencies, no one can be required to give more than that proportional amount without just compensation.

13. That the courts have continually found that the terms "use" and "take" include the concept of impairment. (In other words, the agency cannot claim that enforcing regulations is not "using" or "taking" your property.)

14. That the taking of privately owned property without compensation cannot be justified upon the basis that the private property provides a service important to the public.

15. That an agency cannot violate one's Fifth Amendment rights simply because it would impair the government's efficiency to protect those rights. That is, the courts have decided that efficiency, cost, and administrative convenience are insufficient reasons for ignoring or weakening constitutional guarantees.

16. Courts have rejected the government's claim that its actions are exempt from the just compensation clause because it was preventing environmental harm.

As you may or may not have surmised, the sixteen items listed above constitute the attempts by various government agencies to wiggle out of paying just compensation. Each item identifies a defense some clever government lawyer invented in an effort to keep its agency from paying for taking someone's property rights away from them. Fortunately, in each instance the government lost, giving us these precedents that we can now quote in our demand letter. Most agencies are well aware of these court rulings but a gentle reminder never hurts. By mentioning some of them in your letter, you are, in affect, advising the agency that the courts have already ruled that such a defense will not relieve it of responsibility for paying you just compensation. In other words, you are advising the agency not to try using any of the above as justification for its actions. The court will not accept them.

Once you have selected those items from the above list that meet your particular situation, you may want to directly challenge some additional aspects of the regulations. Items 4, 5, 7, 11, and 16 provide a mechanism for additional attacks upon the agency's action. For instance, if the alleged purpose for the enforcement action was to protect the public health or the environment or was to prevent a public nuisance, you have an additional can of worms you might like to dump upon the agency's lap.

In chapters to come, you will learn that the scientific evidence utilized to support most of the suppressive regulations on the books today is faulty. Almost every regulation uses, as support for its presence, scientific data which was specifically designed to justify the existence of the regulation. This, obviously, is not good science. When you have reviewed the upcoming chapters on the scientific process, you may want to include some of this ammunition in your letter as well. If you think you might want to take the agency to court at some point, however, you might want to save this attack until later. Blowing scientific evidence into small pieces in a court of law is very dramatic and very impressive. In any event, items 4,5,7,11, and 16 provide the ammunition you need to attack poor scientific practices, either in a court of law or in a letter to the agency.

For purposes of developing your letter to the agency you can assume that, without doubt, most of the regulations you were forced to comply with were based on very faulty science. Certainly, any regulation designed to prevent an individual or group of individuals from contracting a disease are very suspect. The agency and the regulations will have failed to address several very important issues. For instance, the regulations will make no mention of dosages or of lengths of exposure, both of which play a major role in determining if there is a possibility of endangering someone's health. Also the regulations will fail to take into account other factors (such as heredity) that probably play a much larger role in the individual's susceptibility to contracting a particular disease than the incident that the agency determined was a violation. Without this kind of scientific backing, the agency will be unable to meet the criteria established under points 4, 5, 7, 11 and 16 discussed earlier in this chapter.

Number 4, for instance, allows the court to explore the agency's actions to determine if these actions were necessary in order to meet the "intent" of the law. Assuming that the intent of the law is to prevent the public from getting ill, the agency must prove that their actions stopped someone (or more accurately, the public) from contracting a disease. This is why your preparation during the inspection process is so important. You now have on tape the inspector's own admission that the regulations you are complying with are not currently causing a public problem. Therefore, the actions could not possibly have been taken to stop an on going public nuisance (health hazard, etc.) which was the "intent" of the law. As I have mentioned a dozen times before, the regulations drafted by the agency unfairly require that you prove you will never commit a nuisance.

Number 5 provides an even more interesting scenario. It provides that even if the agency *can* prove that you or your company is causing a public nuisance, it is not off the hook. The agency must also prove that it could not have accomplished the same thing (met the intent of the law) in some other fashion or it may still owe you just compensation. In the case of a health hazard, the agency might have accomplished the same thing through a vaccination program or a research project rather than by requiring you or your company to comply with its regulations. Where the regulations were designed to prevent the public from acquiring cancer through exposure to a "carcinogen," you should have a field day. Chapter 9 provides you with all the ammunition you will ever need.

Number 7 and number 11 look at the same situation from another angle. They require that the agency prove that a public nuisance (health hazard, etc.) is really *public*. In this court ruling, the agency must demonstrate that the violation was affecting, not just an individual or two, but rather affecting the public in the broad sense of the word. Number 11 explores the concept of what is "public" even further. There have been a number of debates in court regarding what constitutes the "public" and what constitutes a "nuisance" and these debates are continuing. There are some interesting discussions to be found in the law books with regard to this subject for those that are interested in pursuing it further. However, this only comes into play if the enforcement agency insists that they took the action against you to stop an existing public nuisance.

Since we would be dealing with some ground that has not yet been thoroughly tested, I have purposely left out situations where your property or your company might be causing a public nuisance.

This is the reason I strongly suggested that you separate the possible nuisances (hazards, etc.) from those situations that were only preventative in nature. However, I don't want to discourage you from pursuing situations where the agency has decided that a nuisance (hazard) exists. If you don't think the situation you were required to correct was causing a *public* problem of some sort, you certainly have every right to pursue just compensation for the costs you incurred in complying with the regulations. Let the agency prove that it is, indeed, a *public* problem. You have nothing to lose. You have already corrected the problem in compliance with the law. You are only trying to determining who will pay for the costs you incurred in complying with the law.

Other Things it is helpful to Know

The process of asking for just compensation under the rights granted you by the Fifth Amendment should not be confused with possible libelous acts. There may be times when the government takes actions that fail to meet procedural requirements, that are arbitrary or irrational, or that violate any number of substantive rights. Such activities by government would violate your rights to due process and, under such circumstances, the government may not take such action at all and may be libel for damages. In this case, you need to consult a lawyer to determine whether you should be pursuing a liability suit against the government. This, no doubt, is the situation that occurred with Larry Duncan. The Customs Service not only violated his Fifth Amendment rights, it also violated his right to due process. Therefore, he most likely has grounds for a libel suit against the Customs Department as well. However, this is beyond the scope of this book and needs to be discussed with a lawyer.

The "just compensation" clause of the Fifth Amendment comes into play only if the government's action was otherwise permissible. In other words, if the inspector was enforcing legislatively authorized regulations and the inspector was following the proper enforcement procedures, the just compensation clause comes into play. The government undertook no libelous acts.

The courts have also determined that the government cannot change its mind about an enforcement procedure to avoid just compensation. If a property has been taken, it has been taken, regardless of how temporary the taking may be. Once the government has required that you comply with its regulations and you have met the requirements, a taking has occurred.

Now that we have a fair idea of what a "demand letter" should consist of, let's write a letter for some of our friends. Most of the cases we selected to follow throughout this book were still unresolved at the time this book was written. Therefore, we are going to write the letters the way they would have been written had the victims followed the procedures in this book.

Larry Duncan

Since Larry Duncan has chosen to sue the Customs Service rather than pursue just compensation, we will skip him for now and move on the Caytlings who own Wheel Chairs of Berkeley and were accosted by the Food and Drug Administration.

Wheel Chairs of Berkeley

To: Director
San Francisco District
Food and Drug Administration

Dear Director

During the period from March 18 through 31, 1993, Eric W. Anderson, who identified himself as an inspector representing your agency, carried out an inspection of our business. During the course of this inspection, Mr. Anderson identified to us several situations where our company was allegedly operating in violation of certain portions of the Federal Food, Drug, and Cosmetic Act.

As required by law, during the next few months, we

worked very closely with Mr. Anderson in making sure all infractions of this act were corrected to his satisfaction. Enclosed is his inspection sheet in which he has noted that we have complied satisfactorily with all the violations he noted.

This letter is to notify you that, in accordance with the "takings clause" of the Fifth Amendment to the Constitution of the United States, the action taken by the representative of your agency constitutes a "taking." This presumption has been confirmed by the courts of this country. The Fifth Amendment further stipulates that whenever an individual or business suffers a loss of property through a "taking" by a government agency, said agency must pay the individual or business "just compensation" for this loss.

Enclosed is a detailed accounting of the expenses Wheel Chairs of Berkeley incurred as a result of complying with the written orders of your representative. None of these expenses were incurred in an effort to abate an existing public nuisance; therefore, your agency is libel for the full amount. Payment is due and payable immediately. If payment is not received within thirty days of the date of receipt of this letter, the payment will be considered late. Late payments will be assessed interest at the rate of seven percent (7%) per annum until the bill is paid in full. Should it become necessary to hire legal council in an effort to collect this bill, all legal expenses so incurred will become a part of this debt.

To help you understand why the actions of your representative constitute a violation of our rights under the "takings clause" of the Fifth Amendment to the Constitution of the United States, listed herewith is a summary of various rulings by the courts that support this contention.

1) The courts have ruled that police power regulations

can destroy the use and enjoyment of property just as effectively as formal condemnation or physical invasion of property.

2) The courts have ruled that compensation is due even if the regulations are determined to be valid.

3) The courts have ruled that although the court will assume that the agency acted in good faith, even an emergency action does not save the action from being a taking.

4) The courts have ruled that, even though we could have anticipated that we might be regulated at some time in the future, this does not relieve the agency from paying just compensation.

5) The courts have continuously found that the terms "use" and "take" include the concept of impairment.

6) The courts have ruled that the taking of property without compensation cannot be justified upon the basis that the property provides an important service to the public.

There are other court rulings that are undoubtedly relevant to this situation as well. However, the above provide adequate support for our contention that we are due compensation for the actions taken by your representative. If there are any questions in this regard, please do not hesitate to contact us.

Please be advised that it is not our intent, nor is it the intent of this letter, to interfere in any way with the enforcement of your regulations as provided by law. You are welcome to inspect our place of business for compliance with your regulations at any and all intervals and at any and all times the law suggests or requires. The only intent of this letter is to advise you that such inspections may constitute a "taking" as defined by the Fifth Amendment to the Constitution and as confirmed by our courts of law. Further, that when a "taking" has occurred, your agency will be held account-able for paying just compensation for the taking.

Thank you for your attention to this matter.

Sincerely,

John Poszgai

Unfortunately, John Poszgai never complied with any regulatory mandates, so he is not entitled to any compensation from the agency involved. In fact, by failing to comply with the regulations, he committed a felony (according to the Bush administration) and was summarily tried and convicted as a felon. Therefore, by failing to follow proper procedure, he not only ended up paying huge fines and spending time in jail, he forfeited his opportunity to collect compensation from the enforcement agency.

Bob Carpenter

Bob Carpenter, however, followed the mandates of the agency and is thus entitled to just compensation. Bob's only mistake was in not requesting compensation right after the tank was removed. By waiting a year, then asking the agency to "close" his file, he set himself up for further abuse by the agency. While he is still entitled to just compensation, he may go bankrupt before he is able to collect. When an agency knows that you are not going to ask for compensation, their favorite tactic is to keep pushing until you are so financially strapped that you can no longer afford to comply with their mandates. Once this happens, you become a John Poszgai, a felon who refused to comply with the law, instead of the recipient of just compensation. Bob Carpenter could have written this letter to the enforcement agency as soon as the tank was removed:

Director
Alameda County Health Department
Address, etc.

Dear Director:

In order to comply fully with the regulations of the Regional Water Quality Control Board, we filed a plan with your department prior to removing a diesel fuel storage tank from an underground site on our property. On December 26, 1990, our plan was approved by your agency and, shortly thereafter, we commenced the process of removing the tank in accordance with the approved plan. The removal of the tank was supervised by Mr. Gilbert M. Wistar, a representative from your department.

While removal was in progress, I discussed with Mr. Wistar the results of measurements taken from the tank that indicated that the fuel level in the tank had stayed constant for thirty years. He agreed that the measurements were a strong indication that the tank had not leaked any diesel fuel during the period it was confined underground. We also discussed the fact that cars had been parked in the driveway next to the tank and on the ground above the tank for over sixty years. Mr. Wistar agreed with me that these cars would have left a heavy residue of petroleum hydrocarbons in the soil above and around the tank. Records of these conversations can be made available to you upon request.

When removal of the tank was complete, Mr. Wistar provided me with a written report which stated, in part, "Tank is clearly old, but although rust is apparent, no holes are visible. Hole (where tank was removed) is about ten feet deep; no visual or olfactory evidence of leakage or release."

As you know, soil samples taken at the removal site indicated the presence of petroleum hydrocarbons in excess of the amount allowed by law. However, it is our position that leakage from the tank was not responsible for the presence of the petroleum hydrocarbons. This is supported by your own representative, Mr. Wistar, whose observations collaborate this finding. Mr. Wistar has also agreed with me that the presence of petroleum hydrocarbons was most probably the result of hundreds of cars being parked in the immediate vicinity for over sixty years. I would also like to point out that there is no indication that any water table in the vicinity has been contaminated by the presence of or the removal of this tank. Therefore, the tank was not being removed at your request to abate an existing public nuisance.

This letter is to notify you that, in accordance with the "takings clause" of the Fifth Amendment to the Constitution of the United States, the actions your agency required I take in order to remove the tank constitute a "taking." This presumption has been confirmed by the courts of this land. The Fifth Amendment further stipulates that whenever an individual suffers a loss through a "taking" by a government agency, said agency must pay that individual just compensation for this loss.

Enclosed is a detailed accounting of the expenses I incurred as a result of your regulatory requirements. Please note that you are not being charged for the removal of the tank but only for those cost that resulted from your enforcement activity. Since none of these expenses were incurred in an effort to abate an existing public nuisance, your agency is libel for the full amount.

Etc, etc.

To help you understand why your actions constitute a violation of our rights under the "takings clause" of the Fifth Amendment, listed herewith is a summary of rulings by various courts that support our contention.

(At this point Bob should probably quote items 1, 2, 3, 6, 10, 11, 13, 14, 15 and 16.)

Please be advised that it is not our intent, nor is it the intent of this letter, to interfere in any way with your enforcement of regulations as required by law. You are welcome to inspect our property for compliance with your regulations at any and all times the law suggests or requires. The only intent of this letter is to advise you that enforcing your regulations on this property may result in a "taking" as defined by the Fifth Amendment to the Constitution and as confirmed by our courts of law. Further, that when a "taking" has been found to have taken place, your agency will be held accountable for paying just compensation for this taking.

Thank you for your attention to this matter.

Sincerely,

Bob Carpenter

Had Bob sent such a letter to the health department as soon as the tank was removed, I doubt he would have been required to spend an additional $8,400 to remove another three feet of soil and take additional samples. Certainly, he would not find himself hiring a lawyer just to save his house. In the face of a demand for just compensation, the agency would be placing itself in considerable jeopardy by demanding a year later that Bob take samples every five feet until he reached the water table.

The Gorsks

The Gorsks are dealing with an entirely different situation. The Fish and Wild Life Service invaded their property and devalued it without notifying the Gorsks. It was not until Mr. Gorsk attempted to get a building permit that he discovered that his property had been donated to the Stephens Kangaroo Rat. He is never going to be able to build on this property and, since it now belongs to the rat, he will be unable to sell it as a building site and purchase another building site. In order to determine how much the Fish and Wild Life Service devalued his property, he may need to sell it and purchase a legal building site of like kind and size. Otherwise, he may find himself trying to compare the property's current value with its value at the time it was purchased. He would get no credit for the fact that property in the area had appreciated considerably since he originally purchased the property. The "taking" the Gorsks are suffering is probably the most common type occurring today. In a later chapter, we will discuss legislation being proposed around such "takings." The Gorsks letter should probably follow along this line:

Director
Fish and Wild Life Service
Address

Dear Director:

On (date), we purchased a 26 acre parcel of land at (location) and described as (description) for purposes of constructing a new home. At the time we made this purchase, we checked with the required government agencies to be sure that this was an approved building site. We made this purchase only after receiving such assurances.

Unfortunately, at some time between the date we purchased the property and the current date, your agency designated our property as the habitat of a threatened or endangered species of plant or animal. As a result of this designation, our property can no longer be considered a building site.

This letter is to notify you that, in accordance with the

"takings clause" of the Fifth Amendment to the Constitution of the United States, the action taken by your agency constitutes a "taking." This presumption has been upheld in the courts of the United States. The Fifth Amendment further stipulates that whenever an individual or a business suffers a loss of property through a "taking" by a government agency, said agency must pay the individual or business "just compensation" for this loss.

Enclosed is a bill summarizing the costs we have incurred in an effort to replace this lost building site with a comparable building site in a similar area. None of these expenses were incurred in an attempt to abate a public nuisance, therefore your agency is libel for the full amount. Payment is due and payable immediately. If payment is not received within thirty days of the date of receipt of this letter, payment will be considered late. You will be assessed a late charge of seven percent (7%) per annum for late payments. Should it be necessary to employ legal council to collect this bill, all legal expenses incurred in the collection process will become a part of this debt.

To help you understand why your actions constitute a violation of our rights under the "takings" clause of the Fifth Amendment to the Constitution of the United States, listed herewith is a summary of various rulings by the courts that support this contention. (Mr. Gorsk should list items 1, 2, 3, 4, 7, 8, 9, 10, 13, 14, 15, and 16)

(The remainder of the letter would be basically the same as it was for the others.)

The Payoff

As far as I know, there is not a government agency anywhere in the country that has budgeted money to pay you or me or anyone else compensation for invading our property and creat-

129

ing a "taking." Therefore, as you might imagine, there is going to be resistance to your request for "just compensation." At this point, you have the administrator of the agency feeling rather uncomfortable. There is no money set aside in the agency's budget to cover such things, and he or she certainly has no interest in paying you out of his personal finances. In fact, the agency administrator will most likely place an immediate call to the nearest attorney general's office. The Attorney General will probably advise the administrator to sit tight in hopes that the whole thing will eventually blow over. The AG will also tell the agency administrator to cease any further action against you or your business and to make no more inspections until the matter is cleared up.

There is also the possibility that the administrator will advise you by letter or whatever, that he doesn't know what you're talking about. He or she never heard of "takings" and "just compensation" and the Fifth Amendment. However, this does not hold water. All agency heads must be aware of what took place on March 15, 1988. This is when President Reagan issued Executive Order 12630. In this Executive Order, he required federal agencies to consider the takings implications of their regulatory actions and to act to minimize their interference with private property rights to the extent permitted by law. Certainly, they haven't ignored their President.

So far, the only expenses you have incurred in the pursuit of just compensation is the cost of writing the letter demanding payment. It is not my recommendation that you spend any further money on your demand at this point. You have accomplished most of what you set out to do. You have given the agency notice that any actions it takes will be assumed to be a violation of your Fifth Amendment rights and that you will expect just compensation. In so doing, you have protected yourself from any further action by the agency until this matter is settled.

Since the agency is unlikely to pay you without a mandate from a court of law, the matter will remain unsettled until *you* decide to pursue it in court.

As I mentioned previously, no agency is going to continue "regulating" you when they have been notified that they will be libel for just compensation if they do. Should an agency continue regulating you after receiving such a warning, its actions could be construed as an agreement by the agency that you are entitled to just compensation and that it is willing to pay compensation for the privilege of continuing to "regulate" you.

This is a commonly accepted method of assuming legal liability. It is no different than the liability you assume when you ignore a sign in a store that warns "if you break it you buy it" or the liability you assume if you get bitten when climbing over a fence where a sign has been posted stating "Beware of Dog." By disobeying the "warning," you are assuming the legal responsibility. Should an agency ignore your "warning" it must assume liability for its actions.

In the unlikely event that an agency inspector should arrive at your door for another inspection after you have issued your warning letter, you should immediately grab your tape recorder. Your intention, of course, is to follow the same procedures as before. However, before the inspection begins, you need to tape record the inspector's answers to the following questions:

"Are you aware we have advised your agency that any inspections undertaken by your agency will be subject to the 'takings' clause of the Fifth Amendment to the Constitution of the United States?"

"Are you aware that if you undertake this inspection your agency will be liable for all expenses incurred as a result of this inspection?"

"Would you like to discuss these matters with your supervisor or Department Head before we start this inspection?"

Regardless of how the questions are answered, you will have proof that the agency is aware of its liability and that it has determined to proceed with the inspection anyway.

Meeting Our First Goal

Our first goal, of course, is to have the owner of every business and every property in the U. S. send a demand for just compensation to every agency that is currently regulating their business or property. If every owner participated, there would soon be no business or property an agency could invade without admitting liability. When one considers the number of "citations" the average agency issues in one day, you can be assured that the agency will stand up and take notice of this sudden change. Instead of receiving one or two challenges per year, agencies will begin receiving between twenty and 100 challenges per day. If we all participated, the regulatory process as it is operating today, would soon have to make some dramatic changes in order to survive.

Going To Court

We have not, to this point, talked about going to court. The only reason one would go to court at this juncture is to get the court to order the agency to pay you just compensation for the expenses you incurred in complying with the agency's regulations. This is not something most of you should consider at this juncture. There are a lot of variables that must be considered before one considers taking an agency to court and you will be battling a covey of trained government lawyers. You should discuss your situation with a property rights lawyer before considering any court action.

Some of the things you should evaluate before considering court action are the following:

- Has the agency continued to regulate you, your business or your property since you sent your "demand" letter. If so, you should contact a property rights lawyer.
- Has the enforcement of the regulations caused a substantial loss of "property"? While the courts have ruled that taking (devaluing) a portion of your property is a taking, the amount has yet to be determined. The court is not going to look favorably upon awarding compensation for a small or temporary loss. If your loss has been significant, consult your lawyer.

Certainly someone suffering set backs such as those being experienced by the Gorsks or by Bob Carpenter should consider this avenue. However, if you are a ten million dollar business spending $500.00 to comply with regulations, forget it. We have bigger fish to fry, as you will discover in the following chapters.

- Try to discover the attitude of the judges in your area. Some judges always favor the "public good" and some favor "property rights." You don't want to go before a judge that believes that individual rights must always be sacrificed for the "public good."

While collecting just compensation is a worthy goal, it is not going to have any major impact on the regulatory process as a whole. Until the system itself is changed, our job is only half done. Until the regulatory process itself is brought under control, we will continue to function under the dark threat of new agencies with new and stricter regulations. Therefore, permanently changing the system should be the primary goal of all of us. The following chapters will be devoted to discussing how we can bring sanity to the entire regulatory process.

CHAPTER 7

Judgment Day

"The tyranny of a prince in an oligarchy is not so dangerous to the public welfare as the apathy of a citizen of a democracy."

Montesquieu

"The political machine works because it is a united minority acting against a divided majority"

Will Durant

Well, you've done it. You've gotten that troublesome agency off your back; at least until it comes up with another means of imposing its actions upon you. However, as mentioned in the last chapter, in order to keep the government off of your back permanently you, along with everyone else, must take a second, very large, step. There are several reasons why this next step is so vital.

First, since an agency's very existence depends upon its power to regulate, it is not going to give up easily. It will be in an immediate huddle with every government attorney it can locate, looking for a loop hole that will let them back into your life.

Second, as I stated earlier, it is not our goal to eliminate all regulations and all enforcement actions, but to bring a reasonableness to the process. We want them to continue to abate *real* public nuisances just as much as the next person.

Third, we must also remember that there are hundreds of agencies with millions of regulations out there. Just because we managed to get one agency off our backs does not mean that our troubles are over. You could very easily be visited by another agency with as many or more vile regulations you must comply with. There is a small chemical plant in Contra Costa County, California, for instance, that is currently being regulated by 26 different agencies.

Finally, government agencies are very inventive. If one agency is no longer able to enforce its regulations against you, it may request another agency to take up the charge. In Bob Carpenter's case, for instance, the Health Department was enforcing regulations written by the Regional Water Quality Board.

Bringing Reasonableness to the System

There are several reasons why it is important that *all* persons and *all* businesses participate in this second and final process. It is not our goal to beat the government into submission but, rather, to bring some sanity into the regulatory process. However, this will never happen until such time as the government is made accountable for its actions. If the government knows it must pay for its regulatory activities, it will be far more judicious in carrying out its enforcement activities and will be much more likely to undertake a cost-benefit analysis before it abridges our property rights. Therefore, our ultimate goal should be to establish a system where the government, if it wishes, can continue to enforce regulations developed under the guise of "Enabling Legislation," but a system where the government knows that it must bare the cost for this type of regulation. On the other hand, the agency should have the option of eliminating those regulations that are abusive and do what we would all like them to do. That is, get rid of the *real* public nuisances and penalize those that create them. Remember, in the final analysis it is not whether the government's action is proper or improper, judicious or injudicious, relevant or non-relevant. In the end it is a matter of who pays for it. If it is determined by the government that it is taking the action for the public good, then the public should pay for it. If it is abating a *real* public nuisance, the creator of the nuisance should pay for it. This is all we should ask for.

The remainder of this book is devoted to addressing the methods and providing the know how needed to bring this kind of sanity to the entire regulatory process so that it will no longer be necessary for anyone to demand just compensation when the government comes knocking. In order to accomplish this, there are several things each of us must do. Only with the cooperation of all of us can we be totally successful. Following are the various components that must be in place before we can rest assured that our property rights are secure.

Getting Proper Representation

While the Bush Administration has kicked off a campaign directed toward jailing everyone who thinks they have a right to their own property, and while Clinton shows every sign of following suit, there are some clear heads among our politicians. There is currently a lot of activity taking place in our Capitol and in our state houses, much of which needs our support. There are a number of politicians who are on your side and you need to let them know you are behind them all the way.

Several lawmakers in Washington are scurrying around trying to propose "takings legislation," including a number of proposals modeled after the Reagan executive order requiring federal agencies to conduct an evaluation of the proposed rules and regulations to determine their takings implications. Write your Senators and Congressperson and let them know that you are watching them. Tell them you want to keep your property rights and expect their support on bills that help you keep them.

Takings assessment bills have already become law in Washington, Delaware, Indiana, Utah and Arizona although the Arizona bill has been suspended until Arizona voters have their say in a 1994 referendum. You may know the outcome of this referendum by the time you read this book. While not all these bills are perfect, they are much better than nothing. If you are not a citizen of one of these states, you need to get after your state representatives to put forth such a law. While a state law won't guarantee you compensation from federal regulators, it will provide you with compensation from state directed activities. It will also influence court decisions within the state.

Rep. Jimmy Hayes (D-La.) has introduced legislation that would classify the nation's wetlands in terms of their ecological value. If owners of "high value" wetlands dislike restrictions imposed on developing their property, they could force the government to buy their land at the fair market value. Hayes' proposal would also make it far harder for government to strictly regulate other kinds of private property, regardless of the public purpose served. This is a wonderful bill, but not currently well supported in Congress. You need to get after your Congressperson to support this one. It is critical.

Rep. W.J. Tauzin (D-La.) has proposed an amendment to the Endangered Species Act which would provide compensation whenever an action of the secretary of interior would "substantially deprive" a property owner of the "economically viable use" of the property. This is another vitally needed bill that will go down to defeat unless we can all get our Congressperson to support it.

At the present time it is the property owners vs. some very radical special interest groups. Congress is in the middle and will align itself with whatever group it feels has the most political pull. Unfortunately, the special interest groups are very well organized political machines. Property and business owners, while greatly outnumbering the special interests, are not organized. We need to show Congress that we are a strong political force to be reckoned with.

As one might expect, environmental groups are violently opposed to the above two pieces of legislation. The legal departments of the Audubon Society, Sierra Club and other environmental groups are ramping up for the battle to make sure this legislation never passes.

Unfortunately, there are also some lawmakers who are not getting the message. There is just as much or more activity going on that is anti-property rights. For Instance:

In Chapter 1, I mentioned that in 1994, the U.S. Sentencing Commission will hand down a new set of environmental guidelines. One of the advisers to this Commission, Jonathan Turley, recently wrote in the "Wall Street Journal," "Environmental criminal penalties punish individuals and corporations by correctly labeling them as criminals. Nothing serves to concentrate the business mind more than a potential prison stint, even a brief one."

And don't forget, as I also discussed in Chapter 1, Representative Schumer is ready to reintroduce his own environmental crimes bill. This bill, you will recall, would increase the penalty for violating certain environmental crimes to as high as $1 million and prison terms as long as fifteen years. In addition, his bill would permit enforcement agencies to award bounties of as much as $10,000 to citizens who turn in violators. This bounty system should certainly help neighbors get along with each other.

Schumer's bill would make it a greater crime to dump a wheelbarrow full of dirt onto your own property than to rape a woman or to open fire with an Uzi on a playground full of school children. The bounty he proposes is the most despicable affront to our rights ever put forward by a politician. If your congressperson supports this bill, you definitely need a new representative. Obviously, the special interest groups will be fighting to get this bill passed. Just imagine, if this bill passes there will be millions of environmentalists looking over your fence hoping to collect that $10,000 bounty. Can you think of a greater nightmare?

During the last two presidential elections, each candidate tried to persuade us that they would be "Environmental Presidents," as if this would be a good thing. While I view myself as someone very much interested in preserving "the environment," I do not believe it should be accomplished by destroying our businesses, our property or our constitutional rights. However, under our current political climate, in order to be in favor of the environment, one must be anti-business and anti-property rights. We must let our legislators know that it is possible to be pro-environment without stomping on property rights. Each of us needs to write our representatives in Congress and let them know that there is a growing awareness among the public that congress has permitted government agencies to exploit our property rights to serve the political aspirations of a few special interest groups. We must let them know that this will no longer be tolerated. I would suggest something along the following line:

Dear Senator (Representative):

For the last twenty years, Congress has yielded to those special interest groups whose only aim has been to preserve the environment. Unfortunately, there are many among these groups that believe that any form of governmental abuse is permissible as long as it is justified under the guise of "protecting the environment." While I also consider myself an "environmentalist," I do not believe that the burden of protecting the environment should fall entirely upon the shoulders of businesses and property owners. I also do not believe that "protecting the environment" is an acceptable reason for depriving an individual of his or her property rights under the "takings" provision of the Fifth Amendment to the Constitution of the United States.

For this reason, I have joined an ever growing number of individuals and businesses who are demanding that congress look at other options for reaching our environmental goals. I am sure you are aware that there are far more businesses and property owners than there are radical environmentalists. Now that we are in the process of organizing, you will find that we have far more political clout than these radical groups. Those lawmakers who ignore this movement will find themselves replaced by representatives that are willing to be more reasonable about who shoulders the burden of protecting the environment.

On the assumption that you wish to continue to be my representative in congress, I am asking you to do the following:

1) Support Representative W.J. Tauzin's (D-La.) amendment to the Endangered Species Act.

2) Support Representative Jimmy Hays' (D-La.) legislation regarding the classification of the nation's "wetlands."

3) Support current legislation modeled after the Reagan Executive Order which requires government agencies to undertake a cost-benefit analysis of all regulatory activities.

4) Encourage special interest groups who want to control our property to meet with us. We would be happy to sell it to them so they can do whatever they want with it.

5) Solicit the help of your colleagues in defeating the very abusive environmental bill being proposed by

Representative Schumer,

I am encouraging my friends, neighbors, relatives and business associates to take note of your actions on these issues as well. Please don't let us down.

It would not hurt to point out to your representatives that until congress acts, agencies are going to continue to grab power. As we will discuss in upcoming chapters, the EPA is using every trick in the book to justify its existence and extend its power. Also, the Caytlings and their associates are not the only businesses the FDA has its eye on. For instance:

The FDA wants to regulate your cellular phone. It seems this agency just can't find enough to do. FDA Deputy Director Elizabeth Jacobson chastised the Cellular Telephone Industry Association for its "unwarranted confidence" that cellular phones are safe. "Although there is no direct evidence linking cellular phones with harmful effects in humans," she says in a letter to the CTIA, "a few animal studies suggest that such effects could exist." Jacobson obviously feels that cellular phones need the FDA's regulatory touch.

David Kessler, head of the FDA is trying hard to suppress consumer information about nutrients (vitamins and minerals) by forbidding manufacturers from making any health claims without prior FDA approval. In light of the new findings about the critical role nutrients play in preventing chronic diseases that kill modern Americans—cancer, heart disease, diabetes, osteoporosis—as well as cataracts, infectious diseases, neural-tube birth defects and other conditions, this move must be questioned. The potential cost of restricting such information is huge. In effect, he wants to subject vitamin health claims to something similar to the extensive trials that the FDA now requires for drug approvals. This process takes over a decade and costs some $230 million per drug. Imagine what your current over-the-counter vitamins and minerals would cost if they had to undergo this kind of approval system. Considering the reliability of the FDA's own science, I wouldn't feel one iota safer.

Reason Magazine quotes Carolyn Lochhead, Washington correspondent for the San Francisco Chronicle as saying: "Kessler has repeatedly used the L-tryptophan incident as support for his case. In so doing he very conveniently overlooks the convincing evidence that the contaminant was solely to blame. The agency has even gone so far as to say that the essential amino acid itself 'could' be the culprit. Blumberg, the Tufts nutrition professor, himself no devotee of amino acids, says the FDA position is 'very hard to understand. I have not seen any evidence, none, zero, and the FDA hasn't put any forth. They've just made this speculation.' Indeed, the FDA continues to allow L-tryptophan in infant formulas and hospital intravenous feeding—presumably because the ingestion of this suspected 'toxin' is essential to maintaining health. At each congressional hearing on supplements, several unfortunate victims of the L-tryptophan incident testify to the members, who cannot fail to be moved by their tragic stories (each of them linked only to the contaminated batch)."

However, the FDA is exploring an even larger and more terrifying expansion to its empire. It is seriously considering the regulation and ultimate banning of tobacco products. There are currently fifty-five million nicotine addicted people in this country and, as David Kessler points out, nicotine addiction is as powerful as addiction to heron. Such action would make Prohibition look like a Sunday school picnic. The outcome of this adventure in stupidity is discussed in more detail in Chapter 11.

In the 1970's Ralph Nader pushed very hard to get the airlines deregulated, now he (and co-author Smith) are trying to get the airline deregulation reversed and have written a book toward this end. The book contends that deregulation has made the airlines less safe. In the book they argue that cutthroat competition has forced airlines to keep old planes in service, to use inexperienced pilots, and to cut corners on maintenance. They accuse the Federal Aviation Administration of being enamored with the airlines (and of being incompetent). Unfortunately for their thesis, Nader and Smith immediately run up against some inconvenient facts. Every objective assessment of the statistics on airline accidents before and after airline deregulation shows significant reductions in accident and death rates in the years since deregulation became the law of the land. This is probably because the airlines best asset in attracting customers is a lack of accidents, not low fares. Therefore, safety will never be sacrificed for low fares. No one wants to ride on an airline that's had several accidents regardless of how cheap the fares are. I would ask Nader the following: Which airline would he rather fly on: the one that is regulated but has a high accident rate, or an unregulated airline with a low accident rate?

Yes, agencies will lie through their teeth to get more power. You need to let your congressional representatives know that you do not support such activities.

Judicial Appointments

Like the rest of us, judges are far from "impartial." They have their own beliefs and their own agendas that become a part of their baggage when they sit on the bench. For this reason, identical cases can receive opposite rulings in different courts. In the area of property rights there are many federal judges who feel that the public good should take precedence over individual rights regardless of circumstances. Judges who take this stance are going to continue to erode our rights as rapidly or more rapidly than any other force. Given the opportunity, they will side with government every time. Unfortunately, far too many such judges have been appointed to our federal benches in recent years.

As you know, all such judges are appointed to the bench by our politicians. It is up to us to watch these appointments and advise our Congressional representatives of the kind of judges we want in our courts. Special interest groups have been aware of this situation for a long time and have had a significant influence on judicial appointments. As a result, the tide of judicial opinion is currently in their favor. Now it is our turn. With some organization, property owners and business owners can be far more influential than these special interest groups. There are currently many openings for judicial appointments in our federal courts. Don't let the special interests fill them this time.

Remember also, the president fills all openings on the Supreme Court. The next time there is such an opening we all need to find out where the "appointee" stands on individual rights and react accordingly. The public has never taken more than a passive interest in judicial appointments. It is time to let our president and our congressional representatives know that this is no longer true.

In June 1993, the U.S. Supreme Court established a precedent that will give our cause an enormous boost. The court held by a 7 to 2 majority that a judge has to rule on scientific testimony based not on peer review but on the judge's own evaluation of the science in question. Writing for the majority, Justice Harry Blackmun charged judges with the responsibility for examining an expert's credentials, ensuring that "the reason or methodology underlying the testimony is scientifically valid," and determining that the conclusions presented in the testimony are "relevant and reliable." In effect, the court ruled that the admissibility of scientific evidence is too important an issue to be left to scientists. After you have read the following two chapters on the corrupt scientific methods used to support most regulations, you will understand why this is such an important precedent.

In February 1993 the Supreme Court ruled that the forfeiture law as it relates to drugs needed to be reined in. The court ruled the government couldn't confiscate drug-tainted property—land, cars, boats, money or businesses—from "innocent" owners who had no knowledge of or connection to a drug transaction. While this ruling has no direct baring on most of our property rights issues, it does have several indirect benefits. It tells us that the courts now recognize that laws can be very badly abused by the enforcement agencies, which was not always the case. It also tells us a lot about how the forfeiture law is being enforced. If you will remember, the Bush administration convinced the courts that the government need not prove that the property owner was aware that he was committing a crime in order for the government to prosecute.

In June 1993, the court ruled that the Constitution gave a home or business owner the right to challenge confiscation of property as excessive punishment for a minor drug crime.

In December 1993 the court ruled that government can no longer seize property like a thief in the night; it must give notice of the projected seizure and submit to a prior court hearing. Had this ruling taken place earlier, Larry Duncan would not be struggling to get his property back at the present time.

Do not believe for a minute that forfeiture laws only apply to drugs. The government is always looking for imaginative ways to apply it to other regulations as well. It doesn't take much imagination to realize that labeling property as a "wetlands" or as a habitat for an "endangered species" can be another form of forfeiture. Perhaps if the government had been required to notify John Poszgai and the Gorsks that their property was about to be relabeled, their circumstances would have turned out differently. At the least, a court hearing would have been required *before* their property was taken.

In a 9-0 ruling, the Supreme Court has made it much more difficult for special interest groups to use violence and other threatening methods to get their way. Basically, the ruling provides that special interest groups, regardless of their motivation, will be violating the federal anti-racketeering law if they use violence or threats against those whose actions they oppose. If found guilty, these special interest groups can be forced to pay treble whatever damages they may have caused. This should considerably slow down the environmental extremists that nail spikes into trees and damage equipment to stop a business from operating. Now that the cat is out of the bag, it will be interesting to see how the lower courts interpret the terms "violence" and "threaten."

While the courts are beginning to recognize that certain laws can be abused, we have a long way to go before the courts acknowledge that property rights are as important as the "public good." Therefore, we have to take an active part in judicial appointments.

Know Thine Enemy

We have not spent a lot of time talking about the special interest groups that have been the primary political force behind most of the legislation we must deal with today. It is time we had at least a nodding acquaintance with those who have pushed Congress into passing "Enabling Legislation" and who have helped the agencies write the regulations that have stolen our property rights.

Most of the legislation we must deal with today has grown out of a concern for the environment. While this concern existed in the scientific community to some extent since the end of World War II, it didn't become a public issue until the early 1960's when Rachel Carson wrote her book "Silent Spring." This book became a part of the school curriculum in many areas and was, in great part, responsible for the public's attitude about the environment today. The book also became the rallying point for many fledgling environmental groups such as the Audubon Society, the Sierra Club, and Green Peace and a great tool for recruiting members to their organizations. As time wore on, some members became dissatisfied with the actions of these organizations and the more radical groups such as Earth First were born. We will talk more about these radical groups later on.

With the creation of the Environmental Protection Agency in 1968, the environmental groups begin pushing for complete protection of the environment from the intrusions of us humans. It soon became the environmental philosophy that humans and the environment were two opposing forces that could not exist on the same planet together. Taken to the extreme, it appeared that the only means of completely protecting the environment was the extinction of man. (This is still the philosophy held by some of the radical groups.) The general public was not too happy with this conclusion and the environmental movement begin to lose a good deal of support.

In order to recover lost ground, the EPA and its supporters found a new cause. They discovered that they could once again get public support if their declared purpose was not just to protect the environment but to protect the public health as well. The new goal was to persuade the public that we humans and the environment were interdependent creatures. The loss of either entity would be damaging. Further, that protecting the environment was also a means of protecting the public health. The public liked the idea of having its health protected right along with the environment, and public support swelled again. However, organizations such as the EPA and its special interest groups could not survive in a vacuum. They needed something to protect the public health and the environment from. Now that humans were not longer the enemy of the environment, they needed another enemy. They declared that the enemy was now property owners and businesses.

I spent the formative portion of my childhood during the Second World War. Killing other humans, at least at that time, was a very traumatic experience for those young men just out of high school who were drafted into the military service to fight this war. The concept of destroying other humans was unacceptable to them and to those of us who were left at home. In order to make this mayhem more digestible, our government had an on going campaign of dehumanizing the enemy. The perception was that if we did not view them as human beings, it would be a whole lot easier for us to accept the killing. It was a very effective campaign. It was years before I realized that the Japanese were not non-human aliens out to destroy the world as I had been lead to believe.

The environmental movement has taken its cue from the government and has used the same tactics in its program to make the bashing of businesses and property owners an acceptable sport. In order to make it acceptable to steal property and destroy businesses, the public had to be convinced that property owners and businesspersons were greedy, uncaring, environmentally insensitive subhumans that would allow their own mothers to be poisoned for a profit. This campaign has been on going for thirty years and it has worked. As a result, the public not only finds regulating businesses and property owners into bankruptcy acceptable, they cheer at the prospect. We are, indeed, the enemy.

It is time we let the public know who it is really supporting. By now we should all be aware that the regulations the public so wholeheartedly accepts, have put thousands of people out of work. Now we must tell the public. In the final chapter, we will discuss how much it is costing the public to hate businesses and property owners. The public needs to be aware of this as well. The environmentalists have made sure the public is well apprised of the existence of the few obnoxious business owners and property owners that have helped the environmentalist give us a bad name. Now it is time that we reciprocate.

It is time the public met some of the people in the more radical segments of the environmental movement and hear what these radicals have to say.

In the "Earth First. Journal" a Miss Ann Thropy writes that "AIDS should be welcomed as a necessary solution to man's overpopulation and destruction of the earth." I'll bet the general public would be delighted to know it is supporting people who want AIDS to become the epidemic that eliminates overpopulation.

David Graber, a National Park Service research biologist, wrote in the "Los Angeles Times," "Human happiness, and certainly human fecundity, are not as important as a wild and healthy planet... We have become a plague upon ourselves and upon the Earth. It is cosmically unlikely that the developed world will chose to end its orgy of fossil-energy consumption, and the Third World its suicidal consumption of the landscape. Until such time as homo sapiens should decide to rejoin nature, some of us can only hope for the right virus to come along."

Comments such as those just cited are upsetting enough, but I'm sure the public will be equally excited to know that these radical individuals are rapidly exploring methods to take this movement beyond the talking stage and into the implementation stage.

In the January 1994 issue of *Reason* magazine, Gregory Benford writes about his research into minds and activities of those who feel that humans are a plague that must be controlled before they destroy this planet. He wanted to know if creating a world wide epidemic of a fatal disease was within reach of these radicals. Following are excerpts from his article, "The Designer Plague":

The more the North (we North Americans) thinks of humanity as a malignancy, the more we will unconsciously long for disasters. Somewhere, sometime, some eco-activist may see a quite simple solution to the South's runaway growth and poverty: the Designer Plague.

In the development of the Designer Plague, The big advances could lie in virulence. There are newly "emergent" viruses like Ebola that can kill up to two out of three victims, suggesting that influenza could be brought to this level as well. A biologist at the University of California, Irvin, remarks, "I doubt that a single person could come up with the required virus. Certainly it could be done either with a large research team, as in defense labs, or by many individuals trying independently, and one getting lucky." How many? "A few dozen."

Our old enemy Smallpox could fill in. Since it was eradicated in the mid-1970's, few people have been vaccinated. By now most of the world is susceptible again. Smallpox is kept locked away at two heavily guarded sites in the world, while the medical community debates whether those two samples should be destroyed. (One counter argument holds that, after all, smallpox is a species, and we should conserve a species.)

But smallpox is imprisoned in only one sense. Its genome is published in open literature, so in another sense it's everywhere. Like all life, smallpox is at root information. A biological virus in this sense is exactly like a computer virus. All smallpox needs to make its way to virtual reality is for a savvy scientist to translate. A UCLA biologist, when asked, could easily describe how this can be done. He went on to say that "with modified proteins, airborne particles can turn ten or even 100 times more deadly. And in the next few decades, myriad biotech workers will know how to alter viral information."

How many will belong to the Animal Liberation Front? It won't take many. A handful of carriers would suffice to spread such a designer plague. "You should hear the eco-warriors talk when there's no microphone around," an industrial molecular biologist remarked to me. "The only thing restraining them is the technical barriers."

Would anyone be mad enough to kill billions, hoping to stave off the ecological and cultural collapse of nations, of continents, of whole societies? Speculations have already been voiced along these lines by molecular biologists. A specialist in tropical diseases said to me, "I think it's a terrifying possibility. I've met enough otherwise intelligent people who believe a mouse and a deer and a human baby are of equal moral stature. Why not kill one that's out of population balance, to save another?"

Regulation cannot contain the evil potential of the Designer Plague. Rather, we must deplore humanity-as-cancer rhetoric and reaffirm basic humanist values. Not all life is equivalent. We cannot evade the fact that we are now the stewards of the natural world."

Gregory Benford is a professor of physics
at the University of California, Irvine.

It is time the public knew that there are many people out there who firmly believe that the way to save the environment is through an epidemic that will kill off three-fourths of the population of this earth. Some of these people are working in the laboratories where the development of "plague" organisms is being studied. If the individuals Gregory talked with are right, these radicals could have in their hands the tools needed to start such an epidemic in less than ten years. We all know who will be vaccinated against this plague, don't we?

Fortunately, the majority of those who want to protect the environment understand that the elimination of the human race isn't the proper method for accomplishing this goal. However, they do firmly believe that there should be very tight controls on the use of property. They feel that the government is within its rights to take your property to protect a "wetlands" or an "endangered species." I am inclined to believe that they are about half right. I respect the concept that we should save as much of the environment as possible. I grew up being a naturalist and would like to see my children and grandchildren enjoy nature as much as I have.

However, I believe groups such as the Audubon Society, Sierra Club, etc. need to put their money where their mouth is. They are very avid environmentalists as long as you and I are paying to protect the environment. However, I wonder how enthusiastic they would be if they had to pay their share.

I think the final step in this project should be to get the special interest groups to purchase any property they feel should be preserved and leave the government out of it all together. Why should you or I or the rest of the public pay for a piece of property that only a few groups want preserved for posterity? I'm sure if these groups had to purchase any land they wanted preserved, they would be a lot more judicious in their selection of property than the government currently is.

Fortunately, there is already some small movement in this direction. Unfortunately, it is not being practiced by these environmental groups but buy government sponsored entities. Nevertheless, it is worth mentioning what is taking place in this area.

The East Bay Regional Park District in the San Francisco Bay area has had its eye on 1000 acres of an especially prime "wetlands" that would provide potential habitat for several sensitive species including the Delta smelt, the greater sandhill crane and the giant garter snake. Because of its close proximity to a large community, the site would also serve as an excellent location for a science center. The property, currently owned by Porter Estate Co., is also used extensively by migrating waterfowl. Over the years, there have been several proposals to develop this property by building homes with private boat docks such as exist in a few other areas in the county. Under the circumstances, no one would be surprised if the EPA or the Army Corps of Engineers swooped down, labeled the property a "wetlands," and stopped any potential development while making sure the current owners continued to pay taxes and upkeep on the property.

The East Bay Regional Park District, however, is doing things the right way. In cooperation with Contra Costa County, the local sanitation district, and a local community college, they are going to *buy* the property. Through a special assessment and other clever money-making endeavors, the agencies are accumulating the funds necessary to purchase the property to serve the purposes the East Bay Regional Park District has in mind.

If only the environmentalists would take note. There *is* a way to protect the interests of the "public" without stomping all over an individuals constitutional rights. Now if we could only get these "special interest" groups to pay their share, particularly those that think the preservation of "wetlands" is more important than the constitution, justice would indeed be served.

Establishing Precedents

The final and most important component of our plan is to carefully orchestrate legal actions that will establish certain desired national legal precedents in our federal courts. Regardless of how many laws are passed by congress and regardless of how many regulations are written by government agencies, nothing can be finalized until these laws and regulations are tested in court. There have already been many precedents established in our courts of law which have determined that agencies confiscating the properties of private citizens must pay just compensation. However, there are still a number of issues that need to be settled. There are also many issues that have been settled only at the state level but not at the national level. Our goal must be to establish, through our federal courts, certain universal precedents that all agencies would be required to abide by. Once this is accomplished, the agencies will stop challenging the just compensation clause in the courts and begin rewriting their regulations. Furthermore, when the agencies must pay for their "takings," they will undertake a very critical cost-benefit analysis before implementing any sort of enforcement action. Finally, they will begin working on the real public nuisances rather than pestering the majority of us who have previously been required to prevent crimes that will never happen.

As discussed previously, there are many areas in the "takings" arena that have not been settled by the courts at this juncture. Among other things, there needs to be further definition of a "public nuisance." The whole concept of "public" and of "nuisance" is still shrouded in shadows. Until these terms are better defined by the courts, agencies are going to continue to utilize the concept of "public nuisance" as a defense for their actions. Other things at issue concern determining at what point an action creates sufficient loss of property to constitute a "taking." While some courts have ruled that a partial taking of property is a taking, there is little guidance regarding how small a loss you can suffer and still be entitled to compensation. Several courts have ruled that the permit process, when abused, is a "taking," however, the point a which it becomes abusive is still foggy.

Another problem lie in the fact that many current rulings have come from state or regional courts and, while they may serve as precedents, other states and regions are not bound by these decisions. As a result, a very liberal court can still rule in favor of the government, regardless of previous precedents. Certain basic rulings need to be established in the U.S. Supreme Court, so these rulings become the law of the land. Until that happens, government agencies in areas with liberal courts will continue to "test" our rights to our property.

There are several legal organizations and property rights organizations working on this problem while you read (See Chapter 11). However, they are minuscule in size compared to government and they have limited resources. To accomplish our task, every reader of this book must support one or more of these organizations. The organizations need support in two ways. First, they need your financial support in order to hire the lawyers and support personnel necessary to follow key cases all the way to the Supreme Court. Second, they need good, solid, well documented cases of government regulatory abuse to bring before the courts.

For years government lawyers have had all the advantages. They have been representing clients (agencies) that were well trained in the regulatory process. They entered court with a case that had been lawyer proofed by the government employee who performed the inspection. The private sector lawyer was so busy trying to keep his client out of jail he had little time to concern himself with setting earth shattering precedents. However, now that you have followed the procedures in this book, you have made it much easier for a good property rights lawyer to win a precedent setting case. At the least, lawyers representing the private sector and lawyers representing the government agencies will be battling on an even playing field. More than likely, the private sector lawyers will now enter the playing field with an advantage. They will have, by the agency's own admission, evidence that you complied completely with the law. They will also have an admission by the agency that you were not creating a public nuisance. The inspection of your property or business, therefore, was totally discretionary on the part of the agency. The only reason for being in court is to determine who should pay the costs you incurred by complying with regulations that are unconstitutional, abusive, and not in the best interest of the public, regulations whose very existence are highly suspect.

The final step in the implementation of this component is locating cases that have the potential to set the needed precedents. Neither you nor I have the knowledge to make this decision. However, good property rights lawyers and the groups mentioned in Chapter 11 do. Therefore, you just need to get your situation before one of these groups. Obviously, they cannot handle the enormous load of cases that would come in if they received information on every visit made by every government agency. Therefore, you need to be a bit judicious in determining if your situation has the potential for use by these groups. By way of guidance, I would suggest that you contact one of these groups if your situation meets all the following criteria:

1) You have followed the procedures in Chapters 5 and 6 to the letter and have everything well documented.

2) You are willing to write a thorough summary of your situation so the group does not have to try to piece your story together from a bunch of inspection forms, letters, etc.

3a) If your property was devalued through government "labeling," you must have an accurate means of determining the actual loss in property value.

3b) If your loss was due to an abusive permit system, you must be able to show that the costs caused by the delay were substantial and the delay was unnecessary.

3c) If the loss was through the regulation of a business, you must be able to demonstrate that complying with the regulations was expensive and, preferably, disruptive to the operation of the business.

4) You must be willing to testify in court should that become necessary.

At this point, I want to make one thing very clear. These groups are going to be very selective in the cases they choose. If your case is not selected, don't assume that your case doesn't have merit. Cases are generally selected based on their need to establish a particular precedent and not on the person's right to just compensation. Therefore, don't assume that your situation does not warrant just compensation just because it was not selected. You certainly have every right to pursue compensation through normal legal channels and, if you have suffered a substantial loss, I suggest that you do so. Your case may not establish a new precedent but, by forcing the government to pay for its regulatory abuses, you are making a substantial contribution toward our collective goal. Your rewards will be substantial. Not only will you get reimbursed for your loss, but you will have informed the regulatory world that you are not one to blithely roll over and play dead. Finally, you will have helped your fellow travelers by making government a bit more cautious in its approach to everyone. I urge everyone who has suffered a substantial loss and has followed the procedures in this book to consult a good property rights lawyer. It's more satisfying to wrangle with government over who pays the bill than to be fighting to stay out of jail.

Changing Judicial Attitudes

By now it should be apparent that ultimate victory lies in the hands of the courts. Survival will not be guaranteed until the proper precedents have been established. As has been mentioned from time to time, success in establishing these precedents rely, to a great extent, on changing the attitudes of the judges. At first glance, you may think there is little you can do in this arena. However, you would be wrong. The courts decision, as always, will be a balancing act between the public good and the rights of the individual. To this point, the courts have heard mostly from the agencies, environmentalists and other special interests who consistently expound on behalf of the public good. The courts seldom hear from our side and when they do, the information is terribly fragmented. There has been no united effort on the side of business and property owners to present a true picture of what takes place when an agency is allowed to run roughshod about the country enforcing regulations developed primarily to increase the agency's own power and guarantee its existence. The courts are not aware that almost every regulation on the books is justified by faulty science or other misleading information. It is not apparent to the courts that it may be in the public's best interest to demand that the agencies do a cost-benefit evaluation before taking any action. Finally, every judge must understand that if something is truly for the public good then the public should bear the expense.

The judiciary has a record of reluctance when it comes to exercising its role as constitutional guardian. Given the option, the judiciary will champion such government activities as land use planning, environmental protection, and provision of housing. The judiciary must be made aware that, while these may be worthy goals, it is not the courts responsibility to decide these issues. The judiciary's only responsibility is to determine whether the means chosen to accomplish those goals comply with the dictates of the Constitution.

The courts also seem to believe that just compensation will make it impossible for government to achieve public goals. It is

up to us to make the courts understand that destroying someone's property rights is not the proper method for accomplishing
public goals. There are other avenues available for fulfilling
these public needs. I would suggest assessing the special interest groups that were instrumental in promoting the regulations
to begin with. There are also options such as forming special assessment districts, encouraging community projects, calling for
a temporary tax, and similar methods. If you will recall, in Chapter 6 we revealed that there are already court rulings that stipu-
late that the enforcement agency must be able to demonstrate
that there are no other means of accomplishing these public
goals. We just need to help the agencies and the courts find
these other means.

Obviously, judges are not going to be aware of these things
until they are adequately argued in their courts. The opposition
is extremely well organized and has spent years developing a library of evidence in support of their position. On the other hand,
there is virtually no information pool that a property rights lawyer might use in presenting facts that support the rights of the
property or business owner. Therefore, the lawyer has no ammunition with which to attack the enormous pile of lies the
agencies and special interests have used to back their position.
It is up to us, collectively, to provide our lawyers with this ammunition. The information they need is everywhere: in our daily
newspapers, in our libraries, in professional and scientific journals and in all other areas where information is stored. We all
need to start reading this material and saving items which support our position.

Information can be both philosophical and factual. A sampling of the types of information that can be used to argue our
cases is presented in the following chapters. Read them over
carefully until you have good grasp of the types of arguments
that might be presented in court in support of our position. Once

you understand what is needed, you can begin collecting support material. You may think that the following chapters provide an enormous amount of information in this regard. However, while there is a significant amount presented, I have only scratched the surface. If we all begin pooling this type of information, we will soon have a substantial library of valuable information that our lawyers can carry to court. Until a centralized library can be established to store this information, the author of this book will try to serve as a repository for all the information you gather. The opposition has a thirty year head start, but we have the truth and the Constitution on our side. Let's start reading.

Now lets look at how science has been pulling our tails for the last thirty years in order to justify most regulations.

CHAPTER 8

Scientific Hocus-Pocus

"The great masses of the people...will more easily fall victims to a great lie than to a small one."

Adolph Hitler

"The whole aim of practical politics is to keep the populace alarmed (and hence clamorous to be led to safety) by menacing it with an endless series of hobgoblins, all of them imaginary."

H.L. Mencken

Charles R. Knight has had a more profound influence upon the public's perception of dinosaurs than just about anyone else in the world. You would suspect that anyone having so much influence over public opinion would be a leading authority on dinosaurs. However, you would be dead wrong. Charles Knight is not a formally trained paleontologist or, for that matter, a formally trained scientist of any sort. Rather, Charles Knight is an artist, and an extremely good one.

Using his artist's brushes and an exceptional amount of talent, Mr. Knight has created some incredible pictures of what we have imagined our planet to be like during the era when dinosaurs ruled the earth. In an effort to make his pictures as authentic as possible, he has relied on the best available scientific knowledge in the design of each animal and each habitat. However, he will be the first to tell you that accurate information concerning most dinosaurs is difficult to come by. For instance, in order to portray the size, texture and color of each dinosaur's skin he had to depend entirely on guess work. The same problem existed with regard to other aspects of a dinosaur's soft tissue, such as reproductive organs, liver, heart, brain, lungs, etc. In addition, the only thing he had to assist him in developing a habitat for these animals was a good deal of conjecture. Whenever he wished to show one of these behemoths eating or hunting or hiding or running or doing something else we suspect dinosaurs probably did, even the best information was sketchy. After all, there were no scientists around to make scientific observations and take notes during the period when dinosaurs were king. Therefore, the very best we can say for Mr. Knight's pictures is that they are a depiction of dinosaur's life based on limited evidence left over 100 million years ago. Mr. Knight faced other problems as well. In some instances, it was necessary to portray 100 million years of dinosaur evolution in one picture. As a result, dinosaurs that roamed the earth several million years apart, often appeared together in one picture.

Mr. Knight's responsibility was to provide us with the best available perceptions of what it was like back then. However, we will probably never know how close he came to reality. His pictures seem so authentic that even scientists, whose job it is to be totally objective about such matters, have tended to accept some of Knight's works as a "fairly decent" depiction of what life was like 100 million years ago.

We should be willing to forgive scientists for slipping into this world of fantasy every once in a while. They are, after all, humans just like the rest of us. Such a dalliance into the world of make believe isn't really going to hurt anyone is it? At least not when we talk about dinosaurs. Major errors in judgment about things that occurred 100 million years ago aren't going to have any significant impact on decisions made about how we function today. However, when scientific fantasy becomes the major tool in the development of public policy, it is time to become very alarmed.

Unfortunately, a great many public policies have been developed over the last thirty years that have used, as justification for their existence, scientific evidence as unreliable as our knowledge of dinosaurs. This may not be a big deal when painting a picture of dinosaurs, but it can be a major catastrophe when it involves the development of regulations that govern our lives, property and business.

It has been the pattern for the past three decades to use some fancy scientific paint brushes to justify the development of the millions of regulations that sit on the books of the Environmental Protection Agency, Public Health, Occupational Health and Safety, the Army Corps of Engineers, and other government agencies. Unfortunately, this is an expensive practice. The cost of operating enforcement agencies is expensive enough. However, the real cost lies with the property owners, businesses and others who are required to spend billions of dollars each year complying with these poorly justified regulations.

In this chapter we will explore some of the current scientific fallacies that have been used by agencies and others determined to force their wills upon the rest of us. We will also discover how scientists design research for their own use or for the use of an enforcement agency. Later we will look at the means one can use to determine if a regulation is based on solid scientific principles, and what to do when the regulation is based on scientific illusion.

The Predictions Game

The New York Times, August 14, 1975 stated we were heading "toward extensive northern hemisphere glaciation." *Science Magazine* on December 10, 1976 declared that we are facing "continued rapid cooling of the earth" and "the approach of a full blown 10,000-year ice age." Not to be outdone, *Global Ecology* in 1971 and *Science* on March 1, 1975, spouted the same propaganda. *International Wildlife* in July of 1975 along with *Science Digest* in February of 1973 and Newsweek on April 28, 1975, asserted that "a new ice age must stand alongside nuclear war as a likely source of wholesale death and misery" and that "the world's climatologists are agreed" that we must "prepare for the next ice age."

Scientific propaganda of this nature was a part of our daily life during the 1970's. The above quotes will give you some idea of how seriously our press and our nation bought into the notion, based only on scientific speculation, that an "ice age" was imminent. We had only two choices in the 1970's: within the next few years we could either freeze to death or starve to death.

It now seems almost unbelievable that just twenty years ago scientists from all over the world "warned" us that we must take immediate action or the world, as we know it, would cease to exist. The earth was cooling at an inordinate rate and an "ice age" was just a few years away. The cause, we were assured, was of our own making. By producing products in our factories, driving cars, building houses and just plain living, we humans were destroying the very planet that gave us life. Now we were heading into an "ice age" that only a miracle could halt. Drastic measures were called for and drastic measures we got. We were warned in no uncertain terms that all the pollution we were creating had to be stopped immediately. To ensure that all pollution ceased, hundreds of thousands of regulations appeared, governing every aspect of business and almost every aspect of an individual's life.

Were the regulations effective in stopping our plunge into an "ice age"? I'm sure that the environmentalist and their scientific cohorts will agree that there is ample proof that they were very effective. After all, we are no longer in danger of being consumed by gigantic walls of ice. In fact, one might suggest that the regulations worked a little too well. Just twenty years later we are being "warned" by these same authorities that we, and our world, are in danger from "global warming."

Fortunately, any reasonable individual will realize that we need only turn the clock back twenty years to resolve the problem of "global warming." If, indeed, all those regulations devised twenty years ago were effective in stopping the encroaching "ice age," it should be a simple matter to reverse the trend toward "global warming." All we need do is eliminate all those regulations that led us down the path to "global warming" and start over. This time we will sprinkle our society with just enough regulations to keep us from plunging into another "ice age" but not enough to send us back onto the path toward "global warming."

While this would seem to be a most logical solution to the problem of "global warming," many environmental groups will disagree. They feel that the answer to "global warming" is the passage of even *more* regulations. At this point I become very confused. If stringent environmental regulations were necessary to escape an encroaching "ice age" and send us spinning into an era of "global warming," how can more regulations stop this trend?

To me this is analogous to building a fire to get us warm then, when the fire gets too warm, putting more wood on the fire in an effort to cool things off. When this sort of faulty thinking becomes the basis for developing public policies, we should all be very concerned. Certainly, any regulation whose intent is to stop the impending "ice age" or whose intent is to stop "global warming" should be challenged.

If you still feel there is some value in heeding the advice of our environmental alarmists and their scientific cohorts, let's examine some of their most recent proclamations. When it comes to projecting what sort of environmental tragedies will befall earth as a result of various man-made disasters that have taken place, this group seems to be batting a big, fat zero. During the war in Kuwait, for instance, environmentalists warned us of the inevitable destruction of the Persian Gulf ecosystem when Sadam Hussein pulled the plug on Kuwait's oil pipeline. What they didn't tell us is that scientists from the Marine Laboratory of Monaco sampled the surrounding waters shortly thereafter and discovered that there was actually *less* oil pollution in the Gulf than in the period between 1983 and 1986.

Then, of course, there was the widely predicted "death cloud" that was going to do major destruction to the world when Saddam's troops lit all Kuwait's oil wells on fire. The prediction was that the wells would burn for many years creating a "death cloud" that would change weather patterns and cause illness and death. In reality, the wells were capped in six months and no one was able to discover any health or environmental problems resulting from the fires.

Scientists and environmentalists have had a field day trying to get us to change our living habits so as to keep the ozone layer from disappearing and giving us all a bad case of sunburn. What they have failed to mention is that the hole in the ozone layer over the Arctic Circle was twice as severe in 1958 as it is today.

Don't get me wrong. There has been a lot of destruction and tragedy taking place on this old planet in the last few years. Unfortunately for us, the environmentalists and scientists didn't warn us about the ones that really counted. But, then, who can outguess Mother Nature. It was, after all, her erupting volcanoes, teeth chattering earthquakes, 150 mile per hour hurricanes, and twenty inch rain storms that really caused all the damage.

As mentioned in the last chapter environmentalist have, for many years, tried to pin the impending destruction of our planet on the backs of businesses around the country and around the world. The more radical environmentalist have suggested very strongly that the very existence of humans on earth is a major environmental calamity. It is opinions and prejudices such as these that have set in motion the major scientific blunders that we deal with today. Fortunately, the prognosticators are never right. Had Paul Ehrlich's prediction in the book "Population Explosion" been right, for instance, we would be just a few years away from a "standing room only" situation for humans on earth.

Science, unfortunately, has taken a big hit because of this prognostication foolishness. Instead of paying heed to proper scientific principles, science has bent to the whims of panicky environmentalist and the world of science has lost a good deal of its credibility from listening to the wrong people.

As much as I dislike seeing science fall on its face, the realization that it can no longer be trusted will eventually play a big role in the elimination of those ludicrous regulations that used scientific speculation as justification for their existence. As more of those who are regulated become aware that the regulations they must tolerate are based on scientific predictions as unreliable as Charles Knight's paintbrushes, the more frequently the regulations will be challenged. Even the country's courts are beginning to realize that regulations developed around projected health and environmental disasters are often no more than someone's thirst for power.

Unfortunately, although science is still unable to effectively predict the outcome of a horse race where there are just a few variables involved, it insists on trying to predict the future of our planet. It is too much to expect accurate predictions about the future when every earthquake, volcano, hurricane, business, human, plant and animal is going to affect the outcome. To help you understand why, here are some excerpts from the article, "Future Imperfect," by Robert Root-Bernstein which can be found in the November 1993 issue of *Discover* Magazine.

Mr. Root-Bernstein begins by discussing how scientific predictions moved from threatened ice age to threatened global warming in just twenty years, and reviews existing controversies over whether or not global warming is occurring. He then goes on to say that "The seeming paradox in global warming predictions is at heart a problem of extrapolation…. Extrapolation is the process of extending data or inferring values for any unobserved period or interval. Unfortunately there is no science of extrapolation. It is, a best, an art, and a highly fallible art at that."

As an example of "extrapolation," think about the following. One can easily visualize the problem extrapolating creates if one were to try to determine how many people per week used the door on the front of an office building by just observing the door for one hour and using that information to extrapolate future usage. Results would differ greatly depending upon what time of day or night you watched. If you observed from eight to nine in the morning, you would see fifty people use the door, while at three in the morning you would see none at all. If you watched from eight to nine in the morning and extrapolated your data, you would figure that 1200 people used the door every day (fifty people per hour times twenty-four hours) and that 8400 people (1200 times seven days) used the door in a one week period. Had you extrapolated data, based on observations taken at three in the morning, you would extrapolate that the door is never used. And, of course, neither extrapolation would take into account weekends and holidays.

If you think I am being a bit harsh with such an example, remember this. Science is extrapolating the future environment of our planet based on thirty or forty years of current observations while the earth has been around for about three billion years. This is like observing the office door for one second in order to determine how many people use it in one week.

Root-Bernstein points out that, even if there were no prejudice or bias in scientific projections, there is no potential for ac-
curacy. The scientific "models" used for these projections have
far too many faults to provide science with a means for predict-
ing the future. For instance, "we are still searching for what
things should be in our models and what things we can ignore.
In 1989 MIT professor Richard Lindzen made some unpopular
criticisms of global warming predictions based on his analysis of
where current climate models are weak. He claimed that computer models are rife with uncertainties, have not been adequately tested, and ignore feedback systems that will tend to
counteract temperature increases—for example, clouds. Indeed, an independent study published in *Nature* in 1989 compared 14 climate models and found that some predicted that
cloud formation would enhance the greenhouse effect, while
others predicted that it would result in drastic cooling. More recently scientists found a correlation between sunspot activity
and the Earth's temperature. The finding suggests that the
amount of energy leaving the sun directly influences global climate—but no climate models included solar radiation as a variable.

"The long and the short of it is that we cannot accurately extrapolate from a model that does not accurately represent nature. All too often we do not understand the basic science well
enough to make the necessary representations. Faced with areas of science that are too young for accurate modeling, or with
systems too complex for accurate description, scientists tend to
simplify."

Root-Bernstein concludes by saying, "Until we understand
the sciences underlying our extrapolative models, and until we
have some means of evaluating the extrapolations themselves,
we know too little to act rationally or with the necessary foresight to assure us that our actions will not have unfortunate, per-

haps catastrophic, effects we never intended. Instead of acting to change things we do not understand, we should first act to understand them better. Extrapolation, for the present, must remain the tool for analyzing the state of our scientific knowledge rather than a science for directing the tools of state."

Perhaps Ursula LeGuin, an award-winning science fiction novelist, said it best: "Science fiction is often described, and even defined, as extrapolative. The science fiction writer is supposed to take a trend or phenomenon of the here and now, purify and intensify it for dramatic effect, and extend it to the future.... Method and results much resemble those of a scientist who feeds large doses of a purified and concentrated food additive to mice in order to predict what may happen to people who eat small quantities for a long time. The outcome seems almost inevitably to be cancer. So does the outcome of extrapolation."

It is obvious that most of our regulations are base on just such extrapolations. Isn't it nice to know that public policy has been developed around science fiction?

I am sure most judges would be interested to know that many very reputable scientists feel that such poorly understood science should not be used to develop public policy. Yet almost every regulation currently enforced by the EPA is the result of just such extrapolation. The truth is, no one, scientist or otherwise, can predict the future. Nor can anyone determine how man or his businesses are affecting the future of our environment. Under the circumstances, it is painfully obvious that business is being required to pay a very high price to prevent something that no one can determine will ever occur. This does not mean that I advocate abolishing every regulation on the books. However, I certainly believe, in the light of such uncertainty, we should all share the costs of protecting ourselves from this paranoia. What better way to control the abuse of regulations built on this pillar of salt than through just compensation?

Promoting Fear and Hate

In my capacity as a Medical Entomologist, I continually received all the latest information on health issues and research surrounding my profession. We had all but eliminated the problem of mosquitoes carrying diseases to human beings here in the United States, and we were frantically looking around for something else to justify our existence. (We is a collective term for all of the other Entomologists and scientists involved in diseases transmitted to humans by insects.) The boys and girls in the laboratories began looking at all the other insects that share our environment and discovered that many of these insects were capable of hauling around some of the bacteria that can make us sick.

I took this information to my boss, partly for its informational value and partly out of concern. I wasn't really convinced that any of these insects were likely to make anyone sick, but then, why take any chances? My boss took the information to his boss who, in turn, took it to our local law making body. It was then that I discovered that our law makers are great politicians but lousy scientists. My boss's boss was truly eloquent. In short order, he had all those law makers convinced that the public was at great risk if something wasn't done. He fed the politicians a lot of malarkey that violated every scientific principal devised by man. However, he had done his job. The law makers quivered with fear at the spectacle of a disease epidemic and gave my boss's boss the authority to do whatever was necessary to eliminate the menace.

Since I was the expert in such matters, the project was handed over to me. In short order, I had my own budget, a bunch of equipment and several people working for me. In light of my new supervisory responsibilities, the Civil Service Commission awarded me with a nice raise in pay. I wasn't aware of it at the time, but I had started construction on a new promotional ladder within the government "system." Imagine what I could have done if I was really motivated to build an empire and was skilled in the process.

Way back in the deepest recesses of my mind, I realized that I was probably doing absolutely nothing to protect the public health. The organisms our laboratory people had found on these insects were the same bacteria every one of us human beings carry around on our bodies all the time. Deep in my subconscious, I suspected that the only real dangers lie in one human transmitting the disease organisms to another human. However, no one seemed to be interested in giving me the authority or equipment to kill off the real transmitters of these disease organisms (humans), so I had to be satisfied with launching a big campaign to kill off all the insects. What the hell. I wasn't hurting anyone and I might be doing a *little* good. I hoped I was. I was certainly spending a goodly sum of your tax dollars.

It wasn't until some time later that I began to learn more about the nuances involved in presenting information in the fashion most favorable to your own personal cause. For instance, the information you keep hidden is often many times more important than the information you provide. As it turned out, I discovered some time later that the toothbrush each of us sticks into our mouths each morning and evening has far more harmful bacteria on it than there are on the insects I was mandated to destroy. Had this bit of information been revealed at the hearing before our local Legislative body, I don't think my boss's boss would have had much luck persuading the law makers of the need to control those insects I was spending big money to kill. They might have been more receptive to a suggestion that the Health Department undertake a $100,000 program to eliminate toothbrushes.

To fully grasp how the use of FEAR and HATE have evolved, let's examine what would have happened if I had pulled my little escapade in 1940 and how things would have evolved if I had pulled my prank any time after 1970. See if you can detect the difference.

In 1940 you, the taxpayer, would have been totally unaware that some laboratory junkies had found some disease organisms on a few insects. Your only source of news at that time was the daily newspaper and you would never find an article reporting such information in your paper. The newspapers in those days had no interest in reporting "such nonsense." You would hear nothing about our game unless the lab junkies and I were able to prove that some human or group of humans had actually gotten sick from being exposed to these insects. Newspapers in those days were interested in reporting facts, not extremely remote possibilities.

In 1940, I would have had a complete lack of success with the local law makers as well. Even if I could have persuaded my boss's boss to plead my case before the local lawmakers, he or she would have accomplished little. The lawmakers in those days were not susceptible to "scare tactics" and would have demanded proof that the public health was in danger. We would not have been able to document a single case in which one of our constituents had gotten sick specifically from an encounter with one of the insects the "lab boys" had found the organisms on. The lawmakers would have had no interest in funding such a remote probability.

In 1940, any such proposal would have met an untimely death due to a lack of interest. Neither the lawmakers, the newspapers or the public had yet been taught to succumb to "emotional terrorism."

The 1970's, however, is a different story. You (the taxpayer) would have had little choice but to hear about our little discovery. We would make sure of it. All that would be necessary is for either the "lab boys" or me to slip the information to the press and every television station and newspaper in the country would be carrying the story of our "discovery." With a little "tampering" our discovery could become a sensational headline and herein lies a big part of the problem.

The majority of us now get our news from T V, and T V news is not equipped to give you in depth information about a story. Following is a presentation of our discovery as it might be presented on television after 1970.

On your TV screen there would appear a half dozen buzzards soaring through the sky, circling the decaying carcass of a deer, its body bloating in the noon day sun. The carcass has already been torn apart and partially eaten by coyotes. In the hot sun, fumes can be seen rising from the carcass, hinting at the terrible smell of rotting flesh. The camera zooms in for a close up of the carcass where we see hundreds of flies, busily crawling around on the carcass feeding, mating and laying eggs in the putrid meat. After a few seconds, the scene changes and we find an average American family enjoying a meal together in the family dining room. Once again the camera zooms in for a close up and shows a fly (we all assume it is one of the flies from the carcass) crawling across the baby's pabulum or the six year old daughter's mashed potatoes. You are repulsed!

After a few seconds the camera moves to the back of a restaurant where it focuses on a garbage can that hasn't been cleaned or emptied for several months. The garbage is a repugnant mess of slimy, fermenting gunk that you know must smell like a neglected cesspool. Running around the garbage can, feeding on the slim are a number of cockroaches. A few seconds later you are treated to a picture of an innocent five year old girl dining in this same restaurant. A cockroach crawls from under the table and onto the plate of French fries the little girl is eating. You are further repulsed! These wonderful scenes are accompanied by the following commentary:

> Scientists, earlier this week, discovered that several common insects are carriers of many diseases that are dangerous to human beings. Scientists are particularly concerned because many of these insects are found in large numbers around almost everyone's house. It is suspected that some recent cases of "X" disease might have resulted from exposure to these insects. Based on the number of these insects found around the average home, some scientists suspect that we could be heading toward an epidemic that might kill thousands and leave tens of thousands hospitalized. The costs of such an epidemic could be staggering. One of the scientists has been monitoring this phenomenon for several months and now suspects that this sudden increase in disease organisms among the insects may be due to the overuse of insecticides.

Welcome to the land of "emotional blackmail." The fact that cockroaches or flies may have nothing to do with our little discovery is irrelevant. We have gotten your attention and that's what we're after. We will try to follow this up with several short up dates appropriately spaced to make sure you remain fully apprised of our "startling" discovery.

The media, who crave to "out sensationalize" their competitors, is going to have little motivation to check out our story for authenticity. The media reasons, rightly or wrongly, that those "scientists" in the lab and that fine, up standing Entomologist from the Health Department have no reason to lie. Besides, it's the media's responsibility to report the news, not guarantee its authenticity. In fact, the media feels an obligation to make the news interesting, so much so that some of what is broadcast is re-written with little embellishments in order to make sure they have your attention.

Somehow, they failed to mention that our toothbrushes are a far greater health hazard.

If we have done everything right, we have added all the ingredients we need to begin a new dynasty. First, we started our campaign with a liberal dose of *Fear*. Almost everyone is afraid of insects, and now we have insects that are making humans sick and could cause an epidemic. In case you are one of the more hardy souls who is less easily frightened, we have added those wonderful graphics of insects crawling on dead animals, garbage, and finally on innocent children's food. If the insects don't get you, the kids will. Next we flavor our campaign with a couple of tablespoons of *Hate*. Everyone loves a conspiracy, particularly if it involves a perceived public enemy and we just gave you a full dose of both. We know that a large segment of the population is wary of big corporations, especially corporations that have anything to do with pesticides. It's absolutely amazing what that very last little sentence in the T V news broadcast will do if someone *wants* to believe that the pesticide industry is evil.

With these two ingredients well established in the public mind, the rest is simple. We know that we have hit a vital nerve among a number of "special interest groups" that are politically very active. We no longer need to go before our law makers and plea our case in hopes of getting a small budget to control these pests. These politically powerful "special interest groups" will make sure our "discovery" gets the attention of the law makers. The only thing left for us to do is to decided what sort of "empire" we should advise the lawmakers that we need in order to prevent the big epidemic. The lawmakers will pass the "Enabling Legislation" necessary to ensure that we can build one.

The final ingredient is now ready for inclusion in our very successful campaign. To protect our investment from some do good scientist who might think we are stretching the truth a bit, we add *Greed*. This final ingredient effectively immerses our program in a protective cocoon that ensures our program will last in perpetuity. A large portion of the budget we will require from our legislators will include money for further research. There are hundreds of Universities and research institutions out there that are panting breathlessly for research dollars. They will do whatever is necessary to get their share of our research money. Because of this, we can be sure the research that is produced will support the continuation of our program. We can guarantee this through a very simple mechanism. Since we provide the funds for the research we "own" the results and merely require that the results of all research be turned over to us. If we don't like the results being produced by a particular researcher, we can file the results in the waste basket and you will never hear "the other side of the story." We want only research that will continue to "prove" how badly we are needed.

No wonder it took so long to find out that there are a lot more dangerous bacteria on your toothbrush than on the insects we have learned to hate. Who is going to provide the money for such research when there is no empire to build around eradicating toothbrushes?

According to "Smoker's Advocate," the EPA recently undertook similar tactics when it decided that Environmental Tobacco Smoke (ETS) is a carcinogen. When the EPA could not support its predetermined conclusions by using generally accepted statistical practices, the agency simply changed them. Among other things, EPA refused to include several studies that refuted their claim. Among those ignored was the largest and most recent study, the Brownson study, which was funded in part by the National Cancer Institute and published in the American Journal of Health. This study reported no increased risk for non-smoking women married to smokers. Had the EPA included this study in its report, the agency would not have been able to claim a statistically significant increased risk for illness in non-smokers by exposure to ETS.

Investor's business daily commented that "some scientists and policy analysts...are worrying aloud that the EPA report is paving the way for justifying new health-based government regulations and programs without real science behind them." Another scientist commented that it was "rotten science," but for a "worthy cause. It will help us to get rid of cigarettes and to become a smoke-free society."

I suppose, in a way, we should be thankful for this current move by the EPA. It certainly demonstrates what can be accomplished when special interests and a government agency work hand in hand. Whether you do or don't approve of smoking, you should be alarmed. It should make you wonder how many of the regulations you are currently complying with are based on the same partnership of lies and deception.

The majority of the regulations on the books of the Environmental Protection Agency and in Public Health are the result of just such tactics. These agencies and their supporters have used FEAR and HATE as tools to justify their regulations and the current distrust of businesses. Most of these regulations are subject to challenge.

Scientific Fraud

Unfortunately, along with everything else, there is a lot of outright fraud in science. The magazine Issues in Science and Technology reports that researchers from such prestigious schools as Harvard and the University of California Medical School in San Diego have been caught with their hand in the tempting cookie jar of scientific fraud. Even such prestigious scholars of the past as Galileo, Darwin and Gregor Mendel are suspected of scientific fraud.

Fraud differs from the other sins of science because it is committed after the experimentation is completed. Oft times the results of an experiment are not what the scientist was hoping for and it is very tempting to "fudge" the results. Scientists succumb to this temptation for a number of reasons. In many cases, ego plays an important part. With every important discovery comes much prestige, and sometimes a little fudging with the statistics can turn a bunch of insignificant statistics into an amazing discovery. There is a tremendous amount of pressure in most universities for professors to be published in important scientific journals. This pressure will often seduce a scientist into altering the results of an experiment just enough to make his or her work worthy of publication. However, the greatest pressure comes with a price tag. All university research must be financed, either through government or private funds. Those scientists who produce research pleasing to their financiers are the most likely to continue getting financed. The Environmental Protection Agency is especially good at using research money to control the outcome of scientific research. We will be exploring this further in the next chapter.

Unfortunately, scientific fraud is difficult to uncover. It takes hundreds of hours of painstaking study to uncover intentional errors in scientific work. Therefore, you will probably be able to take very little advantage of this knowledge in your fight against unjust regulation. However, it is important that you be aware of its existence.

The Labeling Game

Considering how often we hear and see the words *Toxin, Carcinogen,* and *Mutagen* on TV and in our newspapers, it will no doubt surprise you to know that there are no such things. No.

You don't have to go back and read that last sentence again. You heard me right. There are no such things as *toxins, carcinogens* and *mutagens.* To better understand this proclamation, study the following examples over several times to see if you can find where the toxin or carcinogen or mutagen exists.

If you have ever wanted to help someone just "spit the words out," you know how frustrating it is to listen to someone who stutters. However, you keep quiet because you know it is ten times more frustrating for the person who is doing the stuttering. Stuttering has long been a problem for both science and the people afflicted with the problem. Stuttering is, by definition, the strong, inappropriate movements of the lips, tongue and vocal cords to the point that the vocal cords lock together. To everyone's delight, a Neurologist from Columbia University recently found a drug that would relax the vocal cords and stop the stuttering. However, this drug has to be administered with care. A small overdose would mean immediate death to the patient. This is because this drug is the same botulinum toxin that causes botulism. Is the drug that stops stuttering a toxin or not?

The constant search for drugs to treat those stricken with AIDS has led to few drugs with any real promise. However, this frustration may be coming to an end. In recent studies at Rockerfeller University, researchers found a drug that thwarts the growth of HIV, the AIDS virus, in laboratory cell cultures. If it does as well in humans, it could one day prove to be a powerful treatment for those stricken with AIDS. This same drug is already in common use as a treatment for leprosy. Everyone should be praising science for bring such a wonder drug to our doorstep. Unfortunately, the drug is, by reputation at least, a creature of modern medicine's dark side. Marketed as a harmless tranquilizer, it was unmasked as a poison in the early sixties, when thousands of British and German woman who had taken it while pregnant ended up giving birth to children with serious deformities. This drug, Thalidomide, would thus seem to be an unlikely candidate for the next wonder drug, and yet for some time now it has been making a clinical comeback. Science has found that it has a number of medical benefits, so long as it is not administered to pregnant woman. Is Thalidomide a mutagen that should be forever ban?

Sleepy grass is a tough plant. Not only does it survive in rugged terrain but it has evolved a unique defense against animals that might graze on it. It harbors a fungus which produces a powerful poison that can knock a horse cold for a week. The fungus gets passed on to future generations through the plant's seeds. The isolated chemical poison is an alkaloid called lysergic acid amine. Alkaloids are the poisons in hundreds of poisonous plants, and lysergic acid amine has been found in a few of them, but never in such a high concentration. Lysergic acid amine is a potent sedative in humans as well. Central American Indians are said to quiet crying infants by feeding them a single sleepy-grass seed. In the 1950's, American pharmaceutical manufacturers considered marketing LAA as a prescription sleeping aid. However, the idea ran into a public relations problem. Lysergic acid amine has a close relative called lysergic acid diethylamide, which is more commonly know as LSD. Is LAA a toxin that should be forever banned?

Nitric Oxide has always been considered a very toxic chemical, one of those dangerous chemicals found in the smog that we would all be much better off without. Therefore, scientists were more than a little surprised to find that the immune systems of people with infections were producing large amounts of Nitric Oxide. Did not these people already have enough to deal with in just fighting the infection? Was their immune system turning against them at a most critical time? However, it was found that Nitric Oxide was a friend, not an enemy. It was being produced by the macrophages in the immune system of people with infections, not to harm the patient, but to kill the invading cells. Surprised scientists begin looking for Nitric Oxide in other parts of the body and found it in the brain, nervous system and blood vessel walls. In blood vessels, it seems, Nitric Oxide triggers the production of a chemical that relaxes the surrounding muscles, opening the vessels to more blood flow. One can imagine how this might stop a potential heart attack. In the brain and nervous system, Nitric Oxide was found to act as a neurotransmitter, stimulating neurons to fire. In the intestines, Nitric Oxide combines the properties of neurotransmission and muscle relaxation to regulate peristalsis, the rhythmic contractions that push food along. However, the biggest discovery was how Nitric Oxide affected people's sex life. Nitric Oxide, they found, is a key link in penile erection. Now, aren't we glad the EPA wasn't successful in getting rid of all the Nitric Oxide?

No one would voluntarily suffer from such maladies as mental retardation, convulsions, neurological degeneration, variable body temperature, fragile bones, lack of skin pigmentation and similar problems. However, if we were to make a conscientious effort to avoid those substances that have been labeled "toxic," we would all be suffering from just such maladies. In the human body, there are at least thirty enzymes that require copper to perform metabolic tasks and the lack of sufficient copper will lead to the diseases mentioned above. Other heavy metals such as iron, magnesium, manganese, arsenic, mercury, cobalt and zinc are "highly toxic," yet our body will not function properly if they are not present in our systems. We need constant exposure to these elements in order to live healthy lives. However, too much of any one of them and we will be looking at the world from the inside of a coffin. Should these metals continue to be considered "toxins"?

In the situations we have just discussed, we found that many chemicals or compounds that are considered very "toxic" are also essential to our survival. Other very dangerous chemicals or compounds have become indispensable friends in our battle against human diseases. What makes this all the more confusing is when we discover that many of the compounds we consider to be our friends can become our enemies.

Certainly, one would consider anything as essential to our survival as water to be a very good friend. And, of course, it is. However, as a ten year old boy in the midwestern part of the United States found out, too much of a good friend can be a bad thing. He consumed so much water that his tissues became super saturated and he died of a water overdose. Should we protect this child and others that might overdose on water by banning water?

A San Francisco Bay area newspaper recently reported that a four year old boy died because he consumed some Pine-Sol which is not considered toxic. When he begin to feel peculiar, his mother called the poison control center to find out what she should do. She was assured that the boy had not consumed anything harmful. Give him an hour or two and he will be fine, she was told. She gave him the allotted time only to discover that he had died in his sleep while taking a nap. Would this child have survived if we were not so determined to label things either toxic or non-toxic?

So, what has this all got to do with my earlier statement that there is no such thing as a toxin, carcinogen or mutagen? The purpose of all of this is to demonstrate a very important point. There is no such thing as a chemical or compound that is innately all bad or that is innately all good. For every compound and for every chemical, there are levels of exposure that are harmful and levels that are not harmful. In most cases, there is also a level where the chemical or compound is beneficial. (Probably, with enough research, we will find that all chemicals and compounds have a level at which they are not only safe, but are in some way beneficial to humans.)

Labeling any substance either "toxic" or "safe" can be a very dangerous practice. If people were to live by such labels they could very readily overdose on those substances labeled "safe." However, our greatest danger lies in allowing agencies, such as the EPA, to label something as "toxic" or "carcinogenic" and then remove it from our environment. While we have a pretty good idea of what we can live with, we have very little idea of what we can live without. In its exuberance to protect us from our environment, the EPA could deprive us of certain "toxins" that are essential to our well being.

While we cannot safely label different substances either good or bad, we can label doses of a substance as such. Physicians have been doing this for years. Most of the things our doctors prescribe for our illnesses are subscribed as doses for a very good reason. These medications will do little good if not taken in sufficient quantity. However, they quickly become toxic if taken in large quantities. The rest of our world is no different, and needs to be viewed just as the doctor views our medication. There are no "toxic" or "carcinogenic" substances, but there are "toxic" and "carcinogenic" doses. This is true for all chemicals and compounds.

The next time you hear a news commentator talk about the discovery of a "toxic" substance, remember that they have no idea what they are saying. They can't possibly know if the substance is "toxic" without knowing whether there was a sufficient dosage to make it toxic. However, the commentator's greatest crime is not in labeling something as "toxic" when it most likely isn't. The greatest crime is that by using the label "toxic" the commentator infers that there are substances out there that are *not* toxic. This assumption has killed several people.

The regulatory process is primarily responsible for creating this label-mania. In an effort to control certain substances and activities, particularly as related to businesses, they begin to label certain things as "toxic" or "carcinogenic" or "mutagenic." By so doing, they could regulate such things without concern as to whether there was any real potential harm or not. Besides, it would have been difficult to do things the proper way. To do things properly, the EPA and its scientific cohorts would need to examine each substance and determine the levels that were beneficial, the levels that were safe and the levels at which the substance becomes toxic. This would take a tremendous amount of time, money and effort. It is much easier to just determine that all levels are toxic. This certainly makes enforcement a lot easier. Imagine the problems an inspector would have trying to determine if a particular dilution of a compound could be considered a toxic dose. By eliminating the word "dose," the enforcement person could consider the very presence of a substance as toxic.

Once we understand that the labels being placed on various chemicals and compounds have no validity, we have the means for attacking those regulations that use such labeling. Armed with the knowledge that labeling a compound as "toxic" or "carcinogenic" or "mutagenic" is meaningless unless the dosage is known, you can place the enforcement agency in an awkward position. It then becomes the agency's responsibility to demonstrate that you possess a particular chemical or compound in sufficient amount or sufficient concentration to constitute a toxic dose. If it isn't a toxic dose, you could be eligible for "just compensation" for any costs incurred in complying with the regulations.

The words "pollutant" and "pollution" fall into the same category as those words previously discussed. The only difference is that the words "toxin," "carcinogen" and "mutagen" generally refer to the effect of a substances on humans, while the word "pollutant" generally refers to a substance's affect on the "environment." The principles are the same, however. No substance is a "pollutant" unless it is administered in a dosage that is harmful to the environment. Likewise, there is no substance that is totally safe for the environment regardless of the dosage administered.

There are thousands of different "environments" in our world, each with its own unique characteristics. Each one of these "environments" has certain strengths and weaknesses that make it resistant to damage from certain substances and highly sensitive to damage from other substances. Therefore, the introduction of a particular dosage of a substance in one environment may be beneficial while this same dosage could be extremely damaging to another environment. Because of our planet's tremendous environmental diversity, it is absolutely impossible to label any substance as a "pollutant" without identifying the specific environment where it is placed and the specific dosage administered.

To cover this topic in any detail would require a separate book. However, it is sufficient to know that the mere presence of a particular compound or chemical does not constitute "pollution." Once again, if properly challenged, it should become the enforcement agency's responsibility to prove that pollution of the environment actually took place or you should be paid "just compensation" for the expenses you incurred in complying with the regulations.

The greatest abuse of the scientific method, the greatest abuse in creating public hysteria and the greatest abuse in "labeling" has occurred within the purview of the Environmental Protection Agency. In the next chapter, we will discover how this agency has exploited the word "carcinogen" to promote their agenda. We will determine how the agency has played fast and loose with acceptable scientific principles, misinterpreted data and desecrated the field of statistics to further its cause.

CHAPTER 9

Flawed Science
Uses and Abuses

"Science is nothing but perception."

Plato

"Science is simply common sense at its best—rigidly accurate observation, and merciless to fallacy in logic."

Thomas Huxley

Randolph Wilson stood dangerously close to the edge the cliff and contemplated the 400 foot drop to the rocks below. A millennium of waves had worn the rocks smooth, and although he couldn't see them from his perch on the edge of the cliff, he knew that hundreds of plant and animal forms had made that inhospitable environment their home. He hated to interrupt their solitude but he didn't feel he had a choice. Things had just gone from bad to worse over the last year. First, his son, Elias, had been jailed for selling drugs. And then it was his beloved daughter, Janis. Oh, how he missed her. She had been shot dead by a passing car full of drunk teenagers just a few weeks after Elias was arrested. Although Randolph tried desperately to prevent it, the ensuing grief and the overwhelming guilt at having lost both children in such a short time span tore his somewhat fragile marriage to shreds. Grief stricken, guilty and depressed, Randolph found some solace in alcohol. His drinking, however, soon lead to the loss of his job. Randolph, indeed, had nothing to live for. He took off his jacket as he prepared for his leap into destiny and the end of his pain. Somewhere in his subconscious, he noted the sounds of a passing car just as he took that final leap into eternity.

Randolph was totally unaware that his final farewell to the world did not go unobserved. Dr. Dennis Alcornson had observed the phenomena as well. Dr. Alcornson had, as a matter of fact, been observing this particular spot for several years. This cliff had been the site of several human deaths and he suspected that cars, which also polluted his beloved environment, were responsible. He pulled out his notebook and made several notes. He tested the air currents, studied the angle of the sun and checked his barometer and thermometer. He made some more notes. The pattern was becoming obvious. Seven out of the ten people he observed disappearing over the cliff had done so just at the time a car was passing by. This could no longer be considered a coincidence. He was sure that the wind created by the passing cars was somehow responsible for the deaths of these people. He concluded that the cars created a swirling eddy of air that literally shoved the people over the edge of the cliff to their deaths on the rocks below. He now had a very important scientific paper to write. The scientific community and the public needed to know of the dangers a passing car could create for those standing near the edge of a cliff.

As a result of Dr. Alcornson's research, the Department of Public Health wrote a batch of regulations prohibiting cars from driving along roads that were closer than 300 feet from any cliff (providing a good margin of safety). Meanwhile, relatives and friends of Randolph Wilson have bid him a final farewell at a near by cemetery, unaware that his suicide will do absolutely nothing to help the social condition of this country. Society, instead of exploring what led to the jailing of Randolph's son and the murder of his daughter, have accepted Dr. Alcornson's premise that Randolph was the victim of a passing car.

And thus, another batch of regulations was born on the back of some badly flawed research. Unfortunately, most research involving our health and the environment carry the same flawed baggage as Dr. Alcornson's did.

Perhaps the most important change in the scientific method to take place in the last twenty or so years is in its basic approach to science. There was a time when no scientific works would be accepted by the scientific community if it carried with it a built in bias. In the past, Dr. Alcornson's research would have been laughed out of existence. However, now it is acceptable. The goal of his research was "to determine what effect passing cars will have on people standing on the cliff." Previously, science would have demanded a proposal that carried no bias: a research proposal such as "a study to determine why people fall to their deaths from the cliff."

The differences in the two proposals become quickly apparent.

1. Dr. Alcornson's proposal assumes ahead of time that passing cars have something to do with people going over the cliff. By stating the objective in his way, he isn't obligated to prove that passing cars have some affect on the people, this is assumed in the proposal.

2. Dr. Alcornson can, by only considering the cars, ignore all the other factors that might influence the deadly plunge these people have taken. He does not need to take into account the fact that Randolph Wilson committed suicide or that someone else may have slipped off the cliff.

3. He can be sure that cars are incriminated in the deaths of these people by skillfully avoiding the investigation of any evidence that might lead to other conclusions.

When our politicians and our government agencies use Dr. Alcornson's approach to scientific discovery as a basis for developing the laws of the land, everyone gets hurt. First, many, many other people and other businesses become victims of the faulty research by being penalized for crimes they didn't commit and never will commit. Second, by accepting Dr. Alcornson's research, we have slammed the door on any possibility of discovering the *real* reason people are going over the cliff. Third, we have justified creating a nightmare of regulations under the guise of preventing people from dying by going over the cliff, while the actual problems are left unsolved.

Unfortunately, this type of research is all to common, and has been for some time. This is due, in great part, to the fact that the research process is now controlled by special interest groups and by government agencies. The goal of most environmental groups is to prove that the activities of humans, especially when it comes to businesses, are the major enemies of the environment and the public health. With such predetermined goals in mind there is no hope for honest, unbiased research. The goal of the government agency is to continue to exist and to grow. Adding more regulations intended to control the activities of individuals and businesses meets the agency's goals exceptionally well. Therefore, there is a natural partnership between the special interests and government agencies to push for biased research. By default then, the ultimate goal of all research is to justify the development of more controls through the development of more regulations.

Of course this can't be accomplished without public support. However, finding this support is not as difficult as one might imagination, as we will discover in this chapter.

Horace, Harriet, Morton & Mable

In July of 1993, a Silicon Valley biotech firm announced that it soon expected to receive a patent on a genetically engineered mouse. The company applying for the patent had engineered a mouse that lacked an immune system. While having no immune system can be very traumatic for the mouse, it is a great tool for research into human diseases. Since the mouse has no immune system, anything, including human tissue can be transplanted into the mouse without fear of it being rejected. This allows scientists to experiment with human tissue without involving a human being. The down side for the mouse, obviously, is that it has absolutely no defenses against even the most benign disease organisms.

Although there are 179 animal patents currently pending, this is only the second patent actually issued for an animal. The first such animal patent was issued for a genetically altered research mouse that was engineered to grow malignant tumors. This first mouse was specifically engineered to assist scientists in the study of cancer. Hopefully, these mice will be put to better use in cancer research than was their predecessors. Long before mice had been engineered in this fashion, there were rats and mice around the science laboratories that could function just about as well as their engineered friends. These original rats and mice were the product of selective breeding. Through selective breeding, scientists had developed a mouse that could grow malignant tumors almost as readily as the currently engineered variety. Unfortunately, they were not used for the best scientific purposes as we will discover.

I suspect it is about time that you met Horace, Harriet, Morton, and Mable. If their names don't sound familiar to you, I'm not surprised. There has been no effort to make their existence public knowledge, even though they are the principal harbingers of the *Fear* that makes us tolerate the myriad regulations we live with today. Therefore, I think it only proper that you meet the creatures that, through no fault of their own, have guaranteed the survival of the Environmental Protection Agency and have helped finance the budgets of Public Health and a few other regulatory entities.

Horace and Harriet are a pair of laboratory rats and Morton and Mable are a pair of laboratory mice. It is them, their ancestors and their progeny that have faithfully given their lives time and time again so that you might continue to live in perpetual fear. You must understand that these are not your every day rats and mice. These wonders of the laboratory are the products of hundreds of generations of selective breeding. This process of selective breeding has produce a strain of mice and a strain of rats that are unlike any of God's original creations.

What makes them unique is that Horace, Harriet, Morton and Mable, as well as all their progeny are going to die of cancer. I know, a lot of creatures, humans included, die of cancer. But not like our four friends. *They have been inbred so that their immune systems have almost no defense against developing cancer tumors. They will most likely die of cancer within six to eighteen weeks after their birth.*

By taking advantage of this unique feature, scientists could just about guarantee that cancer would dominate their lives. Having been properly certified, these "warriors" were ready to serve their country as "guinea pigs" in this country's cancer research projects.

The thing that really makes our friends so very special is that regardless of what they are exposed to, they will most likely develop cancer. When you are a scientist frantically looking for research dollars, or when you are an Agency that has pinned its existence on convincing the public that there are millions of carcinogenic menaces in our environment, these four friends are the "pot of gold" at the end of the rainbow.

When the entire process first started, everyone had a field day. Regardless of what was tested, the scientist could be sure that at the end of the experiment, our friends and their progeny would develop tumors. The EPA could then announce that product "A" caused cancer in mice (or rats). The public was duly shocked, the agency and the research dollars grew, and the process continued. In short order, products "B," "C," "D," "E," "F," etc. were all "discovered" to cause cancer in our especially bred friends. Unfortunately, after a while it started to become apparent that virtually everything was causing cancer in Horace, Harriet, Morton and Mable.

All too soon, the public begin to get a little agitated at the fact that everything they were exposed to was causing cancer in mice and the *fear* level begin to slip. The public also begin to question just how important such experiments were in real human terms. It was obviously time for a little more slight of hand. The agency still had a ways to go before it would feel secure that it would exist and grow in perpetuity.

The agency and the scientists were ready to accept the challenge. They realized they had four things going for them. First, they knew that they would not be allowed to actually do research upon human beings. Second, they had some mice and rats that would develop tumors, almost upon command. Third, they would be the one's doing all the interpretation of the data they gathered in their experiments. Fourth, much like my toothbrushes, they would avoid any research that might have an adverse affect on their cause.

The first part was incredibly easy. They just announced that it was not appropriate to conduct experiments upon human beings as this was cruel, inhuman, intolerable, etc. Everyone readily agreed with them that it was not appropriate to use humans as "guinea pigs." This meant that they could continue to use Horace, Harriet, Morton and Mable in their study of how carcinogenic the environment was to humans. They just needed to take the data they were getting from all these cancer-prone animals and extrapolate the data into human terms.

Simple, what?

Interpreting Data

A friend told me about a scientist friend of his who had trained a frog to do something rather unique. This scientist had trained his frog to jump whenever he gave the verbal command. He had done such an excellent job of training the frog that the frog never failed to follow the command. The scientist would yell "jump" and the frog would jump. Every time. Soon he was giving demonstrations all over the country.

However, the game eventually got old and scientific curiosity got the better of the scientist, so he decided to try some experiments on his frog. He severed the foot from the frog's left hind leg and set the frog back on the table.

"Jump!" the scientist commanded.

The frog jumped. Not as good as before, but the frog jumped. The scientist gave the command several more times and each time the frog would give his best effort pushing off with his good right foot. The scientist made the appropriate notes. He then picked up the frog and proceeded to sever the foot from the frog's right hind leg as well. Once again he set the frog on the table.

"Jump." the scientist commanded.

The frog didn't move.

The scientist gave the command several more times but the frog wouldn't budge. Satisfied that the frog wasn't going to react to his command, the scientist picked up his research book and made the following entry:

"When you sever both hind feet from a frog, the frog becomes deaf."

Obviously, there is more than one way to interpret data. In

the above example, I can offer several other reasons why the frog did not jump. Perhaps the frog was mad at the scientist for cutting off his feet and got his revenge by refusing to obey any further commands. Perhaps the frog stored all his energy in his feet and no longer had the energy needed to jump. I'm sure, with a little imagination, you can come up with several other possible reasons why the frog didn't jump. However, I'm sure most of us immediately jumped to the conclusion that the frog had neither the desire nor, perhaps, the ability to push off with the bloody stumps he was left with. However, no one will ever know what our opinion might be concerning the frog's sudden reluctance to jump. This is the scientist's research and he will be providing the interpretation of the data he has gathered.

With this in mind, let us return once again to our friends Horace, Harriet, Morton and Mable. Here we find that the concept of interpreting data gets considerably more complex. In the first place, we know that our friends will most likely develop tumors regardless of what we may or may not do to them. This fact alone makes it difficult to accurately "interpret" how much effect product "A" really had in giving them the tumors. Then there is the problem of trying to make the data extracted from the experiments with H, H, M & M meet the human condition. Our ultimate goal, after all, is to determine how carcinogenic these products are to human beings such as us.

So, why don't we use regular mice, you ask? You know, mice that haven't been bred to die of cancer by the time they're two or three months old? The best answer I have been able to get from the research people is that they want to study the *long term* effects of exposure to various products on humans. Humans beings, they reason, live for 70 years or longer and may be exposed to certain products for their entire lives. Mice, on the other hand, are lucky to make it much beyond six months and rats are stretching it to live much beyond a year. So the problem the scientist faces is how to evaluate what a product will do to a human over a period of 70 years by using an animal that will live naturally for only one year.

As they saw it, they had three options. 1) They could use H, H, M, and M in their experiments. 2) They could use normal rats and mice and increase the dosages to make up for the disparity in longevity. 3) They could abandon the whole project as a bad idea. Option number three was immediately thrown out as totally unacceptable. It would, after all, eliminate millions of dollars in research money.

Unfortunately, there were a large number of problems with option number two as well. How does one determine how much to increase a dosage to make up for 70 years of lost time? Some compounds, they decided, could be very slow acting and show no deleterious effects on humans until forty or fifty years after exposure had begun. How does one simulate such conditions in a rat that only lives for a year? After making many analytical calculations they determined that giving normal animals increased dosages wouldn't cut it. The product had to be introduced to the animal in such large doses that the animal often immediately died of an overdose. Nicotine, for instance, gives one a great high if given in very small doses. However, increase that dose twenty or thirty fold and you have instant death. Under the circumstances, it is difficult to determine how carcinogenic nicotine is over a period of 70 years by introducing a 70 year dose in one sitting. The inconsiderate rats keep dying instantly. Even water resisted being tested in this way. The carcinogenic qualities in water are so minute that you would literally kill the rat by overloading its tissues with water long before its carcinogenic qualities would appear.

This left the scientists with Harold, Harriet, Morton and Mable.

It also left them with a bit of a dilemma. How does one go about running tests to determine the carcinogenicity of a substance when the test animal is likely to die of cancer regardless of what you do? It was at this point that the "scientific method" came back into play. The "scientific method" requires that you test a large number of identical animals, with the animals divided into several identical groups. The object is to be sure that the conditions for each group are identical except for the one factor you are attempting to measure. In so doing, you can evaluate the impact of this one factor by analyzing what happened to each of the groups of animals after a specified period of time.

When evaluating the carcinogenic qualities of a particular product, scientists reasoned, all we need do is inject each group of rats with a different quantity of the product. Each group would receive a different dosage of the product being tested, with one group receiving trace amounts, another slightly more ad infinitum. One group even receives a "placebo" (a "placebo" has none of the product being tested in it). At the end of a specified period of time, each group of rats is examined and the results recorded.

It all seems to be on the up and up doesn't it? For the most part it is. When you run your experiments, you find that product "A" causes cancerous tumors very quickly, even in rats receiving small doses. However, when you test product "B," you find that only the rats receiving very large doses have cancerous tumors and that it took a long time for the tumors to develop. You might assume from the above experiments that product "A" is more carcinogenic than Products "B." Unfortunately, this is only an assumption, since these rats were most likely going to develop cancer regardless of what you did.

More important, however, we still don't have any idea if these compounds will have any effect on normal, healthy rats. Therefore, the assumption leaves a lot of unanswered questions and, at the very least, falls into the gray area with regard to its use as valid research. However, this assumption shines like a beacon in the night when compared to the "conclusions" scientists have reached when extrapolating this data to determine how carcinogenic these compounds are to humans. Let's look at some of the problems scientists have happily ignored in order to bring you their latest findings about how carcinogenic various substances are to you human types.

1) The very essence of pure science must be ignored before the experiments can even start. Pure science demands that all research be conducted with out a predetermined bias. Since the experiments they conducted were designed to "determine the carcinogenic qualities of a product," the research begins with a built in bias. These experiments, in fact, are designed very much like Dr. Dennis Alcornson's research. While his research assumed that cars were responsible for people falling off the cliff, the research on M,M, H,and H assumes that the product being tested is carcinogenic and, therefore, responsible for any tumors that develop in the mice and/or rats. Pure science would demand that the research be conducted to "determine what is causing these rats and/or mice to develop cancerous tumors." Does it seem like I'm nit picking? Well, just think about Dr. Alcornson and his research into why people disappear over the cliff. When you have a predetermined goal in mind, such as "determining the carcinogenic properties of a product," your interpretation of the data is going to be biased in that direction. You will fail to consider any data that is not specifically relevant to your predetermined bias. For instance, by designing his research in his way, Dr. Alcornson could prove that cars were responsible for people going over the cliff by conveniently ignoring all the other factors (such as suicide). In cancer research, the scientists can prove that the product is the cause of the tumors by disregarding any facts that might indicate that the cancerous tumors may be the result, not of the product, but of other factors

such as using rats that are extremely prone to developing cancer.

2) There is an assumption in these experiments that is totally without foundation. It assumes that large amounts of a product introduced over a relatively short period of time (the one year life of a rat) will have the same affect as a small amount of product introduced over a long period of time (the 70 year life of a human). This is absolute rubbish. Every animal, including humans, has the ability to eliminate unwanted materials from its body if given adequate time. We also have a very effective immune system that, if not overwhelmed by an extremely large dose, can attack the unwanted product and render it harmless before it has an opportunity to damage the body. Therefore, if a product is introduced in small amounts over a long period, the body will have gotten rid of the first dose long before the second dose is administered. Unfortunately for the rats and mice in the experiments, they are administered much larger doses than we would normally receive in order to make up for the time disparity (one year vs. 70 years). Because they receive these larger doses and receive them more frequently, their body and immune system will not be able to completely eliminate or render harmless the previous dose before a new dose is administered. Therefore, they will be constantly carrying a much larger dose of the product in their body than we would during our 70 years. We are constantly exposed to compounds that, in large quantities, are deadly to us. However, the exposure occurs over a number of years, so our body can get rid of any excess material rapidly enough to avoid having a harmful dose in our system at any one time. If the body were unable to eliminate unwanted products, the human race would have died out long ago, as none of our ancestors would have lived long enough to reproduce.

3) Their "research" assumes that there are products that are

innately "bad." Again, close examination will relegate this assumption to the garbage heap. Life is not nearly as simple as they would like us to believe. There are many compounds and elements, both natural and manufactured, that are highly "toxic" to humans in relatively small amounts. However, these very same compounds are essential to our survival. We humans would soon die if we did not have these "toxic" materials in our body and if we were not continually exposed to these "toxic" materials so we can replenish the supply. In other words, as we discovered in the previous chapter under the topic "labeling," there is no such thing as materials that are innately "bad," but there are definitely "bad" doses. This principal is very happily ignored whenever the research results are reported. When testing various substances on Harriet, Horace, Mable and Morton, the tendency is to continuously administer larger and larger doses until some sort of negative affect can be recorded. In many cases, the dosage that is necessary to show some effect on our friends is hundreds or thousands of times the concentration that a human would receive from the environment. By ignoring the fact that humans will never be exposed to such a dose, the scientists can label the products they test as "toxic," "carcinogenic," "metagenic" or whatever they wish. However, the label is totally meaningless.

4) The ability of a living organism to survive exposure to potentially dangerous amounts of a material over a long period of time is dependent, to a great extent, upon that organism's immune system. It is the immune system that keeps the foreign material from harming the body and, in many cases, is responsible for helping the body get rid of the material. In this regard, the human immune system is greatly superior to the immune system of Horace, Harriet, Morton and Mable, or any other rats or mice.

However, this is not taken into account when scientists try to determine how the data taken from the experiments on our four friends is applied to the human condition.

Once you realize that the above items are "toothbrushes," you can understand why scientists and the EPA might not want such information made public. You could never build a super-agency and get more research funds by proving that your research was highly flawed and, therefore, meaningless.

There are other reasons why there are problems with trying to use Horace, Harriet, Morton and Mable as models for testing the carcinogenic impact of materials on human beings. However, it was not my intent to write a scientific treatise and I have said enough to help you understand why I take all such reports "with a grain of salt" (which is also bad for us nowadays).

Selecting The Proper Data

As was mentioned in the previous chapter, some enforcement agencies are not above throwing out or hiding scientific data that does not support their enforcement goals. One can find many articles in scientific journals written by prominent scientists accusing the EPA of just such tactics. There are articles in such well known publications as the "American Journal of Public Health," the "Investor's Business Daily," and the journal "Toxicological Pathology" documenting instances where the EPA has concealed research that conflicted with its preconceived goals. In fact, a local newspaper quoted Dr. Walter Williams of George Mason University who wrote in his article, "EPA Lies," that "this is gross dishonesty, and all EPA bureaucrats involved should be summarily fired." Dr. Williams salvo was directed primarily at the EPA's decision to label "environmental tobacco smoke," ETS, (what the general public considers to be second-hand smoke) as a carcinogen before any research was even compiled on the subject.

There is no doubt that second-hand cigarette smoke is irritating to some of us. So is perfume, car exhaust, smoke from a camp fire or fire place, barking dogs, emergency vehicle sirens, people with body odor, and thousands of other things. However, the mere existence of something irritating to a certain segment of the population cannot be allowed to justify the existence of more and more oppressive regulations. Likewise, no agency should be allowed to utilize corrupt scientific data nor should an agency be allowed to disregard scientific data, just to further its unquenchable thirst for power.

In recognition of these principals, there is now a lawsuit pending before the courts in an effort to declare EPA's report (that ETS is a human carcinogen) null and void. If the lawsuit is successful, the agency will find it difficult to get the support needed to regulate "environmental tobacco smoke" which will be a blessing for all of us. However, a lot of the damage has already been done. Three out of four Americans walking the streets today believe the EPA's lie. They believe that second-hand smoke is carcinogenic. I'm not sure who won this battle but I certainly know who lost. Every time we are lied to by our government, we lose in many ways.

One In Ten Million

As we approached the 1980s, tiny voices could be heard from within the research community, objecting to this blatant abuse of the research process. Reluctantly, the Government/Research Community complex had to be a little more specific in how they reported the results of their research. It was no longer adequate to just announce that product "X" might produce cancer in humans. People wanted to know whether they could really get cancer from the product. This was not an easy question to answer.

The other day I heard a Doctor on a "talk show" explain that all Doctors are trained in medical school to never use the term "never." Even if a situation has never occurred once since the inception of the universe, you cannot say that it will "never" happen in the future. Therefore, any honest person is faced with the same dilemma. How do you answer when you are interviewed by a reporter or a "talk show" host and are inevitably asked "that" question.

"Can you honestly say that it will never happen in the future?"

Even though the situation *never* occurred in the past, no one can predict the future, so the answer is always "No." Unfortunately, the interviewer and almost everyone else will interpret this answer to mean that it can and, therefore, will, happen in the future. The EPA and its associated research institutions have taken full advantage of this dilemma. Only in their case the question is:

"Can you honestly say that no one will ever get cancer from exposure to this product at some time in the future?"

What a wonderful question. No one is going to stick their necks out and predict the future. Particularly when it's to their distinct advantage not to. Therefore, that one question alone can guarantee the perpetuity of the EPA and can guarantee that more billions of our tax dollars will be spent on useless research.

The other question frequently asked is:

"Has anyone ever been diagnosed with cancer as a result of exposure to this substance?"

Of course this is impossible to know. As you know, we can't experiment on human beings. However, this does not prevent the EPA and its research cohorts from extrapolating. Tucking in their shirts and pulling up their pants they will look you straight in the eye and advise all who will listen that, based upon their research with rats, they can assume with some authority that one out of every ten million cancer cases could be attributed to exposure to compound "X."

This is the point at which I quickly lift my feet up off the floor. I am not one who enjoys wading in bull pucky and a big batch was just laid at my feet. The above statement is the ultimate misrepresentation of research data.

To understand why, let's go back to Horace, Harriet, Morton and Mable once more. These poor old friends of ours and their progeny are acquiring cancer, not because of the compounds they were exposed to, but because that were bred so as to guarantee that they would get cancer. While no humans are specifically bred to guarantee that they will get cancer, there are certainly those that have a much greater probability of getting cancer than others do. This is why one person can smoke three packs of cigarettes every day for eighty years and never get cancer while someone else can live a perfectly clean life and die of cancer at thirty-eight years of age.

"Ah ha!" responds the EPA type logic. "At least we can determine that product "X" might have been responsible for the fact that the clean living guy died at thirty-eight because of his exposure to product "X." After all, only one person in ten million who lives that cleanly will die of cancer. Therefore, the two numbers match perfectly. There is a one in ten million chance that product "X" will cause cancer in someone, and this guy is the one in ten million who is that sensitive to cancer causing products."

This makes sense only if you ignore several thousand other EPA sponsored research projects. If you review the research you will discover that, according to the research records, Horace, Harriet, Morton and Mable have been very busy. Due to their continually dying efforts, EPA has discovered hundreds or thousands of other materials which, using their logic, have a "one in ten million" shot of causing cancer in someone. They also have found hundreds or thousands of products where the odds are one in a billion, and many more products where the odds are one in a million, and so on *ad infinitum*.

The real question then, is which one of these materials really caused this thirty-eight year old clean living individual to get cancer. Product "X" or one of the other one thousand products EPA has found will cause cancer in Horace, Harriet, Morton and Mable? Perhaps it was more than one. Perhaps it was all of them. Or, perhaps, he was just unfortunate enough to be much like our four friends. He was going to die of cancer regardless of what he was exposed to.

Under the circumstances, how can anyone look you in the face and tell you that product "X" was responsible for his death or that it is even carcinogenic to humans? After all, a product can only be toxic, carcinogenic, etc. if the proper "dose" is administered, and that "dose" is going to be different for every person, plant and animal on this planet. By the same token, EVERY substance on earth, natural or manufactured, is "toxic," "carcinogenic," etc. to every human, plant and animal if a large enough "dose" is administered.

However, all this very expensive research accomplished one thing. It taught us all to *Fear* the words "toxic," "carcinogenic," "tetragenic" and "mutagenic" even though they have absolutely no meaning in the context in which they are presented. The media, in their exuberance to get our attention, use these words liberally without any concept of their meaning. How many times have you heard a television commentator say something like the following:

"The Environmental Protection Agency reported today that it has discovered the *toxic* chemical "X" in a ravine in South Florida."

Hey, television newsbroadcasters, pay attention! There are no toxic chemicals or, by the same token, there are no elements or compounds that are "non-toxic." There are only "non-toxic" and "toxic" *doses* of each. Please report the news more accurately from now on. I am tired of you constantly providing the EPA with further ammunition they can use to pick my pocket. How about being on the taxpayers side for once?

Reversing The Playing Field

Considering the fact that most of the regulations being enforced by the EPA, Public Health and some other agencies are justified on the basis of the highly flawed research discussed above, something needs to be done. Certainly, those businesses and individuals that have gone to great expense to comply with such regulations are due "just compensation" for these expenses.

Unfortunately, we are not currently playing on a level field. The EPA and others have had years to convince the rest of us that all these chemicals, substances and compounds are "bad" and that those who are responsible for manufacturing them or using them are trying to poison the world. It would take years of expensive advertising and a lot of media cooperation to begin to swing public opinion in the opposite direction. In the course of any public debate on the subject, businesses and individuals would be placed in the same position as they are currently. They would be assumed to be guilty until proven innocent. As we discussed in the first chapter, it is impossible to *prove* that you aren't going to commit some sort of problem in the future.

In order to level the playing field, each incident, each substance and each regulation needs to be challenged independently of all others. This is easier than it sounds. If your business is required by regulation to undertake some action to prevent public exposure to a "carcinogen," "toxin" or "mutagen," evaluate the situation. Is this action going to increase the operating costs of the company? If it is, you should challenge the regulation and request "just compensation" for meeting the requirements of the regulation.

This action accomplishes one very important thing. It reverses the roles of the two major players in this action: namely you and the enforcement agency. It levels the playing field and puts you in the position you should be in. Innocent until proven guilty. You are now on the offensive and the agency is on the defensive. They must prove you are guilty, just as would be the case in any normal legal procedure. You will no longer be in the position of trying to prove that you will not commit a crime in the future.

The challenge consists of just a few well thought out questions. These questions are equally viable in a direct response to the agency during the enforcement process or in a court of law if they refuse to pay you "just compensation." Following are some of the questions that should be asked if you are ordered to take some action regarding a "potential" carcinogen, mutagen or toxin and feel you are entitled to "just compensation" for complying with the order. With some thought, you should be able to come up with many more.

At what dosage does this "substance" become carcinogenic (toxic, etc.) to humans?

For how long does a human need to be exposed to this "substance" before he or she has had enough exposure to get ill (cancer, etc.)?

Can you supply me with the name of even one person who got cancer (ill, dead, etc.) from exposure to this "substance"?

Do you have *any* documented cases where an individual became ill (got cancer) from exposure to the *doses* involved in this action?

With so many different "carcinogens" (toxins) in the environment, how are you able to determine which agent was the actual cause of the illness (cancer, death, etc.)?

Have you checked to make sure the people who are in danger of becoming ill (getting cancer, etc.) from the operation of my business are not being exposed to more dangerous substances over longer periods of time from products they are using or storing in their homes?

Are you sure these same people are not getting a more dangerous exposure at their place of work or recreation?

How would you be able to determine that an illness (cancer, etc.) resulted from exposure to substances from this business rather than from the person's home, work or recreation?

When in court, there will be an opportunity to attack the research process itself by questioning who ever is providing expert testimony as to the "toxic," "carcinogenic" or "mutagenic" qualities of the substance. Following are some questions for those providing expert testimony. I'm sure you can come up with many more.

Can you explain to me why one man can live a clean life and die of cancer at age 38, while another man can smoke 3 packs of cigarettes every day for 70 years and not develop cancer?

Will you concede then, that a person's immune system (or heredity) plays a role in determining whether this person is likely to contract cancer?

With so many carcinogens in the environment, how do you go about determining which carcinogen was responsible for a particular person contracting cancer?

Can you document for us one case in which a person contracted cancer from the substance currently under discussion?

If so, what was the dosage to which this person was exposed and for how long was this person exposed?

Can you give us some idea of why this person contracted cancer and others receiving the same or a larger dose did not?

Can you say positively that this person's cancer was not the result of a weaken immune system or heredity rather than the substance in question?

Have you investigated this person's home and work environment to determine that he or she was not exposed to other carcinogens (toxins) that might have triggered the illness (tumor growths, etc.)?

What did you find?

I have here a list of products commonly used in the average person's home that the EPA has determined are (carcinogenic, toxic, etc.). Have any of these products been found in the homes of those people you feel might be affected by exposure to the product on trial here today?

If so, are the people in question receiving greater exposure to these home products than to the product on trial?

Note: If the product in question is one of those that the EPA has declared will cause one person in one hundred (or one in a thousand, etc.) to get cancer (ill, etc.) the following questions would be appropriate. Since there are currently over 250 million people in the United States, any substances that causes less than 2.5 million cases of cancer (illness, etc.) is going to affect less than one percent of the population.

What percentage of the population do you believe would be at risk for developing cancer (becoming ill, etc.) if they were exposed to the dosage of this substance under discussion at this time?

Why isn't the other 99.99% of the population at risk?

At such a low percentage and with so many other carcinogens in the environment, how can you be sure this product is the culprit in the cases you claim would result from exposure to this product?

Most of us, I suspect, remember Ivan Pavlov's dogs. They were the ones that were trained to salivate when they heard a bell ring. Every time Pavlov rang the bell, he would feed them their favorite food until they finally associated the ringing of the bell with being fed. At that point, the dogs would salivate when they heard the bell, even thought there was no food offered. Not to be out done, today's scientists have come up with a mouse that can do something much more dramatic. Operating on the same principle, scientists from John Hopkin's University have trained mice to turn off their immune systems whenever they taste saccharin. Such mice, the researchers tell us, are much more likely than untrained mice to grow tumors when both groups are fed saccharin.

I find this information both interesting and a reason for some concern. For years now scientists and the EPA have been telling the public about all the toxins and carcinogens that exist in our universe. It is difficult to do anything or go anywhere without risking exposure to one or more of these hazards. I'm sure most people must feel, as I do, that we are surrounded by toxins of various sorts. They are in the air we breath, they are in the water we drink and they are in the food we eat.

We also know that the mind plays a significant role in how our body functions. How big a role is yet to be determined, but we do know that the mind plays a key role in the body's ability to fight off diseases. We know that the mind has some control over the actions of the immune system, and we know that a person's attitude affects their ability to fight off illness. Considering how easily the scientists at John Hopkins got the mice to suppress their immune systems, I can't help but wonder if all of the public concern over toxins, carcinogens and mutagens isn't creating a similar problem in some humans. Is it possible that all this worry about the constant exposure to cancer causing chemicals is just another form of saccharin? Can certain people become so distraught with concern over the possibility of getting cancer from the environment that their immune system becomes suppressed? Could just hearing the words "toxin," "carcinogen" or "mutagen" over and over again cause these sensitive individuals to subconsciously develop tumors by suppressing their immune system?

These are questions that I think are well worth answering. I would be more than willing to pay my share of the tax dollars necessary to find the real answers to these questions.

CHAPTER 10

Finding Truth in Science

"Nature does not complete things. She is chaotic.
Man must finish, and he does so by making a garden
and building a wall."

Robert Frost

"A new scientific truth does not triumph by convincing its opponents and making them see the light, but rather because its opponents eventually die, and a new generation grows up that is familiar with it."

Max Planck

Unfortunately, when the research process is severely abused, offensive regulations are not the only by product of such abuse. As mentioned in Chapter 8, when we accept this type of science, we deprive ourselves of the opportunity to discover the truth. In the case of carcinogens and cancer, our failure to observe and recognize the truth can allow the development of millions of cancer cases and cost thousands of lives. While the EPA and its myriad supporters and scientists continue to promote the agency's enforcement program, other scientists, not tied to EPA research dollars are discovering the real cause of cancer and are taking positive steps toward real prevention and cure. Following are some of their discoveries.

Genetics And Cancer

Since we have been held responsible for producing most of

the carcinogens in this country, it is only proper that we have at hand all the facts. Although I don't pretend to have found nearly everything in this area, here are some facts to help refute the current propaganda. I'll leave it to you to dig up some more.

When evidence of this nature is presented in court, I don't think you'll have much trouble persuading a judge that trying to eliminate carcinogens in the environment is a very expensive waste of time. Money spent to eliminate a single carcinogen from the environment is money very poorly spent. It will prevent no illness and will save no lives. This same money spent on projects such as those listed below could save thousands of lives. This *is* our country's priority, isn't it?

A recent article in the Oakland Tribune newspaper reported that an estimated one in 200 women—i.e. 600,00 women in the U.S.—carry a gene that makes them highly susceptible to breast cancer according to Sarah Rowell, researcher and Mary-Claire King, Geneticist at the University of California at Berkeley School of Public Health. Such women may have as much as a fifty-fifty chance of developing breast cancer before age fifty and an 80 percent chance of getting the disease by age 65. About 182,000 American women will be diagnosed with breast cancer this year and 46,000 will die of the disease, according to the American Cancer Society. Researchers suspect that the same gene that is linked to breast cancer is responsible for ovarian cancer, which is far more deadly. (Just how is all the billions we are spending to eliminate carcinogens in our environment going to help these women?)

It was recently announced that a defective gene has been found to be responsible for 90% of the acute leukemia cases in infants and 40% of the cases in older children.

Scientists have discovered there are a couple of genes that, when they mutate, trigger cancer. They also discovered that this situation is inherited. Fortunately, a new test has been developed in Massachusetts General Hospital which can detect whether a person has a dangerous defect in one of these genes. This gene, called p53, is a so-called cancer-suppressor gene. P53 is the most commonly known genetic defect to cause human cancers and can contribute to the development of leukemia, breast, lung, bladder, colon and liver cancers among others. When all goes well, p53 acts as a kind of genetic watchdog. If a cell's genes somehow become damaged, p53 shuts everything down until the mix-up is fixed. Thus cancer is avoided. However, when p53 itself is harmed, the cell loses this built-in control, and it makes new copies of its genetic mistakes. Making copies of genetic mistakes is, of course, what cancer is all about. Therefore, those that inherit a damaged p53 gene will get cancer. Removing all the carcinogens in the world will not change the fate of those who inherit this defective gene. However, research designed to correct this genetic flaw would save their lives.

According to the *Contra Costa Times*, Dr. Bert Voglestein of John Hopkins University along with others has discovered a flawed gene that causes colon cancer. They are preparing a test so those with a family history of cancer can be tested to see if they have the flawed gene and are thus prone to contract colon cancer.

Meanwhile, the FDA has given physicians at the San Diego Regional Cancer Center in La Jolla permission to treat 9 patients with genetic therapy as a treatment against colon cancer. The patients will receive three genetic injections to boost the patient's immune response to attack colon cancer. "People don't have a good immune response against their own tumors, so there needs to be a little help," said Dr. Ivor Royston, the cancer center's scientific director. About 57,000 Americans die of colon cancer each year, and 152,000 new cases are reported annually. (This small program in La Jolla will save many more lives than all the enforcement activities by the EPA in the next ten years.)

Our local newspaper recently advised us that scientists are zeroing in on the gene that causes melanoma, the deadly form of skin cancer. This year the American Cancer Society predicts that 6,800 Americans will die from melanoma. The paper quoted Dr. Darrel Rigel of New York University as saying, "However, the rate on melanoma is increasing faster than any other cancer in the U.S. At the current rate, approximately one in five Americans will develop melanoma during their lifetime." Dr. Laurence Meyer of the University of Utah said scientists believe they have narrowed the search for the responsible gene to a small stretch of one human chromosome.

In some cancer-prone families, people inherit one damaged copy of a cancer suppressing gene and one good copy. If the good copy becomes scrambled, cancer occurs. Cancer is much less common among those born with two good copies of the gene, because they stay cancer-free unless both copies are damaged.

When our courts become aware of this type of information they are going to begin to understand the realities of the cancer scare. When we spend billions of dollars trying to eliminate compounds in our environment that the EPA claims gave Harriet, Horace, Mable and Morton cancer, we are wasting enormous resources. If these same resources were directed toward projects like those just discussed, millions of cancer cases could be eliminated.

Remember those optional items we talked about placing in our letter to the agency when we demanded just compensation? The above situations would certainly apply to the court ruling which held that "the court may explore the statute's purpose, its operative provisions, the extend to which other means could have been used to achieve the same purpose, and the rights it sought to abridge in the process." Since the alleged purpose of most EPA regulations against businesses is to prevent cancer in humans, it is obvious that the same purpose could have been achieved more effectively and with less expense in other ways. Armed with the information from this and the previous chapter, a good lawyer should have no trouble proving to the court that genetic research is a far superior method of eliminating cancer.

One of the greatest obstacles standing in the way of good medical research is a generally negative attitude about the concept of differences among humans. Being different is looked on as a negative and this has kept society from discussing differences that could save many lives. Whenever anyone suggests their might be differences between races, for instance, the roof falls in.

This perception, unfortunately, plays havoc when dealing with diseases that are hereditary. Research money is spent in this area very grudgingly although it is apparent that the eventual cure of most chronic diseases will be through this medium. Also, in our effort to "standardize" everyone, we are hurting certain groups. Race and sex, for instance, are not taken into account when administering drugs and this could create a problem.

Because we fail to recognize and admit to individual weaknesses, we try to pretend they do not exist. We can then blame society, or our businesses for illnesses and deaths. This is the tack that was used in whipping up the carcinogen scare. Instead of approaching cancer as a problem of heredity, we approached it as a social problem with a bunch of bad guys creating poisons that would eventually kill us all.

The problem is, we have people dying from every imaginable type of exposure. In February of 1994, an 8 year old girl died from exposure to the fumes from a pot of cooking garbanzo beans. She was allergic to beans and inhaled mist from across the kitchen when visiting a friend. While this is allergy in the extreme, there are a lot of people who die from exposure to substances that are either benign or beneficial to the rest of us.

Society needs to face this issue head on and make a decision. Do we continue to create giant agencies whose goals are to eliminate any substance that might be harmful to one or more groups of humans? Or do we begin to recognize our differences so we can start finding a real cure for those of us who have inherited a special sensitivity to some aspect of our environment?

Armed with the above information, it should not be hard to come up with some very clever questions for your demand letter or questions in court that challenge the justification for the existence of a regulation. Especially when applying the court ruling that requires an agency to determine if there is not a better way of meeting the "intent" of the regulations. Here are a few off the top of my head.

"Are you aware of the research currently being undertaken at the University of California, Massachusetts General Hospital, the San Diego Regional Cancer Center, John Hopkins University, New York University, the University of Utah and else where that have determined that most cancers occur as a result of inherited factors such as a damaged p53 cancer suppressor gene?"

"In light of the current research on genetics and cancer, how can you determine that the cause of these cancer cases was not of genetic origin?"

"Don't you think we could do much more toward saving the lives of these people by finding a means of eliminating this inherited susceptibility to cancer than by reducing (NO2 admissions from cars by 1%)?"

"In light of these current studies don't you think that the money currently being spent to reduce emissions, such as the ones we are discussing today, could be better utilized by undertaking real cancer research?"

Can you state positively that this person's cancer was not the result of a weaken immune system or a hereditary factor rather than the substance in question?

"Is it possible for someone with a healthy p53 cancer suppressor gene to get cancer from exposure to the (chemical and dosage) we are discussing here?"

"Is it possible to stop someone from contracting cancer by removing this (chemical and dosage) if their p53 cancer suppressor gene has been damaged so that it no longer functions properly."

More Genetics In Action

As I mentioned previously, genetics has turned out to be the major culprit responsible for a great many human diseases that were previously blamed upon some factor in our environment. Progress in this area will depend, to a great extent, upon educating the public to the realities of these diseases. To do this, our country must over come two obstacles. First, we must overcome the decades of brainwashing by special interest groups. Second, we must overcome our fear of recognizing our differences.

In a recent issue of the magazine *Issues in Science and Technology*, James D. Watson, Nobel Prize winner, director of the Cold Springs Harbor Laboratory and founding director of the National Center for Human Genome Research at the National Institutes of Health is quoted as saying, "I suspect we underestimate the effect genetics is going to have on medicine and on human life. What we're witnessing is evolution in action. And evolution often isn't kind to the individual."

In the same magazine Michael S. Brown, 1985 Nobel Prize winner and regental professor at University of Texas-Southwestern Medical Center warned: "Social policies that are designed for one group may actually harm another group who are genetically susceptible to whatever manipulation occurs."

Severe Combined Immunodeficiency Diseases (SCIDS), are a group of devastating genetic disorders that afflict one in every 100,000 babies. Several gene defects are at fault.

The Oakland Tribune reported that a recent study demonstrated that genetics controls 50% to 60% of a woman's susceptibility to alcoholism, with cultural and environmental factors accounting for the rest. Same for men.

Scientists have now found a third genetic defect that is involved in the development of Alzheimer's disease.

L-tryptophan is an essential amino acid that is found naturally in milk, turkey and other foods. Unfortunately, a small number of people with abnormal immune systems will develop EMS, an auto-immune disease, when taking L-tryptophan supplements. As a result, L-tryptophan has been removed from store shelves. However, it is still allow in baby formulas. People who are sensitive to this natural product are now suing because the product *was* on the market. Should they win? Should they be allowed to have a product removed that is essential to the survival of most other humans? When pondering this question don't forget, there is always a small number of babies born each year who are allergic to milk.

A group of scientists will attempt to find the genetic basis for manic-depression, a disease which strikes 1% of all Americans.

Scientists have found that as many as 7% of the population may have a natural immunity (or resistance) to the AIDS virus and do not get AIDS despite having the virus. They are able to fight off the virus in some manner yet to be discovered. This is probably a genetic factor.

American Journal of Medicine reported that genetics, not diet, is the determining factor in determining a person's cholesterol level. About one percent of the population have a condition called hypocholesterolemia which can be passed on to their offspring. Those people that have this condition can eat all the McDonald's French fries and hamburgers they want.

The Journal of Drug and Alcohol Dependence recently advised its readers that Kenneth Blum, a professor of Pharmacology at the University of Texas Health Science Center in San Antonio, and Ernest Noble, a professor of alcohol studies at UCLA have found a gene common to cocaine addicts. Dr. George Uhl, chief of molecular neurobiology at the National Institute of Drug Abuse, said the findings confirm other recent research. It had previously been reported in relation to alcohol addiction. Many now believe that those with the gene will have what some have labeled an "addictive personality," and there is a very strong correlation between the gene and family histories of alcoholism, the use of more potent forms of cocaine and early childhood conduct disorder.

An article in *Discover* Magazine mentioned that University of California scientists have discovered a gene defect responsible for Menkes disease, a disorder that kills one of every 50,000 newborn males. UC-San Francisco researchers feel their discovery will lead to improved prenatal testing for the inherited disorder, which prevents the body from using copper and causes severe mental retardation and other abnormalities.

Maple Syrup Urine disease is a genetic disorder in which certain amino acids are not properly metabolized causing a whole array of neurological problems. Although rare in the general population, it is a thousand times more common among the Old Order Mennonites of Pennsylvania thanks to generations of inbreeding. The genetic defect that originated with a single Mennonite couple in the eighteenth century now affects one baby in every 176. Those babies invariable die if not put on a special diet within a week of birth. Many of them die anyway. One fifth die even on diet therapy, and most others have low IQs and are underdeveloped. The only cure is gene therapy. They have now learned to fix the genetic defect in laboratory cell cultures.

Five generations of aggressive men in a Dutch family have led researchers to a gene that seems to lie at the root of the violence. They found a gene, passed from mother to son on the Z chromosome, that causes low intelligence and violence in the son. This discovery is not going to be very popular in most social circles.

Myotonic dystrophy is a degenerative muscle disorder whose victims can grip but can't let go. They may suffer from such bewildering and seemingly disparate symptoms as cataracts, abnormal heartbeat, diabetes, and metal retardation. But what has puzzled doctors most about this inherited condition is that the disease gets worse with each generation: children tend to be more severely afflicted than their parents; grandchildren suffer even more. This pattern of escalation has been an utter enigma to physicians. The genetic rules they learned in medical school simply can't explain a disorder that gets more severe from parent to child.

The immune system is the ultimate arbiter of which substance is dangerous to the body and which is benign, what is self and what is not-self. But when that judgment goes awry, a biological civil war called autoimmune disease breaks out. Perhaps the most infamous autoimmune disease is systemic lupus erythematosus, which afflicts tens of thousands of Americans (90 percent of them women) and is sometimes fatal. In lupus, the body inexplicably begins to attack its own DNA, setting off a chain reaction that leads to inflammations in the connective tissues of the skin, kidneys and other organs.

The National Institute of Diabetes and Digestive and Kidney Diseases in Bethesda, Md. published an article in the *New England Journal of Medicine* announcing the discovery of a genetic defect that causes hyperactivity in children. Scientist found attention deficient-hyperactivity disorder can be from a flaw in a gene regulating thyroid hormone use. Three to ten percent of children are estimated to have attention deficit disorder. They found that 70 percent of children and fifty percent of adults who inherited the bad gene that causes the thyroid disorder also had attention deficit-hyperactivity.

About one in every 100,000 babies are born with a disease (X-linked SCID), which results in the child having a severely crippled immune system. Such children have no defense against even the slightest infection, and will die of an infectious disease if not protected by an almost sterile environment. This disease is the result of a defective gene that is passed from mothers to sons on the X chromosome.

One in 500 people carries a defective gene linked to extremely high blood cholesterol levels and early death from heart disease. Untreated, the disease, called familial hypercholesterolemia, can cause cholesterol levels of 350-450—twice normal—and lead to death by age forty-five for men and fifty-five for women. Drug treatment costs $500 to $3000 per year and there is currently a project under way to locate, test and treat families carrying this defective gene.

Dr. Markku Linnoila of the National Institute of Health has discovered that people with low levels of the chemical serotonin are prone to impulsive, violent acts. Serotonin is a neuro-transmitter that modulates emotion. The low level of serotonin in these people is suspected to be genetic in nature and a search is currently underway to identify this genetic defect.

His work challenges long-held assumptions that social and environmental factors—poverty, joblessness, discrimination, lack of education—are sole causes of crime and violence. It would also explain why only a small percentage of those who are socially and environmentally disadvantaged are violent. It, too, might help us understand why there is violence among those that are not socially and environmentally disadvantaged.

Other diseases of genetic origin include: Cystic Fibrosis, Neurofibromatosis, Huntington's disease, Downs Syndrome, Fragile X gene, Spina bifida, Schizophrenia, Spinocerebellar ataxia, Myotonic dystrophy, Spinobulbar muscular dystrophy, Type II Diabetes, Lou Gehrig's Disease (ALS), Lorenzo's Disease (ADL), Hemophilia, and—highly suspicious but not yet proven —Homosexuality.

When all is said and done, human diseases come from one of two places:

1) An invasion of the human body by some outside entity such as a virus, bacteria, chemical or other product of our environment.

2) A defect in our genetic make up that allows the body to attack itself or a defect in our genetic make up that prohibits our immune system from functioning effectively.

Over the last three million years humans, in order to survive, have developed an immune system that can fight off most external invaders very successfully as long as the invading alien does not occur in overwhelming doses. Science and the medical community have done a rather effective job of protecting those of us living in the U.S. from most diseases caused by biological invaders. Smallpox, cholera, malaria, typhoid fever, polio and other killers of the past are all but history. For the most part, we are just left with those obnoxious colds and the flu. Once in a while a new form arrives, such as Legionnaires Disease or Lyme Disease, but it takes little time for science to discover the culprit and begin work on a vaccine or a drug that will help our immune system fight the infection.

However, our immune system does a much better job of destroying and eliminating various foreign "chemicals" that would be toxic or carcinogenic in large amounts. Over millions of years, our bodies have not only learned to protect us from such invasions, but our bodies have learned how to put them to work for us. As a result, our bodies have not only learned to eliminate these chemical invaders with dispatch, they have learned how to utilize them in "trace" amounts. Chemical invaders are less dangerous than biological invaders for another very important reason. Biological invaders (viruses, etc.) can mutate into a form that the body does not recognize and is not equipped to defend against, thus creating another disease epidemic. Inert chemical invaders cannot mutate.

However, our struggle to conquer those diseases resulting from genetic factors has not been nearly so successful. Much of this failure has occurred because we do not want to take responsibility for these diseases. We do not want to admit that the disease is the result of some human weakness. We do not want to admit that the human species is not perfect and that it is, in fact, still evolving. As Nobel Prize winner James D. Watson said, "Evolution is not kind to the individual."

For this reason, we are willing to buy into the propaganda championed by the EPA and its cohorts who would like us to believe that these diseases are not inherited but are the result of invasions from an outside entity. Unfortunately, there will be no relief from the ravages of these diseases as long as we are willing to pretend that their source is the product of some business or other environmental factor that is invading our bodies. We can spend billions and billions of research dollars trying to prove this fallacy and can spend billions and billions of dollars enforcing regulations, but we will not prevent one single case of these diseases. However, we could well eliminate many of these diseases forever by spending just one tenth this amount on research that will identify the real causes of these diseases.

The truth is, Horace, Harriet, Morton and Mable got cancer because of hereditary weaknesses, not because they were exposed to any chemicals that the EPA would like us to believe are carcinogenic.

Is Saving Lives Our Priority?

We are told over and over again that all the regulations we must deal with are there to prevent illness and death in humans and to prevent damage to the environment. Under the circumstances, I don't think it is too much to ask for the establishment of some priorities in these areas. After all, neither this country nor its citizens have the resources to eliminate all sources of illness, death and environmental harm at one time. Some of these forces have been around for hundreds or thousands of years. Therefore, it seems only logical that some priorities be established. If saving human lives is our greatest concern, common sense would dictate that our first priority be to eliminate that which is taking the most human lives.

This does not seem like such a huge task. We just need to determine if saving human lives or saving the environment or some other goal is the most important. Once resolved, priorities can be established and realistic goals set. The option, of course, is to capitulate to every special interest group that demands an immediate solution to their pet project and establish no priorities whatsoever. This option is, obviously, the road to chaos. When we try to solve all problems at once, we solve none of them. A country pulled a thousand different ways has no direction. This, unfortunately, is the path our country (i.e., our lawmakers and policy makers) have chosen to take.

Whenever another special interest group begins to holler, congress passes more legislation and another agency appears at the doorstep of property owners and businesses. While such action will not solve the country's problems, it does solve congress's problem. It gets another special interest group off its back. Since property owners and businesses have become the fall guys for solving all the country's health and environmental problems, we certainly have a right to determine if we are being pushed in the right direction. On the assumption that saving lives is a priority, the remainder of this chapter is devoted to information that could help our courts set priorities in this area. Helping the courts learn the truth should improve our chances of getting useless regulations off our backs.

This information is by no means complete. As I suggested in Chapter 7, we all need to search for additional information that will support our position. The material I've provided in this chapter will, hopefully, jump start our campaign. More important, however, it will help you identify the kind of material you should be looking for. Our ultimate success will depend upon the information we gather in support of our position.

Public Health, the EPA, OSHA, and other agencies that have used saving lives as the primary justification their existence, will claim that savings lives should be our priority. I'm not going to quibble with that. Let's see if they are putting their resources where their justifications are. Following is some of the information that has been recently published about causes of death in our country. Finally, at the end of this chapter is a list of the twenty-five leading causes of death in the U.S. Are the agencies achieving what they claim they set out to accomplish?

Murder was the leading cause of death in the work place in five states and the District of Columbia. In all, 7,603 Americans were slain on the job in the last decade. Construction and transportation/utility workers accounted for the most fatalities. Most likely to be murdered at work were taxi drivers, police officers and retail workers.

The Centers for Disease Control and Prevention in Atlanta warned that tractor pulls, truck jumps and mud racing can be dangerous to your health. A study of such events over a two year period in Cincinnati demonstrated that carbon monoxide reaches dangerous levels in the arenas where these events are held. Levels were found to reach 283 parts per million, over twice the level where carbon monoxide can start causing symptoms. How would a regulator explain to the court why this is not regulated while much less harmful doses produced by other businesses are? Could it be that no priorities exist?

Talk about walking the tightrope. Iron is an essential nutrient found mainly in red meat and fortified grains. Too little can cause medical problems, from anemia to retardation. However, too much might be even worse. The largest study to date shows iron to be a cancer risk in men when the amount of iron in their bodies is only 10% higher than average. Some choice, huh? How would you regulate this out of existence?

There were 15,529 auto accidents in Contra Costa county in 1992. Of those, 72 or 0.46% were caused by equipment failure. The other 99.54% were caused by driver error. This same ratio exists throughout the country. Why do we spend ten times as much trying to eliminate the cause of 0.46% of the auto accidents as we do on trying to prevent the cause of the other 99.54 percent? Is this a case of misplaced regulation?

As terrible as it may be, AIDS is not the predominant threat to life that everyone seems to have portrayed it as being. Nation wide it doesn't rank among the top twenty-five killers. Even in California, where AIDS victims are more prevalent, it ranks fifth as a cause of death. According to state Department of Health services data, AIDS caused about 5,000 deaths in 1990, the last year for which comprehensive numbers are available. Cancer caused three times as many deaths and heart disease twice as many. More people died of accident-caused injuries or in homicides than from AIDS. The Library of Congress says that more federal money is being spent on AIDS research—some $2.1 billion—this year than on any other disease, including cancer and heart disease. Not only does political activism on behalf of AIDS mislead the public about the disease and its support, this activism cheats the victims of other diseases of their rightful share of research money. Is this the way we establish priorities?

In the 1940's and 50's measles, mumps, polio and TB were the primary targets of public health. Now, being poor is a primary health problem. Poor people get most of the problems facing us today. AIDS, drugs, gunshot wounds, fetal alcohol syndrome. Are we heading in the right direction? Could we be more effective in handling these problems if we weren't so busy chasing our tails around the regulatory bush?

Scientists have decided that soot is responsible for tens of thousands of deaths each year, making it the most deadly air pollutant. Affected are those that already have respiratory problems such as asthma and emphysema, bronchitis and pneumonia. How do they really know? Those people with respiratory problems could be living with a smoker or have a fire in their fireplace every night. Unfortunately, this is another unverified statistic that will probably come back to haunt us in the near future.

Meanwhile, the new Clean Air Act Amendments will raise the cost of a new car $1,000 to $1,500 but will just reduce auto induced smog by .5%. Is this a rational cost-benefit regulation? It's especially depressing when we remember that soot is now considered the most dangerous air pollutant.

According to a study by Bookings Institute economist Robert Crandall and Harvard Univ. professor John Graham, current federal fuel economy standards will cause each year between 2,000 and 4,000 additional deaths and an additional 11,000 to 19,000 serious injuries. This is because the cars must be made smaller and lighter. Is this economical? Is our goal *really* to save lives?

An architect claims stairs are one of the worlds most dangerous products. He could be right. In the U.S. one million people
seek medical treatment for falls on staircases. About 50,000 are
hospitalized and 4,000 die. Where should this fit in our priorities?

Many newspapers across the country carried the story about
Clark R. Chapman of the Planetary Science Institute in Tucson
and David Morrison at NASA's Ames Research Institute in Mt.
View, California who determined that your odds of being killed
by an asteroid from outer space are one in 20,000. (You're better
off being exposed to carcinogens. Your odds are about one in a
million with carcinogen exposure.)

Secondhand noise from traffic, airplanes, lawn mowers, leaf
blowers, chain saws and stereos may be more dangerous than
second-hand smoke, according to a professor of neurophysiol-
ogy at the University of Wisconsin. Now here is something I
could agree with. I could use a little less noise in my environment. EPA where are you?

Harper's Index reported that
- The number of emergency room admissions in 1992 for inju-
  ries involving house plants: 2,421
- The number of admissions for injuries involving pillows: 5,840
- The number of U.S. citizens robbed or assaulted in 1992 by
  people impersonating police officers: 25,000

On August 27, 1928, the KellogBriand Pact was signed in
Paris, outlawing war and providing for the peaceful settlement
of disputes.
The percentage of war fatalities in the last 500 years that has
taken place since the beginning of the century: 75%. This pact

seems to have been just about as effective as most others.

The Coalition for Consumer Health and Safety put out a pamphlet listing ten "hidden hazards" in everyday life that we ignore:

1. Rollover crashes in sport and utility vehicles
2. Failure to use car lap belts
3. Infant drownings in five-gallon buckets
4. Falls from playground equipment (200,000 injuries per year)
5. Falls and burns caused by baby walkers
6. Poisoning from improperly cooked food
7. Secondhand smoke
8. Excessive drinking
9. Sexually transmitted diseases from improper contraceptive use.
10. Not wearing bike helmets

I don't know whether these were prioritized or not, but even if they weren't, EPA and Public Health should look into the unregulated selling of five gallon buckets and baby walkers. It also appears that all household cooks should be required to attend cooking school.

Is Nothing Safe?

Finding the twenty-five top killers in the United States is not as easy as it sounds. Basically we are dealing with a bunch of statistics which, I have discovered, can be used to prove almost anything if bent in the right direction. For instance, in one of the situations mentioned above, scientists claimed that soot kills tens of thousands of people every year. They then go on to say that it only kills those that are suffering from asthma, emphysema, bronchitis and pneumonia.

The first question that arises: "what really killed these people, the soot or the asthma, emphysema, bronchitis and pneumonia?" Certainly, if one were to look at the death certificate, it would list the disease.

The second question that one should then ask is: "would these people stop dying if soot were removed from their environment?" We know that not every one dying of these diseases was exposed to soot. Therefore, we know that they can die either with or without exposure to soot. We can, therefore, conclude that removing soot from the environment is not going to stop them from dying.

The final question is: "would these people stop dying if they did not have the disease?" The answer is yes, even if exposed to soot. Therefore, we can conclude that the real causes of death are asthma, emphysema, bronchitis and pneumonia; not soot.

The soot scare then, like carcinogens, is just another excuse for regulating our lives.

Finding statistics without such built in bias is difficult these days. The following list was compiled by Dr. Ernest L. Abel, Professor of Obstetrics and Gynecology at Wayne State Medical School. Of all the information available on this subject, his seemed to be the most well researched and least bias. Here is Dr. Abel's list of the top twenty-five killers in the United States.

1. Heart Attack—causes one of every four deaths
2. Cancer
3. Pneumonia, Influenza and Tuberculosis (Outside invaders of our lungs) Not soot.
4. Car Accidents—#1 killer of children
5. Diabetes—Attacks the child and kills the adult
6. Hypertension—Most common disease with thirty million cases
7. Suicide—#3 killer of children
8. Liver disease—(alcoholism is most common cause)

9. Cerebral Thrombosis & Embolism
10. Atherosclerosis
11. Kidney Disease
12. Cerebral Hemorrhage
13. Murder—#4 killer of children
14. Leukemia—Affects one child in 100 (#2 killer of children)
15. Septicemia (Blood poisoning)—Affects mostly infants and elderly
16. Emphysema
17. Heart Valve Disease
18. Sudden Infant Death Syndrome (SIDS)—disease of infants only
19. Rheumatic Fever—damages heart of children who then die prematurely as adults from a weakened heart
20. Ulcers
21. Hernias
22. Asthma—#8 killer of children
23. Chronic Bronchitis
24. Anemia
25. Birth Defects

The first question most people will ask is, where is AIDS? Dr. Abel's statistics was based on information available through 1990. At that time he predicted that AIDS would reach the top twenty-five within a few years. However, recent information indicates that the AIDS epidemic has topped out, and the number of annual deaths is beginning to drop. Anyway, a discussion of AIDS should fall under the topic of how research dollars are spent, not on the topic of regulations.

However, in looking at Dr. Abel's list, it is obvious that the agencies that have justified their regulations on the basis of saving lives have been terribly misguided. I don't see where any of the activities currently being undertaken by these agencies is attacking any of the top twenty-five causes of death. Perhaps if we took the money currently used to enforce these useless regulations and coupled it with properly dispersed research dollars, we *could* save thousands of lives.

CHAPTER 11

The Environment
Endangered Species
Special Interests
And More Real Victims

"Let me make the superstitions of a nation and I care not who makes its laws or its songs either."

Mark Twain

"The penalty good men pay for indifference to public affairs is to be ruled by evil men."

Plato

The Truth About the Environment

Property owners and especially businesses have been accused of being the major enemies of the environment. However, when we look at all the facts, we see a different story emerging. Certainly any judge who professes a concern for the environment needs to be aware of facts such as those that follow.

Many researchers strongly suspect that the recent ozone losses and the surprising coolness share a common cause: the eruption of Mount Pinatubo. Pinatubo released four billion pounds of chlorine when it erupted. In other words it did basically the same thing science has claimed that CFC's do, release chlorine. Because of this fact some people claim the CFC-ozone link is a hoax. They argue, that if it was true, volcanic eruptions should long ago have wiped out the ozone layer.

In any event, volcanoes must be taken into account when evaluating ozone depletion. After Pinatubo's eruption, ozone concentrations in the stratosphere dropped unusually fast. In the summer of 1991, the ozone layer was ten percent thinner over the United States. This would permit a twenty to thirty percent increase in the type of ultraviolet radiation that causes skin cancer. Ozone concentrations were twenty-five percent below normal over Russia and ozone levels decreased around the world in 1993. If, indeed, the release of Chlorine is the culprit in the thinning of the ozone layer, then volcanic eruptions must be the heavies. All the man-made CFC's in the world are a pittance beside the eruptions of Pinatubo, St. Helens, and the many other eruptions that have taken place in just the last twenty years.

Finding the real culprit in the ozone depletion saga is not as clear cut as science and the regulatory agencies would like us to believe. Volcanic eruptions would certainly help explain why the ozone over the south Pole was thinner in 1958 than it is today.

It has been discovered that the ice age climate warmed abruptly at least ten times in the last 40,000 years, stayed warm for 500 to 2,000 years, then chilled again. That's about a 4,000 year cycle. Every time this cycle occurs, those plants and animals that are unable to adapt to the sudden change in climate perish. All this has happened without the aid of humans or our current industrial practices. Such awareness makes it difficult to take seriously the harbingers of "global warming." During an ice age, when much of the earth's water is tied up in ice sheets, the sea level is 400 feet lower than today. What happens to those species that were living near the seashore during an ice age? When the earth warms up and the ocean raises 400 feet higher in elevation, do they evolve or disappear? Look at all the animals that now flourish in the first 400 feet of ocean depth. What will be their fate when the next ice age comes. When viewed in this perspective, it is hard to get all upset about the insignificant little things you and I "do" to the environment.

Discover Magazine advises us that Paul Olsen, paleontologist at the Lamont-Doherty Earth Observatory in New York, has a new theory about global warming and ice ages. He feels that they result from the ongoing battle between plants and animals. Olsen's exploration has now taken him to a hypothesis encompassing not just dinosaurs but the entire history of life on land. In his view, herbivores evolve to eat plants, the plants evolve ways of eluding the herbivores, and the herbivores evolve again. As each side gets the upper hand, it steers the planet between balmy and cold climates. When the plants are winning, CO_2 is removed from the air and cold ensues. When the herbivores are winning, CO_2 accumulates in the atmosphere creating the hot house affect. This theory seems to fit well with fossil records and the geological records of rock weathering. Why not? It makes more sense than claiming that businesses are doing it.

The Biomass Energy Research Association, The American Scientist (July-August 1990) and Forbes Magazine have all printed articles refuting the global warming hysteria. They conclude that burning fossil fuels account for no more than 5% of total global carbon dioxide emissions. What would the American public think if they knew that this country is spending billions of dollars and eliminating thousands of jobs each year in order to attack man-made carbon dioxide emissions that have absolutely no affect on the environment? The first two cited groups also concluded that it would severely dampen the panic profits being realized by the media in their coverage of the alleged global warming phenomena if this became widely accepted public knowledge. Certainly the media is a special interest group.

Common wisdom has it that the deserts of the world are on the march, steadily expanding, permanently converting pastures and croplands to sand dunes, and that human mistreatment of the drylands that flank the deserts is responsible. However, scientists, using the most up-to-date investigative techniques, have found no evidence that this is true, at least in the Sahara and its immediate environs, everyone's favorite example of what is called "desertification." In view of the lack of evidence, many experts suspect that the threatening image of encroaching deserts may be more myth than fact. The findings, based on satellite measurements, are forcing a reassessment of just what is happening in the arid and semi-arid drylands along the desert's perimeter, which has turned out to be more resilient than once thought. Long term rainfall records show that the climate in Africa's drylands has shifted back and forth between periods of extended draught and higher rainfall for at least 10,000 years. Rainfall patterns, not humans, influence the ebb and flow of the desert into the drylands, it has been discovered.

Paul Erlich, in 1968, predicted that "the battle to feed humanity is already lost...we will not be able to prevent large-scale famines in the next decade." Erlich also bet economist Julian Simon $1,000 that in a decade the prices of five resources (copper, chrome, nickel, tin, & tungsten) would rise. The prices of all five fell. In a recent issued of *Reason*, Stephen Moore of the Cato Institute reported that, contrary to predictions that increased population would produce scarcities, by every objective measure natural resources became more plentiful in the 1980's.

On January 5, 1993, hurricane force winds slammed

the disabled Liberian tanker "Braer" onto the craggy shores of Grath's Ness, a small peninsula at the southern tip of the Shetland Islands. The tanker broke apart during the week, bleeding 24.6 million gallons of Norwegian light crude into the turbulent waters. It was the 12th largest oil spill in history, and the world braced for another ecological disaster. The worst never happened. A conventional oil slick never formed; the churning seas dispersed the slow leak, and much of the crude was blown on shore, where it coated the landscape with a thin veneer of oil. It degraded quickly. Its more volatile components evaporated, and microbes fed on the rest. Cleanup crews never even had to go to work. "After two weeks even the press left."

Discover, January 1994

One would expect environmentalists to be pleased at seeing mother nature clean up a man-made disaster so quickly. However, certain groups would prefer you didn't know. The truth is, mother nature is very adept at healing environmental scars, man made and otherwise. Unfortunately, this fact takes some of the "bite" out of their predictions of gloom and doom.

However, as George Will, nationally syndicated columnist, commented recently in the Oakland Tribune: "Various reasons for gloominess come and go but the supply of gloominess is remarkably constant. A recent Science magazine editorial, 'The Attractiveness of Gloom,' satirically offered a new version of Murphy's Law: 'Things are worse than they can possibly be.' It quotes Dr. Noitall, who says his fellow gloom-mongers are handicapped by the fact that standards of living, and life expectancy, keep rising. However, he takes comfort from the fact that anxiety will remain high because 'expectations always increase more rapidly than productivity.' And he contentedly anticipates 'the panic that will spread through the population when they read about the epidemic of deaths through natural causes'."

Another favorite area of attack for certain groups is man-made chemicals. They would like us to believe that any man-made chemical isn't "natural" and is therefore bad. Even if the manufactured chemical is a duplicate of a natural one.

In response to this claim Roald Hoffman, *Discover* Magazine, August 1993, tells us the truth about chemicals made in our laboratories:

> Chemists make molecules for many reasons:
>
> First, to see if they can make the same molecules as nature does.
>
> Second, chemists want to make things that aren't found in nature.
>
> Third, they want to make molecules that resemble natural ones but are better in some respect. There are now polymers stronger than steel, and fats that are calorie-free to fry your onions in.
>
> Fourth, chemists want to make molecules that are sort of like natural ones but a little different, so as to fool bacteria and viruses. To trick them into committing suicide or not reproducing.
>
> Fifth, chemists make synthetic molecules to understand nature—its highways and byways, how it got to be the beautiful way it is.
>
> The natural-unnatural distinction is an illusion. Your MSG headache is equally well induced by synthetic or natural MSG. Your pneumonia is cured by an antibiotic made in a laboratory or by a mold. There is no distinction between "natural" and laboratory produced molecules.

Despite the fact that man has been able to enhance many things offered by nature, certain groups continue to believe it is impossible to improve upon nature. They say this, of course, while eating a slice of bread made from a genetically engineered wheat plant, spread with peanut butter that came from George Washington Carver's laboratory and while drinking a glass of milk pasteurized courtesy of Louis Pasteur.

In the end, perhaps it is as George Will suggests in one of his columns: "Some environmentalists (usually at comfortably endowed universities in developed countries) dislike economic growth, and many environmental measures hinder it. But growth is a prerequisite for environmental improvement. The world wide pattern is that environmental damage increases until per capita income increases to a point where people enjoy a social surplus and feel they can ask government to trade some growth for environmental healing."

Perhaps, as property owners and businesses we are the heroes of the environmental movement and not the goats the environmentalist would have us believe. Property ownership and businesses are certainly the road to economic growth and increased per capita income.

Endangered Species

One of the greatest government land grabs to ever hit this nation is taking place as you read this book. This new enterprise is taking place under the guise of protecting endangered and threatened species of plants and animals. You need to understand the reality of this issue and be aware of some of the enforcement programs the Department of Interior has planned for you under the Endangered Species Act. The National Wilderness Institute is currently keeping a log of incidents where the enforcement of this act has created havoc with someone's life and or property, therefore, I won't list any here. If you want to reference specific incidents of abuse from the Endangered Species Act, the address of the National Wilderness Institute is listed with other contacts near the end of the book.

In July of 1993, several farmers in the San Joaquin valley received disturbing letters from the Interior Department's Bureau of Reclamation. The letters informed the farmers that the bureau intended to look for endangered species on their land and asked permission for inspectors to enter the property. As much as many farmers would have liked to deny the bureau permission, this wasn't a real option. If the landowners refused to participate voluntarily, the letter warned, "uncultivated parcels will likely be labeled as habitat if absence of species cannot be confirmed by inspection." In other words, if you don't let us look for species, we will take your property outright.

Farmers panicked and rightly so. They knew that in either event they could lose the use of their land because the feds always took a big "bite" whether an endangered species was found or whether their land was just labeled as a habitat. Among other things, when land can no longer be cultivated, banks will no longer make the farmers loans to grow next year's crop.

As Jeff A. Taylor, national political reporter with Evans and Novak pointed out in the January 1994 issue of *Reason* Magazine: "This project is a top priority of Interior Secretary Bruce Babbitt and he has created a new agency called the National Biological Survey to carry it out."

"The idea of the NBS is straightforward enough. Rep. Gerry Studds (D-Mass.), one of the agency's chief sponsors, says the NBS has 'a simple, yet awesome mission—catalog everything that walks, crawls, swims or flies around the country.' To do this, NBS agents must enter every parcel of land in the country. And, unlike the U.S. census, the NBS won't fan out just every decade; its mission has no down time. Although supporters note that a complete count could prove that some species are *not* endangered after all, landowners fear that the net effect will be the transfer de-facto of control of thousands of more acres of land to the federal government."

The Gorsk family was an obvious victim of this principle of government. It would be difficult for anyone to demonstrate to the Gorsks how they are better off because there might have been a Stephans Kangaroo Rat on their property that needed protection. It is difficult for them to understand why they are required to spend $5,000 to determine if such an animal exists on their property. If would seem far more logical to require the special interest group that petitioned to get the "rat" listed as endangered, pay the $5,000 needed to determine if a rat was present. More important, the petitioning group should have been required to get a search warrant to inspect the Gorsk property.

Had the Gorsks been growing marijuana or cocaine on their property, the enforcing authority would have been required to actually find the Gorsks breaking the law (growing the illegal drug) before any action could be taken. In order to make this discovery, the enforcement agency would need to get a search warrant and, in order to get a search warrant, the enforcement agency would have needed to show a judge that there was probable cause to believe that the Gorsks were breaking the law. However, in the case of the Kangaroo Rat, the enforcing agency didn't need to go to all that trouble. It just needed to label the Gorsks' land as a probable habitat for the rat and all the Gorsks' constitutional rights flew out the window. No search warrant, no search, no crime discovered. Guilty!

This is the most far reaching attempt to abuse the Fifth Amendment that one can imagine. It is difficult to understand how anyone could so blithely propose stomping on the property rights of absolutely every individual in this country who owns property. Those of you living in Massachusetts take heed. Gerry Studds needs to be replaced. The rest of us need to contact our representatives and make sure they stop this National Biological Survey. Remember, their goal is to inspect every inch of land in the United States. If they can't inspect your property, they will "assume" you are harboring an endangered species and label it accordingly.

Perhaps the most common and dangerous feature of the radical environmentalists, is their failure to think things through. In their mad dash to diminish or banish the major enemy of the environment from this Earth, that is you and me, of course, they have taken into account only those things that favor their position. With the eternal banishment of humans from earth, they would like us to picture a planet revived, bounding with an unending variety of species, sun perpetually shinning, clear streams unceasingly running, grizzly bears frolicking in a meadow. And, no doubt some of this would take place. However, they fail to admit to several important points.

First, such things do occur with the human species present on the planet.

Second, they would like us to believe that every species that has disappeared from this planet was a reaction to a human presence. This denies the existence of evolution. Far more species of plants and animals disappeared prior to the appearance of humans than has disappeared since our arrival. While our presence may have caused the disappearance of some species, many were on the brink of extinction anyway, and probably had only a few decades left even if man had not made an appearance. To think otherwise, is to believe that the evolution of our planet ceased the moment man appeared on earth.

Third, many species of plants and animals have gone through such a sophisticated evolution that they can now only survive in a very specialized environment. A minor alteration of this environment and they cease to exist. Many of the species that have disappeared have departed earth because specialization has made the species vulnerable to very small changes in the environment. Whether this change is "natural" or man made, the results are the same. They have lost the ability to adapt to change. There is strong evidence that the presence of man has prevented the demise of some species that, left to mother nature, would have departed this earth by now. The list of species that man has rescued from extinction is constantly expanding. Some of these species would now be extinct without the help of humans.

Fourth, nature abhors a void. Whenever, an environment changes, one species may die out but there is always a new one to take its place. Environmentalists, in order to make their point about man's destruction of the environment, insist that everything stay "status quo." Any alteration of the environment, they claim, especially if occasioned by humans, is bad. The perception that the earth's environments should never be altered in the slightest may prove to be the most dangerous thing that could happen to our planet. Change is beneficial and refreshing. It is a form of renewal. The favorite saying of environmentalists is that the earth is a living organism. All good biologists know that living organisms need to replace the old, worn parts of its system with new, invigorated parts. Look at the dynamic recovery that has taken place in the few short years since the eruption of Mt. St. Helens in Washington State. To suggest that the earth stagnate could lead to its death. Stagnation in a living organism is devastating.

However, the biggest failure of these radical environmentalist is the failure to recognize that the human species is an environment unto itself. Humans are host to hundreds of plants and animals that would become extinct without the presence of humans. Many species of mites, lice, fleas, parasitic worms, bacteria, viruses, yeasts, fungi and other organisms depend on humans for survival. To cause the extinction of humans would be to cause the extinction of these species as well. In addition to those species to whom we serve as host, there are others that might find it difficult or impossible to survive without the presence of humans. Horses, cattle, dogs, pigs, cats, chickens, peas, beans, wheat, rice, and thousands of other species would find it impossible to compete in today's "natural" environment without the help of us humans.

It is fervently possible that man, often viewed as a species destroyer, is actually responsible for the fact that a number of species continue to live. Many species are very habitat specific and their habitat is often very limited. Man's efforts to fight fires, manage water flow in rivers and streams, his agricultural endeavors and his undertaking of other "environmental management" projects has probably saved a number of species that were on the brink of extinction. Take the El Segundo Blue butterfly, for instance. Had Chevron not decided to protect this butterfly and its existence had been left to the whims of nature, a fire might well have burned its scarce habitat into oblivion by now. The Colorado Potato Beetle was a very rare species when first discovered in the early 1800's. All indications were that it was well on its way to extinction. However, when man introduced potatoes to the American agricultural scene, this beetle not only was saved from extinction but has become a major pest.

Yes, it is possible that a few more species of plants and animals might have survived for a longer period of time without the presence of humans, but the price for their survival might be staggering. Thousands of other species might perish without the presence of humans.

Mother Nature can be the unintended destroyer of a species that is on the brink of extinction. There are many species of plants and animals, such as the El Segundo Blue and the Lange's Metalmark, that now exist only in one small, very specialized area. Left to nature, these areas might well be sweep by a fire or other disaster that would destroy these fragile habitats.

The 1993 flooding of the Mississippi River and its tributaries helped us understand how nature can both devastate and revive environments. The January 1994 issue of *Discover* reported: "Some of the plants and animals living in the river and around it were also hard hit. Scores of the oldest, tallest cottonwoods, favored roosts of the endangered bald eagle, toppled in the fast water. Nests of the endangered plover were also swept away by the flood. Jody Miller of the U.S. Fish and Wildlife service in Rock Island, Illinois, reports that forty percent fewer birds than normal passed through that area in the fall. Other organisms rolled with the flood's punches, and some even managed to thrive—among them the paddlefish, walleye, and the Northern pike. The flood may have turned out to have helped some of the native species reclaim territory they had lost to invaders. For years now a European invader, the purple loose-leaf, has been displacing native marsh vegetation in the Mississippi region. After the flood, the European invader never even poked its head out. Apparently it can't stand extended submersion. Zebra mussels, which have been crowding out native mussels in many areas, also may have suffered."

The huge wildfires near Sydney, Australia have destroyed large colonies of animals, including some rare animal species such as the black-faced bats. Whole colonies of different species have been wiped out.

No human, no group of humans, and no business can create the havoc created by nature. It is absurd to assume that nature cannot readily repair the small amounts of damage man, in his quest for survival, might cause.

Unfortunately, not every species can or, perhaps, should be saved. There are times when the cost-benefit ratio is so high on the cost side of the ledger that we must examine what it will take to allow a species to survive a little longer. Those species that are extremely rare, or that are confined to one very small, very specialized environment, are undoubtedly on the road to extinction anyway. To severely damage the economy of this country in order to extend the life of such species for a few years or a few decades may not make sense financially or environmentally. To preserve such a specialized environment in perpetuity could well be preventing natural evolution. By stopping change, we might be preventing the arrival of those species of plants and animals that were destine to fill the void when the environment changed. To save one species, we might be preventing the emergence of many others.

Smallpox will live to see another year. Scientists in Atlanta and Moscow were scheduled to simultaneously destroy the world's last remaining smallpox virus on New Years Eve 1993-94. However, it got a last minute reprieve because of a scientific outcry. Dozens of researchers opposed deliberately destroying an entire species, particularly one that might teach them how to fight other diseases.

In Maryland, a toad that hasn't been sighted in the county since 1986 stopped a road-widening project because it is listed as endangered. How long must an area be "free" of an "endangered species" before development is no longer "endangered"?

A small fly in a very specialized environment is about to stop a project slated to provide jobs to about 10,000 people in San Bernardino county where the jobless rate is 13%. A group called the California Public Interest Research Group is attempting to stop the project and protect the fly. I have no qualms about this, just a question? Who will pay the property owner for the loss of property value and who pays the 10,000 people who will be without jobs? I elect the 70,000 members of the California Public Interest Research Group.

During the recent fire storms in southern California, endangered species could well have been responsible for some of the fires' horrible damage. The Endangered Species Act prevented the firemen from starting backfires because the backfires would have been started in areas where an endangered species allegedly lives. Mother Nature saw to it that the areas occupied by the endangered species burned anyway. Unfortunately, without protection from the backfires, the fires progressed way beyond the proposed backfire area and burned thousands of acres that might otherwise have been saved. Who is responsible for reimbursing those people who lost homes as a result of the firemen not being able to use a backfire? Who is going to revive the endangered species that were lost?

The U.S. Fish and Wildlife Service recently protected 6.4 million acres of habitat for the desert tortoise. This stirs up a lot of questions. For instance, if a species is found in an area of that size, can it really be considered endangered? After all, tortoises are not the fastest moving creatures in the world. There would need to be enough animals so they could find each other in this 6.4 million acre paradise or there would be no reproduction. What would happen to the U.S. (or for that matter, the world) if we set aside this amount of land for every endangered or threatened species? If a species is considered endangered or threatened, should every parcel of land where it is found be labeled to prevent any further human activity? Is an animal that requires that 6.5 million acres be set aside for it really worth saving?

When we begin asking humans to step aside for species that are already extinct or that are on the brink of extinction, we may be doing those species that have a chance of survival a great disservice. If the movement to protect species looses support, every species will lose.

Special Interest Groups

You must always remember what a "special interest" really is. Regardless of what banner the "special interest group" flies or what cause it portents to champion, such a cause is going to fly in the face of the public good. By its very nature, a "special interest" can never serve the best interests of the public at large. Whenever a "special interest" gets its way, someone else is going to get hurt. Whether they are stealing money from another worth while program or regulating your business out of existence or are pilfering more of your hard earned money in the form of taxes, they are serving only their agenda. Not the public agenda.

I think it is time that the judiciary was made aware that laws that serve "special interests" can never serve the "public interest." This would certainly take the starch out of the claim by most agencies that they are acting on behalf of the "public good."

I strongly advise that you try to determine just who is benefiting from the enforcement of those regulations you are being required to comply with. Is it some environmental groups? Is it a union? This information should become useful to you at some point during your efforts to beat the regulatory process. I have always believed that if someone or some group insists on imposing their will upon others, this person or these groups should be responsible for the outcomes that result from their actions. Until special interest groups are made to pay for their political transgressions, they will continue to force you to live by their "special interest" standards. Certainly, Eagle Hardware (remember them?) would like to see BROIL made financially accountable for all the grief it caused.

Even if you decide not to pursue this particular aspect of the regulatory process, you will have learned to see through the smoke screen and will have learned who your real antagonists are. It never hurts to remind the enforcement agency and the courts that you are being forced to bend to the will of a special interest group that does not represent the public good.

Most environmental groups are aware of the takings implications of their actions. In an article that appeared in "Issues In Science and Technology," the legal council responsible for the property rights project for the National Audubon Society stated that, "The protection against takings, like other guarantees in the Bill of Rights, is designed to prevent the government from unfairly singling out an individual to bear a burden the public as a whole should share."

And later on in the article: "Especially today, governmental action is so pervasive, and its effects on property values so common, that it would be virtually impossible to keep track of, let alone compensate, every economic harm."

Unfortunately, although they recognize the problem, their answer to this problem is to keep on doing what we have always done. They determined, in the end, that protecting the environment is far more important than protecting individual property rights. Therefore, they conclude, property owners and businesses should continue paying the bill.

Groups such as the Audubon Society are certainly all for protecting the environment as long as they are spending someone else's money. However, I never see them volunteer to relieve a beleaguered property owner by offering to purchase a critical piece of property on behalf of the public. I have a difficult time taking the Audubon Society's concern for the environment seriously when they are unwilling to make any substantial financial sacrifices on behalf of the environment.

Here are some of the other things our government has accomplished by following the whims of special interests:

125 workers who work in a factory that produces coats agreed to take a 6% cut in pay even though they were making very little as it is. They accepted the cut in pay because the only other option was to have the plant shut down. The bill for workman's compensation for the company, a jump from $55,000 per year to $187,000 per year, was about to bankrupt the company. While everyone seems to recognize that this is happening because of a highly flawed workman's compensation system, attempts to reform it have been unsuccessful. There are just too many special interests with strong political power that are making money off the system the way it is. Therefore, these poorly paid workers and their employers will continue to pay for the excesses of a few special interests.

The Federal EPA logged 300,000 state and federal violations of the Safe Drinking Water Act in 1991 and 1992 affecting the water supplied to at least 100 million people (or almost one half our population). The alarmist group, Natural Resources Defense Council, is proposing better enforcement. However, they have not documented a single case of illness or death as a result of these 300,000 violations. Who should pay for the increased regulation and for the expenses incurred by complying with the increased regulation? I know who I would vote for. I hope the Natural Resources Defense Council has a lot of money.

After putting thousands of people out of work to protect the "Spotted Owl," local newspapers recently reported that far more owls have been discovered than originally thought. Who should compensate the people put out of work, the Fish & Wild Life Service or the Wilderness Society who was in the forefront in urging government to take this action to begin with?

The disease with the loudest activist wins. Research money for breast cancer has increased 450 percent in the past few years while money for lung cancer has diminished to feed the breast cancer frenzy. Unfortunately, lung cancer kills far more women than breast cancer. The women activists are shooting themselves in the foot. This is what happens when we listen to special interests instead of setting priorities.

For years, special interest groups have been criticizing this country for the use of fossil fuels as an energy source and have touted wind power as the way to go. Wind power, they claim, is safe for the environment and all of nature's creatures. However, just the opposite is turning out to be true. Hawks and Eagles, know for their keen eye sight and adept flying are being killed in large numbers by the rotating blades of wind power units. Estimates from a California Energy Commission study showed that around 400 birds of prey, including 39 golden eagles, a federally protected species, are killed each year at Altamont Pass east of San Francisco. Bird deaths have also been noted at other wind-farm areas including the Montezuma Hills in Solano County and the San Gorgonio Pass in Southern California.

As one possible method of solving this problem, the study suggested eliminating the ground squirrel population in the area so the birds are not attracted to the blades. Not a single eyebrow was raised at this suggestion. Can you imagine how environmentalists would react if it was suggested that a ground squirrel population be destroyed to solve a problem being created by fossil fuels?

The movement of humans from place to place has been a prime factor in the spread of diseases and agricultural pests throughout the world. During the era when travel was restricted to ships plying the seven seas, the movement of pests and diseases from place to place took months or years. However, with the advent of air travel, more people are traveling and doing so more quickly. Months have been reduced to hours. Air travel, therefore, has had a profound affect on the spread of unwanted pests and diseases from one country to another. In an effort to curb the introduction of devastating pests and diseases, most countries have some sort of protective mechanism in place. Since most such pests arrive as undetected "hitchhikers" on airplanes, it has been a common practice to spray an insecticide of low toxicity to humans throughout the plane just prior to landing. That way, even if the unwanted "hitchhikers" are not found, they will be dead, and thus rendered harmless.

Unfortunately, a few American tourists have a special sensitivity to this spray and, while the spray is not by any means fatal to them, it is irritating. These sensitive individuals have raised enough complaints that the Clinton administration is considering steps to discourage other nations from spraying the insecticide during flights into their respective countries. The threat of losing U.S. tourism dollars is enough to make some of the poorer countries consider this threat to their economy. It is unfortunate that a few rich American tourists have the power to put less fortunate countries at risk to pests that could spread disease or destroy crops. It is also extremely selfish. Yes, even selfish tourists can become a special interest group.

Other Incidents

In the introduction, I promised you a number of other examples of regulatory activities gone wild. We need to document as many incidents such as these as we can. Somewhere, there will be an example that will help a property rights lawyer win a case for you and for me. The following will give you some idea of what is going on out there in the regulatory world and will help you identify the kind of material we need to support our fight.

The twenty-six agencies that are trying to regulate a small chemical company in Contra Costa County, California just had a special meeting. Each agency had its own agenda for the company and each agency agenda conflicted with the other twenty-five agency agendas. The goal of this meeting? An attempt to coordinate their enforcement activities.

The San Francisco Bay Area recently purchased two brand new state-of-the-art $7 million tug boats, specifically to prevent oil spills. Unfortunately, they are sitting unused. The crew suits up every day and the tugs are readied for service. However, the danger of oil spills remains because the tugs are too advanced for state regulations. They must sit idle until state regulators get around to upgrading regulations so the tugs can be "tested."

Norman Smith, President of ADL Circuits got a regulatory edict that read: "Generators of Transportation Treatment Units conducting onsite treatment of waste streams currently eligible for PBR, and not specifically identified as conditionally authorized, may be authorized under the PBR tier." Norman could not decipher the message so he asked the agency that issued it to provide an interpretation. The agency was unable to explain what it meant. Nevertheless, Norman Smith was required to pay $1,100 to meet its conditions.

The DeBest Company of Garden Grove, Idaho, got fined $7,875 for saving someone's life. Two of DeBest's employees heard a cry for help and found a man buried in a trench (not De-Best's trench) because the wall of the trench had caved in. The two heroes jumped into the trench and dug the man out, saving his life. The Occupational Safety and Health Administration was so pleased to see that the man's life was saved that they fined the DeBest Company $7,875 for going into the trench without 1) putting on approved hard hats and 2) taking steps to ensure that other trench walls did not collapse, and water did not seep in.

Pro-line of Dallas, Texas, at one time employed about sixty-eight women and six men. That is until federal OSHA cited them for having too few bathroom facilities for the number of employees. The company was too near bankruptcy to build additional facilities so it had to dismiss around thirty-two of their employees. Reluctantly, the company laid off those who were the least productive or the least skilled. This turned out to be about twenty-eight women and four men. In other words, they laid off 41% of the women and 67% of the men. Unfortunately, the feds weren't through with them at that point. The Equal Employment Opportunity Commission, which apparently got an "F" in math, filed a lawsuit against the company for laying off more women than men. When asked how EEOC came to this conclusion, Jeffery Bannon, EEOC regional attorney replied the company must treat men and women equally. "It's the company's job to figure out how to do that." It's always fun to be caught between two agencies with two opposing agendas, isn't it?

Owners of property near high-voltage power lines can be awarded damages when "cancerphobia" lowers property value, even without proof of a health risk, New York's highest court ruled. The Court of Appeals decision could prove expensive for New York Power Authority, which has been involved in long-running litigation with forty-seven property owners over damages stemming from completion of an extensive power line project. The potential danger from high-voltage power lines is a subject of heated debate. Earlier this year, the federal Environmental Protection Agency called for more research into whether electro-magnetic fields around high-voltage power lines pose a danger to health. A 1992 Swedish study showed the possibility of a cause and effect relationship between magnetic field exposure and childhood leukemia. (We know better, don't we? Ninety percent of all cases are hereditary.) The State's Court of Claims had said earlier it would allow property owners to be compensated for physical damages caused to the property by construction of the power lines. That court rejected any compensation for a loss in property values caused by the flight of potential buyers. But the Court of Appeals, in reversing the rulings, said the loss in property value is real even if the danger is undetermined. "Whether the danger is a scientifically genuine or verifiable fact should be irrelevant to the central issue of its market value impact," Judge Bellacosa wrote in the 6-0 ruling. Before Tuesday's ruling, property owners seeking damages had to prove both that the value of the property had been lowered and the presumed health risks had a scientific basis in fact, according to court papers.

Here's a court that really needs a reality check.

It is suspected that the Americans With Disabilities Act will wreak havoc with small retail firms. For instance, a small hardware store forced to widen its aisles to accommodate wheelchairs will have to pay for remodeling and construction, reduce its inventory of goods, and raise prices. The likelihood of such a store staying in business is minimal. It would make better sense for employees to bring the goods to the wheelchair-bound person. This is a good example of government needing to find another way of meeting the "intent" of the law.

A large study of rent control showed the following: rent control is a malignant social force with the greatest damage concentrated on lower income renters who have been literally driven out of town by stringent rent regulations. Ironically, these victims are largely minorities, students and single parents, the very people rent control was enacted to "help."

To meet new state air quality standards, the Bay Area Quality Board is making employers carry the burden of reducing commutes by car. It is estimated that it will cost the average employer $200 per employee and that the reduction in air pollution will be so small as to be immeasurable. Every Bay Area employer should demand just compensation from the Bay Area Quality Board for this one. I wonder how many people will lose their jobs over this? The law went into effect June 1994.

The Fair Labor Standards Act requires that overtime be paid for more than forty hours work per week. Some schools can't afford to pay teachers overtime pay so this requirement has stopped highly qualified and willing teachers from teaching classes for students that can't attend school during normal school hours. As a result, these classes now are taught by unqualified part-time people. The school, the students and the teachers all lose because of this act. The teachers would have liked the extra money, even if it wasn't time and a half.

Following an employee complaint of discrimination, a government investigator ordered a company to analyze four years of company payroll records by age, sex, creed, marital status and disability. Employers, of course, are not allowed to ask these questions and, therefore, having such information would be breaking the law. However, the inspector informed the company that if they could not produce the information, it would be assumed that the company discriminates and the "appropriate" action taken. Another catch twenty-two between agencies?

According to Hugo Blasdel, software developer and expert on U.S. export regulations, our export policies do more to hinder our balance of trade than all the trade barriers erected by other countries. In our effort to prevent the export of any technology that might help an enemy, millions of dollars in goods languish on our docks every day. Every item destine for export is held hostage by a Customs Inspector until he or she deems the product safe for export. Everything is subject to the inspector's judgment although no inspector has the appropriate technical knowledge to exercise such judgment. The inspectors become particularly abusive when exercising their powers under the guise of "items having a duel purpose." Such things as a stainless steel mixing bowl and a can of Coca Cola have held up large shipments for months because some inspector decided that they could have a "duel purpose."

Some of the most abusive policies come from the Department of Labor whose actions often put employees out of work rather than protect them. Labor Laws that were designed to keep large companies from taking advantage of their employees often put small companies out of business. After reviewing a number of cases, I have come to the following conclusions about the Department of Labor. (1) They like to enforce actions against small companies because these companies do not have the legal wherewithal to fight the Department's actions in a court of law. (2) One can surmise that the Department has little concern for the plight of the employee since, in almost every instance where it investigated a complaint against a small company, most of the employees ended up worse off. Usually because the company was forced to shut its doors or layoff a number of people. (3) Small companies are easy to intimidate and Department personnel will often call a company's customers, ruining those relationships so important to a company in maintaining a business. For specific horror stories of this nature, talk to Marge Meyers, owner of Vicom in Moline, Ill., or Kathy Carver of Tuscalusa, Ala.

In 1987 Charles Donahoo's company, Charlie's Wreaking and Salvage Inc., demolished a plastics plant, releasing one pound of asbestos fibers from the insulation into the atmosphere. In 1989 Donahoo made history. For not telling regulators about the pound of fibers, he became the first person convicted of a felony under the Comprehensive Environmental Response, Compensation, and Liability Act, better know as Superfund. He was sentenced to three years in prison for that crime, plus another year under the 1970 Clean Air Act. However, things could have been worse. Fortunately, he was sentenced before the Sentencing Commission's new guidelines went into effect.

Nevada rancher Wayne Hage faces a potential five-year sentence under the Clean Water Act for "redirecting streams" by hiring someone to clear brush from irrigation ditches on his property. The ditches have been in use since the turn of the century.

Todd Ross Shumway, an Arizona construction worker, received eighteen months in state prison for dumping two loads of construction debris in the desert. A state environmental regulator said the debris wasn't hazardous waste but "a lot of sheet rock, some metal, wood boxes, and broken brick and tile."

Rich Savvoir, owner of the US 1 Auto Parts Store in Bethpage, New Jersey, faces a possible one-year prison term and a $10,000 fine because he didn't post a sign stating that his store accepts waste motor oil for recycling. Savwoir claims that on the day in question the sign was down because a window-washer was working on the store. The state Department of Environmental Conservation says Savwoir's arrest in April 1993 was the agency's first attempt to enforce the law, which took effect January 1, 1992.

Harvey Van Fossan was ordered by the city of Springfield, Illinois to get rid of the pigeons that were creating a nuisance on a vacant lot near his home. He put out some strychnine-laced corn which got rid of most of the pigeons as well as two common grackles and two morning doves. After an autopsy by the Smithsonian Institution, local officials decided Harvey was in violation of the Migratory Bird Treaty Act because, while it is okay to shoot these birds, it is not okay to poison them. There are, after all, only some 400 million such birds in North America. Harvey was fined $450 and given three years probation. Harvey, like Donahoo was fortunate enough to have been sentenced before the new sentencing guidelines were in force.

Bill Ellen was a savvy environmental engineer who took the precautions of applying for and receiving thirty-eight separate permits from various government agencies before beginning a large project. While he was in the middle of developing his land, the Bush Administration did to Bill what they had done to John Poszgai. They changed the definition of a "wetland" and Bill's almost completed development suddenly was labeled a "wetland" and he was ordered to cease any further development. Unfortunately, Bill moved two truckloads of dirt after receiving the order to cease further development of the property. This act cost Bill six months in prison.

As with most states, the state of Washington has laws regulating boilers. This, they feel, is necessary because those big boilers in the basement of buildings can blow up and kill a bunch of people and do a large amount of damage. Unfortunately, one savvy electrical inspector discovered an estimated 10,000 boilers that were currently not being regulated. The question needing an answer was, should the state impose the same standards on these boilers as on all other boilers. Normally this would be an easy question to answer. Boilers are boilers! Go get them! However, cooler heads finally prevailed. The Board of Boiler Rules decided to exempt these 10,000 boilers because they would put the espresso coffee carts out of business. These 10,000 tiny boilers were being used to steam milk for latte. Congratulations to an agency with a sane approach to the regulatory process.

The world famous San Diego Zoo is having its problems with various regulatory agencies as well. It has been the policy of the zoo to prohibit visitors from bring guide dogs or other animals into the exhibit areas for fear they would frighten zoo animals.

However, the U.S. Department of Justice has begun an investigation to determine whether the zoo's policy violates the federal Americans with Disabilities Act. The probe was launched when an epileptic woman who relies on a dog for assistance filed a complaint with the Justice Department.

The zoo is now considering giving guide dogs limited access to the zoo. However, the Department of Agriculture has threatened to cite or fine the zoo if the presence of a guide dog results in injury to an animal.

Why is it the two government agencies can't get together and work this out instead of placing the zoo in an untenable position?

A case well worth watching is the trials and tribulations of

Ocie Mills of Florida. Ocie, much like John Poszgai, tried to take on the Army Corps of Engineers by claiming that his perfectly dry lot was not a "wetlands." Even though the judge agreed that his property "does not have the appearance of what most lay people think of as a "wetland," Ocie spent 21 months in federal prison for dumping some dirt on his lot. Upon noting that the Corps seemed to have excessive power, the judge added that this "is enough to make a judge pause and question what has happened to old principles of the separation of powers." The Pacific Legal Foundation is about to use Ocie's circumstance to test this very concept. However, it comes out, its national implications will follow us for years to come.

Other government agencies that have severely damaged or put small companies out of business:

- Small Business Development Council (Utah)
- Department of Transportation (Utah)
- Internal Revenue Service
- Department of Public Health

Well, if you don't see your name among these examples, don't give up hope. That knock on your door could come any day now!

It's unfortunate that the companies and individuals just discussed didn't have a copy of this book in hand before the government came knocking. Fortunately, you do.

CHAPTER 12

A Nation Going Bankrupt

"The theory of Communism may be summed up in
one sentence: Abolish all private property."

Karl Marx

"If we desire respect for the law, we must first make
the law respectable."

Louis D. Brandeis

Many analysts today believe that the fall of Communism in the former Soviet Union was, in good part, the result of the State, rather than individuals, owning all the property. Property in this instance meaning not just real property but businesses, contracts and other forms of wealth. The concept proposed under this theory is that only an individual will get full use out of any particular piece of property while the State is going to squander the property on unproductive or arbitrary activities. The ultimate outcome is that a Communist State will inevitably go bankrupt because it failed to get full use of its property.

There are, I am sure, many who will argue to the contrary. However, one need only take stock of what is occurring in the United States to suspect that this theory may have considerable credence. While individual citizens continue to be allowed to own property in this country, the right to put it to its best use is rapidly eroding. What makes the theory plausible is that the general economy and wealth of the United States is eroding at the same pace as the erosion of property rights.

In his book, *Grand Theft and Petit Larceny*, Mark Pollot points out very explicitly that taking a person's right to *use* their property is little different than taking a person's property outright. While our government has avoided walking up to us and taking the deed to our property forcefully from our hands, it has taken over almost complete control of how we use our property. This action has not only considerably reduced the value of the property but has made it impossible to put the property to its best use. If the theory about the bankruptcy of Communism has any credence, the United States is well on its way to the same fate. The name may be different but the game is the same. Government control of property is a sure road to national bankruptcy.

To demonstrate this premise, let's assume that you have purchased 100 acres of land located within a mile or two of a new industrial plant that is in the process of hiring 1000 new employees. You paid a large sum of money for this land because you felt you could develop it and, at a minimum, recover your investment. Your goal is to build 250 single family dwellings and a shopping center on your land to support the people who will be working at the new factory. The town of Highville is excited at the prospect of your development. The town realizes that the tax base on that 100 acres is going to increase many thousand fold with your development. The taxes collected on the vacant land are only three thousand a year while that same 100 acres, when fully developed will bring in over a half million dollars in taxes to the city coffers every year. The addition of 250 new families will also contribute to the town through sales taxes and the spending of additional income. With the development of your land the town can look forward to providing more police and fire protection, better emergency services and upgrading their schools, roads and other civic responsibilities.

Just about the time you are turning over your first shovel full of soil, someone discovers an *Andropedia stunopsis* on your property and an official from the Fish and Wildlife Service orders you to immediately stop any further development on your land. You are advised that *Andropedia stunopsis* is a tiny beetle on the endangered species list and that your land supports a population of this endangered beetle. The regulations developed under the authority of the "Endangered Species Act" prohibit the development of any property which supports a population of an "endangered" or "threatened" species of plant or animal.

Whether you do or don't agree with the tenets of the "Endangered Species Act" is not the relevant issue here. No matter how important it may be to preserve this population of *Andropedia stunopsis*, its preservation is going to cost you, the town of Highville, the state, and the country some wealth. The value of the property for both you and the town of Highville has diminished many thousand fold by not being put to its best use. Government has also lost all the payroll taxes and sales taxes it would have collected from these 250 families. With a little imagination, you can picture the kind of economic impact actions of this nature have on the economic fabric of a city, state or country when they are repeated several million times each year in every corner of the United States.

Unfortunately, this practice comes with a double edged sword. While government is adding more and more restrictions that continue to reduce the value of property all over the country, two other factors are rearing their ugly heads. First, as we have already mentioned, when a property's value is reduced, the tax revenue generated from this property is reduced in like proportion. That means there is less revenue from this property going to the government coffers to support needed government programs. Second, the population of this country is increasing and with this increase is a proportional increase in the demand for government services. The obvious question that arises then, is how can a country hope to survive if it is decreasing its tax base in the face of an increasing demand for services?

Those that believe the collapse of communism in the Soviet Union was due to just such factors will tell you, "You can't." They will tell you this country is only a few steps short of bankruptcy at the present time. Even those that are concerned about our growing national deficit will agree that you can't go on forever reducing your tax base and hope to keep government services in line with our growing population.

People who are suffering from ever larger income tax increases often wonder why the more taxes they pay, the less services they seem to get. The tendency is to blame entitlement programs such as welfare and social security for this growing discrepancy. Few would ever guess that the real culprit is the federal regulatory process. However, it is not difficult to understand once you've seen how the system works.

The federal government is the entity which passes legislation such as the Endangered Species Act or the Clean Water Act or the many other acts purported to protect the environment. However, it is not the feds, for the most part, that enforce these acts. This responsibility is passed on to the states, counties and cities. The feds, however, do not give the states, counties or cities any money with which to enforce these "acts." Therefore, the money you paid your city or county for police and fire protection may go toward enforcing these laws instead. To add insult to injury, your local governments must then go around "labeling" your land as a "wetlands" as they did to John Poszgai or as an area harboring a "threatened species" as they did to the Gorsk family. Each time one of these labels is applied to such property, the value of the land plummets as does the taxes on the land.

The passage of these laws then, has increased the costs of operating local governments while, at the same time, lowering its tax base. Obviously, something has to give when the cost of operating a government increases while that government's revenue is reduced. Until recently, your local government's response to this dilemma has been to raise your state and local taxes. When people begin to object to constant raises in taxes, the local governments response was to endanger your life by reducing police, fire and emergency services. This, they decided, was preferable to trying to tackle the federal government. However, when local governments begin closing fire stations, pulling policemen off the streets and closing libraries, the citizens begin to mumble. When this action was accompanied by an increase in taxes, the mumble became a roar. In 1993, local politicians were finally forced to complain to the feds about the predicament the feds had placed them in. The feds listened politely but nothing was changed.

Nobody has been able to accurately determine the loss in the value of real property that has already occurred nationwide as a result of the actions taken by government regulators under the guise of protecting the environment. However, estimates have ranged into the trillions of dollars. The loss in tax revenues to local governments must, then, run into the hundreds of billions. The hypothetical town of Highville lost over $500,000 in property taxes and thousands of dollars in other taxes because of one small beetle. If Highville were a real town, we might be able to translate this loss into actual injuries and lives lost because of reduced police and fire protection, as well as poorer roads and less emergency services.

In order to understand the full impact of what is taking place in our country you need to understand that when we talk about "property," we are *not* just talking about real estate. We are talking about anything that can be owned, anything that can be sold or anything else that can generate revenue. In a society such as ours, where almost everything we do is taxed in one fashion or another, reducing the value of anything is going to take money away from government services. For example, if a government regulation reduces the value of the car you wish to sell because it fails to meet certain air quality standards, the government will collect less taxes from you when you sell the car.

Government, however, looses the most revenue in its effort to control the actions of businesses. Every time a business is forced to spend money to meet the requirements of a regulation, it makes less profit and pays less taxes. Every time a business is required to hire another employee whose only function is to address the concerns of a regulatory agency, it makes less profit and the government loses taxes. Every time a business must pay a lawyer to defend it against unreasonable government interference the government looses revenue. Regardless of how the government goes about forcing its will upon business, government is going to lose revenue.

However, when it comes to the economic destruction created by the regulation of businesses, we have just scratched the surface. Government interference with business has created a much larger economic problem for this country. As we suggested in the introduction, regulations have been responsible for closing down some businesses while others businesses have escaped to countries where they won't be buried under regulations. The end result has been a significant loss of jobs. Government, through regulation, has not only lost taxes from those businesses that no longer exist or that have moved out of the country, but has lost uncountable revenue by eliminating jobs. All the income taxes, social security taxes, sales taxes, unemployment taxes, and other taxes these jobs produced are gone. Instead of collecting taxes from those people who worked for these vanishing businesses, government must now support ex-workers through unemployment insurance or some other form of government aid.

The Thomas R. Roe Institute report says: "Even by a fairly conservative estimate, there are at least three million fewer jobs in the American economy today than would have existed if the growth of regulation over the last twenty years had been slower and regulations more efficiently designed." If one were to assume that the average salary of those lost jobs was just $20,000 per year, we are talking about a loss of about $240 billion to our tax base every year. If those who lost these jobs, instead of paying taxes, are collecting unemployment insurance or welfare, we have not just lost $240 billion a year from our tax base, we have added about $45 billion to our tax burden.

However, regulations can have a major impact on our economy in other ways as well. For instance:

According to a study by Bookings Institute economist Robert Crandall and Harvard University Professor John Graham, current federal fuel economy standards will cause each year between 2,000 and 4,000 additional deaths and an additional 11,000 to 19,000 serious injuries on our streets and highways. These people will be sacrificed just so the regulators can reduce smog by just one half of one percent. Even if we are calloused enough to believe that the world is overpopulated and a few human deaths may be a blessing, we cannot ignore the cost created by this relatively minor change in our regulations.

To begin with, we will have lost from society between 13,000 and 23,000 productive, tax paying individuals, some for a year or two, some forever. In addition, between 11,000 and 19,000 people are going to require extensive medical care. The average cost of medical care for individuals receiving serious injuries in automobile accidents has been estimated to run around $500,000 per injury. When we add it all together, we discover that this regulation will cost us about $200 million in lost taxes each year and will add $75 billion to our tax burden. This small addition to the Clean Air Act will also add between $1,000 and

$1,500 to the cost of a new car. This is quite a price to pay for a reduction in smog that only a very sophisticated instrument will be able to detect.

During my excursion into the world of regulations I discovered there were many more agencies playing havoc with individual property owners and businesses than I ever imagined. I received calls from business owners that had incredible stories to tell about such government entities as the Internal Revenue Service, the Department of Transportation, the Department of Labor, the FAA (hundreds of cases), Occupational Health and Safety, etc.

The future does not look any brighter. In fact, if anything, we could be moving toward national bankruptcy at an even greater pace in the future. This is due, primarily, to the fact that there are still hundreds of "special interest groups" in this country who have designs on controlling the behavior of certain people or businesses they feel are threatening the environment, themselves, or some moral or ethical code.

For instance, I quit smoking cigarettes two years ago. My wife continues to smoke and, although it isn't always pleasant to be constantly assaulted by her second-hand smoke, I would never want a law passed that would make it illegal for her to smoke. On the surface, it seems that passing a law outlawing the smoking of tobacco would end what some consider to be our greatest health risk. However, under this surface a very damaging scenario emerges.

Among other things, we would lose the $19 billion in direct tax revenues the tobacco industry donates to this country each year and the $5.8 billion it contributes to the plus side of our balance of trade with other countries. However, our economy would take its biggest hit through the loss of jobs. Approximately 690,000 people directly depend on the tobacco industry for their jobs. It is estimated that another 1.2 million jobs are indirectly dependent on the tobacco industry. The impact of this loss on our country's economy is difficult to measure. Quite obviously, those that cannot find another job will end up at the government "trough" and those that do find another job will be taking a job away from someone else.

In the case of tobacco, there is going to be other costs that could amount into the billions. I know what it is like to be addicted to tobacco. Many medical experts have determined that breaking an addiction to nicotine is as difficult as breaking an addiction to heron. There are currently fifty-five million smokers in our country and not all of them are going to be willing or able to go through the difficult process of breaking this addiction. The result will be the appearance of a huge underground "tobacco cartel" that will provide these smokers with cigarettes that are more costly and far more dangerous to their health. This "cartel" will grow tobacco in other countries and sneak the tobacco across our borders or will grow it in secured areas much as marijuana growers do today.

In order to enforce this anti-smoking law, the government will need to launch an enforcement program that will make the current campaign against cocaine look like amateur hour. The turf wars among the tobacco "dealers" will escalate to all areas of our cities subjecting everyone to the possibility of death from a stray bullet. Bodies of innocent victims could liter the streets of our cities. While the current tobacco industry is forbidden from soliciting and selling to minors, the underground industry will specifically target this group. The cost of enforcing such a law will not only be in billions of dollars but in thousands of human lives.

Those individuals who wish to impose their moral or ethical standards on other individuals in this country, will cost us far more than all the other special interests combined. Those that are opposed to the exercise of individual rights, which is the next point of assault by special interests, will make the environmental movement look like kindergarten play.

In June of 1993, my wife and I received two letters. One was from the U.S. Senator representing our area and one was from our Congressperson in the House of Representatives. Both letters advised us that they were supporting President Clinton's plan for reducing the federal deficit. After a quick review of the few spending cuts proposed by the plan, the letters went on to say:

> The budget, however, cannot be brought under control by spending cuts alone—not without starving investment programs, making deep cuts in benefits that citizens have fairly earned, and inflicting hardship on people already suffering. Even if Congress were to cut every penny of domestic discretionary spending, the federal government would still run a deficit and the interest on the debt would continue to escalate. The President's plan is solid and balanced and spreads the burden of sacrifice. The tax increases are aimed primarily at corporations and the well-off, those who profited the most during the 1980's. Almost two-thirds of the tax increases will be borne by families earning more than $200,000, and almost three-quarters will come from those with incomes above $100,000—about six percent of the American taxpaying public. Those families with incomes from $40,000 to $50,000 would owe only $23 a month more than now, and those with smaller incomes would have even less of a tax increase. The deficit reduction package will slash the debt burden of the average American family by eight dollars for every dollar they spend.

I'm relatively sure that my representatives were thinking of the poor and the homeless when they suggested we not inflict additional hardship on people who were already suffering. However, for me this sentence brought to mind Bob Carpenter, Doe and Andy Caytling, John Poszgai, the Gorsk family and the millions of others who worked hard all their lives only to have everything they worked for stolen from them by over zealous government employees enforcing overly stringent regulations. That, to me, is really suffering.

If only the government would allow the Caytlings and their counterparts to stay in business and if John Poszgai, the Gorsks and the hundreds of thousands of others like them were only allowed to develop their property, there would be no need for a tax increase. Such people would happily make up the difference, and then some, if we would just leave them alone.

According to my best estimates, just by bring reasonableness to the regulatory process, we could eliminate the national deficit in less than three years. Of course I wrote to my representatives offering them this very suggestion for eliminating the deficit. The response, so far, has been an overwhelming *silence.*

There is a large contingent of modern day Constitutional scholars who believe that our founding fathers were well aware that government ownership (or control) of property would lead to national bankruptcy. This, the scholars believe, is why the framers of the Constitution were so concerned about protecting the rights of property owners from the greedy hands of government. If this be the truth, then the Framers of our Constitution had a far better knack for foresight than our current politicians have for hindsight.

Now that we all know how to keep the regulatory process from bringing our country to its knees, let's do it!

Books You Should Read

ECO-SCAM: The False Prophets of Ecological Apocalypse by Ronald Bailey (St. Martin's Press, 175 5th Avenue, New York, NY 10010)

Free Minds and Free Markets, Pacific Research Institute for Public Policy (755 Sansome St. Suite 450, San Francisco, CA 94111)

GOVERNMENT RACKET: Washington Waste From A to Z, by Martin L. Gross (Bantam Books, 666 5th Avenue, New York, NY 10103)

Grand Theft and Petit Larceny: Property Rights in America by Mark L. Pollot (Pacific Research Institute for Public Policy)

TAKINGS: Private Property and the Power of Eminent Domain by Richard A. Epstein

Organizations That Can Help You

Following are organizations that can evaluate your situation and determine if it has the potential to establish an important precedent in court. They have the capacity to take up arms and fight your battles in court if they feel your case has the proper merits. These organizations need our financial support in order to carry on their vital work.

Defenders Of Property Rights
 Nancie Marzulla, chief consul and president
 6235 33rd Street NW, Washington, DC 20015
 (202) 686-4197

Pacific Legal Foundation
 Headquarters: 2700 Gateway Oaks Dr., Suite 200
 Sacramento, CA 95833
 Alaska: 121 West Fireweed Lane, Suite 250
 Anchorage, AK 99503
 Oregon: (503) 241-8179
 Washington: 10800 NE 8th St., Suite 325
 Bellevue, WA 98004

Institute for Justice
 Mr. William H. Mellor III, President
 1001 Pennsylvania Ave. NW Suite 200 South
 Washington, D.C.
 (202) 457-4240

Organizations Supporting Our Cause Through Research And Other Means

(These organizations also deserve our financial support.)

Reason Foundation
3415 S. Sepulveda Blvd. Suite 400,
Los Angeles, CA 90034
Robert W. Poole, President
Publishers of *Reason Magazine*

CATO Institute
William A. Niskanen, Chairman
1000 Massachusetts Ave. NW
Washington, D.C. 20001
(202) 842-0200

Institute for Objectivist Studies
David Kelley, Executive Director
82 Washington St. Suite 207
Poughkeepsie, NY 12601

Competitive Enterprise Institute
Fred L. Smith, President
1001 Connecticut Ave. NW Suite 1250,
Washington, DC 20036
(202) 331-0101

Institute for Humane Studies
George Mason University
4400 University Drive
Fairfax, VA 22030-4444

Nation Inholders Association
  Mr. Charles S. Cushman, Executive Director
  P.O. Box 400
  Battle Ground, WA 98604
  Mr. John J. Miller, Associate Director

Manhattan Institute
  52 Vanderbuit Ave.
  New York, NY 10017
  (212) 599-7000

National Wilderness Institute
(Endangered Species Act)
  25766 Georgetown Station
  Washington, D.C. 20007

Information Resources

Civil Disobedience Library
2442 Cerrillos Suite 230
Santa Fe, NM 87501

Conservative Book Club
Harrison, NY 10528

RESOURCES

Discover Magazine
114 Fifth Ave., New York, NY 10011

Reason Magazine
3415 South Sepulveda Blvd., Suite 400,
Los Angeles, CA 90034

Issues in Science and Technology
The University of Texas at Dallas
Richardson, TX 75083-0688